PENGUIN BOOKS

FIRST CONTACT

Robin Anderson and Bob Connolly are Australian writers and filmmakers based in Sydney. They began working in the highlands of Papua New Guinea in 1980, and are at present working on a film about cultural change in the Nebilyer Valley region. *First Contact* was written while the authors were visiting fellows at the Australian National University in Canberra.

FIRST

BOB CONNOLLY

CONTACT

& ROBIN ANDERSON

PENGUIN BOOKS

PENGUIN BOOKS
Published by the Penguin Group
Viking Penguin Inc., 40 West 23rd Street, New York, New York 10010, U.S.A.
Penguin Books Ltd, 27 Wrights Lane, London W8 5TZ, England
Penguin Books Australia Ltd, Ringwood, Victoria, Australia
Penguin Books Canada Ltd, 2801 John Street, Markham, Ontario, Canada L3R 1B4
Penguin Books (N.Z.) Ltd, 182–190 Wairau Road, Auckland 10, New Zealand

Penguin Books Ltd, Registered Offices:
Harmondsworth, Middlesex, England

First published in the United States of America by
Viking Penguin Inc. 1987
Published in Penguin Books 1988

Grateful acknowledgment is made for permission to reproduce the following material:
Photographs of Michael Leahy and extracts from his book, diaries and letters by
permission of Mrs. Jeanette Leahy.
Photographs from the Daniel Leahy Collection.
Extracts from letters from the archives of the New Guinea Goldfields Limited.
Extracts from Hector Kingsbury's letters by permission of Donald Kingsbury.

LIBRARY OF CONGRESS CATALOGING IN PUBLICATION DATA
Connolly, Bob.
  First contact.
  Bibliography: p.
  Includes index.
  1. Ethnology—Papua New Guinea.   2. Man, Primitive—
First contact with Occidental civilization.   3. Papua
New Guinea—Social life and customs.   I. Anderson,
Robin.   II. Title.
[GN671.N5C66   1988]   306'.0995'3   88-5850
ISBN 0 14 00.7465 1

Printed in the United States of America by
R. R. Donnelley & Sons Company, Harrisonburg, Virginia
Set in Palatino
Designed by Camilla Filancia

Acknowledgments

The authors are very much indebted to the men and women of Papua New Guinea's highland valleys, whose recorded recollections form the basis of this book. Had it not been for their unstinting cooperation, generosity and patience, *First Contact* would never have been written. In particular, we would like to thank the following:

In the Wahgi Valley:
Mokei Nambuka Wamp Wan, Kopia Kerika Kubal, Ndika Komp Nikints, Yamka Maepkang Miti, Mokei Andagalimp Wak, Kentiga Amp Kwimbe, Nengka Amp Dau, Ndika Komp Amp Meta, Yamka Amp Wenta, Mokei Akelika Yaga, Mokei Kominika Kubal Nori, Towa Ulta, Mokei Kominika Korua Kolta, Ndika Opramb Rumint, Mokei Nambuka Titip, Tupia Osiro, Ndika Mukuka Wingti, Kopia Kerika Rebia, Penambe Wia Tugl, Penambe Wai, Mokei Kominika Kwipi Nembil, Mokei Nambuka Amp Nemong, Ndika Komp Amp Kenga Kama, Kopia Rompinjimp Nangambia, Nopornga Mare, Maasi Pinjinga of Nongamp, Dan Leahy, Clem Leahy and Joe Leahy.

In the Chimbu:
Ulka Wena, Mirani Gena, Gaima Yokumul, Korul Korul, Kimba Kopol, Gerigl Gande, Onguglo Komugl, Kumai Kama, Aglem Ker.

In the Bena Bena, Goroka and Asaro valleys:
Kirupano Eza'e, Gavey Akamo, Sirizo Gavey, Gopie Ataiamelaho, Kize Kize Obaneso, Koritoia Upe, Ewunga Goiba, Gasowe, Sole Sole, Isakoa Hepu, Agolave, Okame, Seriate, Jim Taylor and Jim Leahy.

In the Enga:
Naia Imulan, Petro Piscin, Gabriel Kane Miok.

During our field research, spread over 1981, 1982 and 1983, we recorded nearly one hundred hours of interviews, spoken in eight quite separate languages. We relied on many interpreters and translators, but we would like to single out for special thanks Magdalene Wilson of Mount Hagen. The bulk of our research time was spent among the Melpa and Temboka speaking people of Mount Hagen, and Magdalene Wilson, fluent in both languages, proved an invaluable collaborator and friend. Her deep local knowledge, wide circle of acquaintance, language skills, tact, unfailing good humour, keen appreciation of what we were trying to achieve, and above all her close relationship with the Hagen people, played an indispensible role in the preparation of this book.

In the Goroka Valley we leant heavily on the translating skill of George Gavey, and our special thanks go to him, and also to Hilan Pora-Schmidt, Peter Palme, Jimmy Tine, Robert Nonggorr, Paul Pora, Peter Pena, Peter Koin, John Endemongo, Dixon Kombagle, Jo Gande, Michael Pal, Ruth Ingalio, Wera Mori, Kainaro Kravia, Thomas Pupun, Yanopa Kai, Fabian Pok, Kumi Kispe, Joseph Ot, Peter Peng, Brown Sinamoi, John Kepagane, and Peter Peone.

We are deeply indebted to Dick Smith, whose generosity and faith in us made *First Contact* possible—both the film and the book. To Peter Munster go our thanks for alerting us in the first place to the wonderful reservoir of memory in the highlands. We also thank Chris Owen, Professor Andrew Strathern and the staff of the Institute of Papua New Guinea Studies for their unfailing support and encouragement, along with Vice Chancellor Elton Brash and the staff of the University of Papua New Guinea in Port Moresby.

We owe special thanks to the Leahy family in Papua New Guinea and Australia, in particular Dan Leahy, Sr., Biam and Mancy and their family; and Robin, Clem, Agnes, Joe, Rhona, George, and Dan Jr. and Tom Leahy.

We are particularly grateful to Papua New Guinea's tourist airline TALAIR for their unstinting support over a period of five years.

For their invaluable help in Papua New Guinea we would also like to thank Lyn Giddings, Rick Giddings, Paul Mason, Malcolm Morton, Bob Fulton, Gail Fulton, Rick Murphy, Keith Wilson, Christine Bourke, Ian Fraser, Janet Fraser, Bob Fraser, Edith Watts and the late John Watts.

On our return to Australia in 1983, Professor Gavan Daws offered us visiting fellowships in the Department of Pacific and Southeast Asian History, Research School of Pacific Studies at the Australian National University in Canberra, where we completed our research and writing. We are very grateful to Professor Daws, and to Marilyn Strathern, Hank Nelson, Jim Griffin, Dorothy Shineberg, David McDougall, Michael Rubbo, Muriel Hussin, Mary Hussin, Donald Denoon, Bernard Narokobi, Sandra Anderson, Roger Millis, James Sinclair and Anne Whitehead for their skilful help and advice during the preparation of the manuscript. For their valued help during this period we would also like to thank Catharine Santamaria, John Thompson and Barbara Perry of the Australian National Library in Canberra, and David Patterson, Peter Hussin, Tony Reid, Ian Willis, Ian Hughes, John Pateman, Pamela Warren-Wilson, John Warren-Wilson, Dorothy McIntosh, Karin Haines, Tim Curnow, Julie Gordon, Charles Marshall, Jannette Greenwood, Sue Rider, Donald Kingsbury, Jobina Gankin and Tim Bowden.

Finally we would like to thank Amanda Vaill and Lisa Kaufman of Viking Penguin, New York, for their invaluable editorial work, encouragement, and unfailing good humour.

Contents

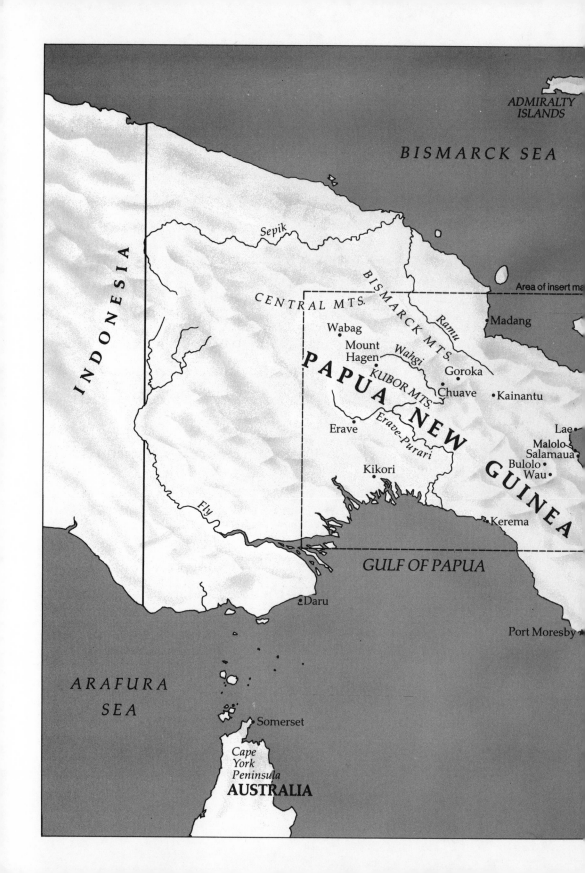

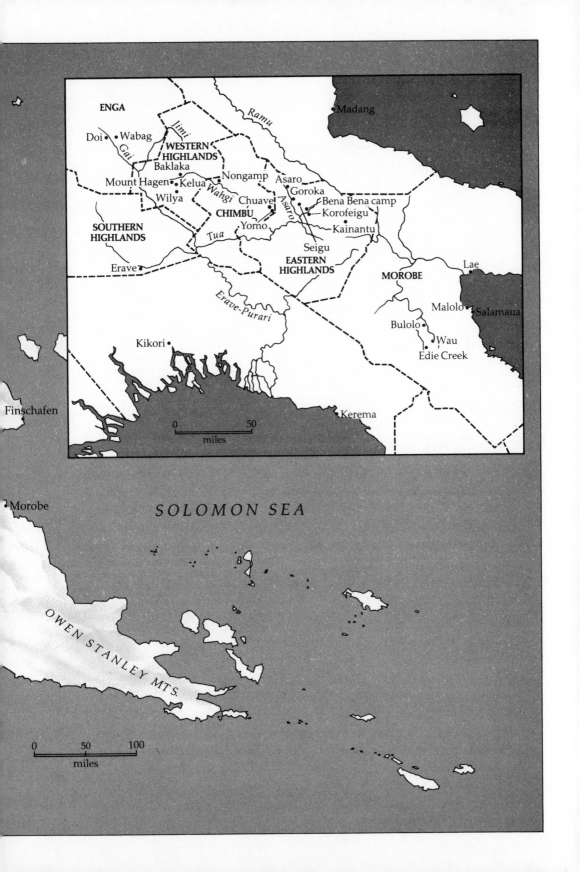

ENGA

Doi • Wabag

Jimi

WESTERN
HIGHLANDS

Ramu

• Madang

Baklaka

Gai

Mount Hagen •• Kelua • Nongamp   Asaro

Wilya   *Wahgi*   Chuave   Goroka

                CHIMBU   • Bena Bena camp

                        Asaro • Korofeigu

            Yomo   • Kainantu

SOUTHERN
HIGHLANDS

Tua

        Seigu

    EASTERN
    HIGHLANDS   MOROBE   • Lae

Erave •

                                    Malolo •• Salamaua

        Erave-Purari   Bulolo •

                                    • Wau
                                Edie Creek

Kikori •

Finschafen   • Kerema

        0   50
        └────────┘
           miles

• Morobe

SOLOMON SEA

OWEN STANLEY MTS.

    0   50   100
    └────┴─────┘
        miles

FIRST CONTACT

Chapter One

WHAT IS BEYOND?

Certain extraordinary events remain engraved forever on the conscious memory. In the highland valleys of Papua New Guinea, old men and women recollect with utter clarity the very day, the very hour, what they were doing, where they were. Questioned in a group, the old people will look around carefully before pointing out the boy or girl whose age they were when news first arrived of the coming of the white people.

More often than not the news came first through the air—sung and echoed from hilltop to hilltop in the eerie melodic wail the highlanders still sometimes use to project messages across their valleys. Coming into new country for the first time, the Australian gold prospector Daniel Leahy remembers the thin mountain air full of sound. On and on into

OVERLEAF: *First contact. A group of Chimbu men, photographed by Michael Leahy on his 1933 expedition into the Wahgi Valley.*

the distance the calls would be taken up and repeated, as word spread of an event beyond all experience.

"I saw them with my own eyes when they first came," says Kirupano Eza'e, "and I've not forgotten it. We were living in our old village then. My mother had stopped breastfeeding me, I was walking around like any other boy. I was with my father when I first saw them."

Kirupano Eza'e, now retired, lives quietly in Seigu Village among his clanspeople. A few miles away is Goroka, capital of the Eastern Highlands Province, with its schools, university teachers' college, police barracks and courthouses, tourist hotels, movie house, supermarkets, beer garden, coffee-processing plants, churches, airport, bowling green and cricket pitch, highlander coffee barons, labourers and lawyers, pavements red with spat betel juice, streets lined with Japanese four-wheel-drive vehicles, a hospital that treats highlanders for heart attacks and arrow wounds. This is Papua New Guinea in the 1980s—a decade after independence, five decades after first contact in the highlands.

Kirupano's village is several mountain ridges distant from Goroka and is very quiet. Occasional coffee trucks grind their way along a nearby dirt road, leaving behind a diesel haze and a trail of juice from the squashed coffee berries. A woman stands waiting with her bucket of berries—cash income, picked daily from her few dozen family trees, sold daily for imported tinned fish and rice—to add to the load. Aside from this, Kirupano's village is more or less as it would have been fifty years ago in 1930, before the Australians arrived, when there was no Goroka township, when news went not by telephone, but was shouted through the air.

Kirupano has dressed carefully in grey trousers and blue jacket. There are wartime medals across his chest; he helped his now-departed Australian overlords in their 1940s fight against the Japanese. The brass emblem of village court magistrate, a holdover from the colonial past, hangs from his neck on a string. He is joined now in the brightening morning by two very old men—stooped, dressed in dirt-stiffened tatters, carrying bows and arrows from force of long habit and, it must be said, occasional present necessity. Some things cannot be left to the police, the courts and the jails. The three men stand at the centre of their village: twenty circular, split-log houses with roofs of kunai grass. The houses have three-foot entrances, perpetually cool and gloomy interiors, no electricity; the ceilings are crusted with shiny soot from open cooking fires. Smoke rises unchanneled and seeps out through the ku-

An Asaro man, probably photographed in February 1933. The man appears to be holding an empty film carton.

nai roofs. In Kirupano's village the houses enclose a cleared area of packed soil, picked clean by wandering fowl and pigs. Children and women peer from doorways and gradually gather round.

Kirupano begins his story. He speaks in Melanesian Pidgin, lingua franca of the colonial times, an amalgam of German, English and New Guinean languages that has defied its detractors and been evolved by the Papua New Guineans into a language of subtlety, beauty and expressiveness. The two old men standing next to Kirupano, since they were not singled out for any form of colonial service in their youth, were not taught pidgin, so the conversation with Kirupano is unintelligible to them. Neither could they converse with Kafe-speaking people twenty miles to the east, or with the Kuman people twenty miles to the west. The two old men speak Gahuku, the language of their region, and that is all they know.

Kirupano, straight backed and serious, turns and gestures towards the two old men flanking him, and then speaks. *"Na dispela taim, dispela ol lapun i sanap ia, ol yangpela tru ol ino bin marit yet. Na ol ino sev yet. Na dispela taim waitman pastaim ikam."*—"At that time, these bigger men— they're old now—were just young men, and unmarried. They hadn't shaved yet. That's when the white men came."

"I was so terrified," continues Kirupano, "I couldn't think properly, and I cried uncontrollably. My father pulled me along by the hand and we hid behind some tall kunai grass. Then he stood up and peeped out at the white men."

Kirupano's first white men were on the march and did not stop at his village. "Once they had gone," he went on, "the people sat down and developed stories. They knew nothing of white-skinned men. We had not seen far places. We knew only this side of the mountains. And we thought we were the only living people. We believed that when a person died, his skin changed to white and he went over the boundary to 'that place'—the place of the dead. So when the strangers came we said: 'Ah, these men do not belong to the earth. Let's not kill them— they are our own relatives. Those who have died before have turned white and come back.' "

Forty miles to the west of Kirupano's village, as the crow flies, is the small town of Kerowagi in the adjoining province of the Chimbu— a school, a church, government offices, local council chambers and a public produce market. Old men and women from several surrounding villages gather in the wooden council chambers to tell their stories. They talk in Kuman, a language as distant from Gahuku as English from German.

Rain patters on the corrugated iron roof, spots the ground outside and sharpens the ambient valley smells of wood smoke and newly turned earth. Children locked outside press up against the windows. Word spreads. More seamed old faces appear and are admitted until thirty people pack the room. Each old man and woman waits patiently to talk, and the session goes on all afternoon. Whereas Gahuku rolls breathily off the tongue, Kuman sounds epiglottal, indrawn. The old man Onguglo Komugl begins.

"We heard the white men were in the Waugla people's country. We couldn't go and see them because we were enemies of those people. But we were very keen to meet them. We were so anxious that night we couldn't sleep at all. We met them early next morning—there were many of them, advancing in a line. All dressed in white. At first we

The men's shocked expressions indicate that this photo was taken very soon after first contact. Leahy places it in the Mariefuteger/Chuave region and dates it 1932.

First contact. Having just sighted the strangers, the men turn in shock and run away. Taken during the 1933 Wahgi expedition, somewhere in the vicinity of Chuave in the Chimbu.

thought they were our enemies, coming with new-made shields. They came down to the river—there'd been heavy rain and it was flooding—and as they crossed the river all of us gathered around them. We were howling and shouting in excitement! And we were saying—these are our dead people, come back!"

Kirupano Eza'e of Goroka saw the first representatives of the outside world on November 6, 1930. Onguglo Komugl of Kerowagi describes events that took place two and a half years later, on April 4, 1933. Like most of New Guinea's highlanders, they assumed the newcomers were spirit beings. In fact, what both men encountered were Australian gold prospecting expeditions, led in each case by the Queenslander Michael Leahy. And what Leahy and his companions were encountering in the highland valleys of New Guinea's interior were members of the last significant population uncontacted by the outside world—nearly one million people, who for hundreds of generations had lived in ignorance of the world beyond.

Between 1930 and 1934, Michael Leahy spearheaded the west's penetration of these highland valleys. He was not the first to stumble upon their hidden populations: before him, German Lutheran missionaries encountered those on the eastern boundaries. Nor was he the last: Australian government patrols were still meeting pockets of uncontacted highland people in the 1960s. But during his five years of active prospecting, Leahy set the pace of exploration and typified its character. He was the archetypal white adventurer—ruthless and determined, searching for riches in an alien landscape among alien people, driven on by the lure of gold, sustained by an unshakeable conviction in the validity of his presence and purpose—a twentieth-century conquistador, arriving just as Europe's great colonising explosion had all but subsided.

But Michael Leahy was not an ordinary prospector. In addition to keeping a daily diary, he took movie and still cameras with him on nearly all his prospecting expeditions into uncontacted territory, and so managed to document on film something that will never again take place—the confrontation, on a large scale, of one race by the exploring representatives of another. Along with this visual documentation of first contact half a century before, there are many highland men and women alive who actually lived through those events and can vividly recall their experiences.

Of all the colonised peoples of the earth, New Guinea's highlanders must surely rank among the most fortunate. Colonial domination came late in the day and was short-lived—a mere half century of foreign rule. The Australians arrived in 1930, and left in 1975—not a long time in the scheme of things. Largely because of this, the highland people were spared many of colonialism's more manifest evils.

The highlanders owed their long isolation in part to the nature of their own society, the geography of New Guinea, and the fact that European colonialism tended to apply itself to where there was a ready profit. For hundreds of years after New Guinea became known to them, the Europeans left it alone. There were no obvious riches, and for its size the island had more mountains, swamps and jungle than any comparable region on earth. It was thought highly unsuitable for European settlement, and, right up until the midnineteenth century, proved to be so. The advance guards were scattered pockets of missionaries and odd, aborted trading settlements—all clinging to the coast, melancholy victims, mostly, of tropical disease and indigenous violence. In one Dutch mission outpost the toll of missionaries who had fallen victim to fever and warlike New Guineans after twenty-five years of earnest endeavour outnumbered the converts.

By the turn of the century, the Dutch had claimed the western half of the island, while the Germans and Australians divided the eastern half between them. German New Guinea sat north of Australian Papua. But the political boundary lines were drawn through an interior the colonisers had never seen. High mountains discouraged access inland, and white settlement remained restricted to the coast and outer islands. German, Dutch and Australian missionaries and colonial officials set about the task of saving and civilising "heathen" souls and minds, while the planters put their bodies to work.

The mid-1920s saw the Australians in control of the whole eastern half of the island. They had seized German New Guinea at the outbreak of the Great War, and at Versailles their occupation was confirmed. Australian New Guinea was not, legally speaking, a colony like Papua to the south, but a mandate assigned by the newly formed League of Nations. As a fledgling member of the white man's club of nations that still dominated world affairs, Australia had a "sacred trust" to extend European civilisation to the Mandated Territory's inhabitants, and to "guide them towards eventual nationhood."[1] Given the New Guinean's brief association with Europeans and the prevailing white notions of innate racial superiority, the Australians considered this latter attainment so remote a possibility that they regarded New Guinea and its people as their possession, one which they had no great interest in developing. Their own country—a huge, empty, undeveloped continent—occupied their full attention and swallowed up their energy and finances. But the Australians did fear invasion by Asian "yellow hordes" to their north, and they saw New Guinea's primary function as a defensive buffer against them. So they acquired from the Germans a large slice of the world's third largest island with no firm policy of administration or development.

The few hundred resident Australians—colonial administration officers, planters, traders, labour recruiters—sweated away in the tropic coastal enclaves hacked out of the jungle by the Germans and established themselves in the vacated German coconut plantations. Apart from these, New Guinea's most valuable resource was its people. Their cheap labour made the plantations economic propositions, and they

First contact. A European hand stretches out in greeting. The man wears on his head the feathers of what Michael Leahy, in **The Land That Time Forgot,** *dubbed the "dollar bird" (after the dollar-size round spot of brilliant blue which appears on its wings), along with a band of giri giri shells. This photo was taken by Leahy in 1933 in the vicinity of Ulka Wena's village in the Chimbu.*

provided missionaries of half a dozen persuasions with souls aplenty to save. Colonial control extended between ten and forty miles inland. And the Australians were quite convinced—right up to 1930—that the island's interior was largely uninhabited.

There are reasonable explanations for this extraordinary demographic error. Looking inland from the north coast, the interior seems to consist of a huge and continuous series of mountain ranges, running almost the entire length of the island. The same view presents itself from the Papuan side on the south. The Australians believed that these ranges—visible from both sides—were part of one solid, mountainous mass, peaking in the centre. Both flanks looked jagged and precipitous, suggesting that no significant population could inhabit such a region.

Much of this long mountain chain lay in Australian New Guinea, the Mandated Territory, where the new administration—quite separate from that which had been operating in Papua since the turn of the century—had its hands full consolidating its position. The Australian government gave no money at all to the Mandated Territory, and the impoverished colonial administration saw no pressing need to mount the sort of elaborate and expensive expeditions required to examine the interior thoroughly. If it was almost certainly barren and uninhabited, what was the point?

What the Australians did not realise was that New Guinea's central interior consists not of one solid mountain chain, peaking in the centre, but (at the risk of a geographic oversimplification) of two—running parallel with each other. Much of the massive plateau that lies between these northern and southern mountain chains was indeed sparsely populated, but spaced along its length are a series of large fertile valleys. And here lived the highlanders.

Beginning about forty thousand years ago, succeeding waves of people began migrating into New Guinea from Southeast Asia. They settled the swamps, the jungles, the coast and the outer islands. They penetrated inland, scaling the mountain barriers, lodging in the highland valleys and plateaus, five and six thousand feet above sea level. Here the climate was temperate and healthy compared to the equatorial heat of the lowlands and coast, and the soil was fertile.

Emerging archaeological evidence suggests the highland New Guineans were among the world's first agriculturalists. Some of them were growing vegetables in gardens drained by ditches at least nine thousand years ago. Perhaps most critical of all, the malarial mosquito found it hard to survive in these high altitudes. In fact virtually none of the diseases that had served to limit the lowland populations of New Guinea had found their way into the highlands at the time of contact. Encouraged by good soil and favorable climate, the highlanders thrived and multiplied in lofty isolation. At the time of contact they were among the healthiest and most vigorous people in all of New Guinea. And their addition to the island's population almost doubled it.

Just as there are reasons why the world took so long to come to the valleys, there are reasons too why the highlanders seemed never to have ventured outside. In 1876, a French sailor named Trégance wrote a strange and fraudulent account of his adventures in the New Guinea interior. Capitalising on the world's ignorance (his London publisher was quite respectable), Trégance told of his shipwreck on the island's cannibal-haunted north coast and of his desperate march inland over high mountains to escape the pot. He emerged in a great valley, peopled by a race he called the "Orangwoks." They lived in cities, mined and smelted gold, rode horses and were united under a powerful king.

The reality turned out to be very different from Trégance's mythic kingdom. There was no unified, hierarchic society. The populations of the highland valleys were splintered into thousands of tiny, isolated enclaves, ranging from a few hundred to a few thousand people. Each enclave had its allies and its enemies, and it was the presence of these enemies that determined the pattern of life and made freedom of movement, and therefore wide-ranging travel, impossible. Men and women lived out their lives knowing nothing but the familiar environment of their own tribal territory. Travel more than ten miles was difficult and dangerous. Travel from one end of the valley to the other was impossible. Travel beyond the valleys, to the outside world, was inconceivable. There was no outside world.

Along with this restriction in movement was a restriction in information. There was no common tongue, but rather a multiplicity of separate languages. This effectively prevented any free flow of information from the outside in, and the inside out. Certainly there were well-established trading routes, extending from both coasts into the highland valleys. Coastal items of value—particularly seashells but also the odd piece of steel—were traded through innumerable hands in innumerable transactions from the coasts into the interior. But by this time information about the origin of the goods was lost. In much the same way, Medieval Europeans enjoyed the exotic products of the Far East without knowing where they came from.

Despite this extreme political fragmentation, the culture of the highland people had evolved along broadly similar lines. They were a settled, agricultural people, living in villages or clusters of family homesteads. The basic food crop was the sweet potato, supplemented by a wide variety of other vegetables. The benefits of soil, climate and agricultural skill produced more food than was needed for subsistence, and the surplus went into raising domestic pigs. But these were no mere food source: pigs were slaughtered to mollify the spirit world, and they were objects of wealth.

Ambitious men competed for prestige, and prestige came from the accumulation and distribution of traditional wealth—pigs and, more importantly, seashells of various sorts, traded in from the coast. More of seashells later. They are integral to this story—paving stones of the Australian march into the highlands.

Highlanders shared a general belief in the spirits of the dead and in their capacity to exert a good or evil influence over the living. And they shared a more diversified belief in a pantheon of gods, ghosts, ogres, giants and mythic ancestors, who, like the spirits of the dead, had to be placated by ritual and sacrifice.

There was no wheel, no beast of burden, and no knowledge of gold or any other metal. Reciprocal obligations and loyalties between kith, kin and ally were the foundations of social morality. Ritual and ceremony accompanied the human transitions of birth, coming of age, marriage and death. Highland people found creative expression in music, dance and the decoration of the human body. They were confident, sure of their position at the centre of things but acutely aware of their vulnerability to the inhabitants of the spirit world.

It was a society that had evolved in extreme isolation. "We only knew the people who lived immediately around us," say Gerigl Gande of Kerowagi. "For example the Naugla, they were our enemies, and we couldn't go past them. So we knew nothing of what was beyond. We thought no one existed apart from ourselves and our enemies."

In Gerigl's Chimbu province, numerous hills and ridges limit the horizon. In the broad valley of the Wahgi to the west, the people enjoyed a longer view. "We used to see smoke in the distance," says Kopia Kerika Kubal from Korabug, "and we assumed people were making the fires. And we'd say to each other—I wonder who that is. I'd like to meet those people one day. So we would look into the distance, as far as we could see, gaze at the distant smoke, and wonder—what is beyond?"

It is possible that in every generation of highlanders there were those who asked themselves that question—what is beyond. Kopia Kubal, Gerigl Gande, Onguglo Komugl and Kirupano Eza'e were among the first generation who learned the answer, and they lived through extraordinary times as a result. Their enlightenment in the 1930s was due to various factors, but perhaps the most crucial one was the speculation by the Spaniard Torres, who sailed along New Guinea's northern shores in the seventeenth century, that since the coastline looked uncommonly similar to that of Peru, it might therefore contain gold. He was eventually proven correct. In 1926, massive deposits of gold were discovered on a tributary of the Bulolo River called Edie Creek—only thirty-five miles inland from New Guinea's northern coast. This was the spur for further exploration inland, and the ultimate discovery of the existence of the populated highland valleys.

News of the Edie Creek strike reached Australia in August 1926. Reports told of miners digging sackfuls of gold every day. Hundreds of footloose Australians immediately took ship for New Guinea in search

Michael Leahy in the early 1930s.

of a quick fortune, among them a Queensland timber cutter named Michael Leahy.

His parents were Irish born and Roman Catholic. They migrated separately to Australia before the turn of the century in search of a better life, met and married in Queensland, and over the years produced Eileen, Molly, Patrick, Michael, Tom, Kathleen, James, Erin and Daniel. Patrick, Michael, James and Daniel would spend much of their lives in New Guinea, and of those four only Daniel survives.

While rearing his nine children, Leahy senior earned a very modest income as a railway guard based in the inland town of Toowoomba. Home was a timber cottage on four or five acres. "We had ten or twelve cows," says Dan Leahy. "My mother used to milk them, and we sold the milk to supplement the family income. We never had money, like a bank account or anything. My father just carried on from week to week.

"Schooling was quite different to what it is now, and none of us finished secondary school. Mick joined the railways when he was fourteen or fifteen. He used to sell tickets. He worked at that for about eight years. I don't think he liked it at all.

"He was a great outdoorsman, Mick. We had a wood stove in the house, and instead of getting sawn wooden blocks like most people, Mick would ask my father to get a truckload of wood from the country—long pieces of it. He'd come home from work and saw up all the wood. That was his exercise, and then he'd be out hunting all around the ridges."

When Leahy senior was laid off from his job, it had a salutary effect on his son Michael. "My father was still a young and healthy man when they put him off," recalled Jim Leahy, who died in 1982. "And in those days there was no pension or anything else, and Mick had been in the railways six or seven years then as a clerk, and he summed up the situation saying: 'Bugger this, if this is what they're going to do to me after a lifetime coming in and out the same old gate, they can have it.' So he came home and told my mother, 'I'm leaving.' She said, 'It's a job for life.' He said, 'That's the bloody trouble.' "

Heading north from his boyhood town, Michael Leahy worked hard to accumulate capital, mostly at jobs requiring great physical labour. When the siren call of New Guinea gold came in August 1926, he was cutting railway sleepers with an axe. He was twenty-four years old. Within days of hearing the news he was on board a ship sailing north along the Queensland coast to New Guinea. He left his axe behind, and his model T truck, parked at the dockside. He had fifty pounds to his name. "Mick wanted to get out and do something for himself," says Dan, "and make his own way. There was quite a lot of publicity about New Guinea at the time. A lot of people made a lot of money very quickly. Just people like ourselves."

At the end of August 1926, Leahy and his fellow hopefuls—sailors, rural labourers, clerks—found themselves surveying the mountainous northern coastline of New Guinea, rising up from the sea. Thirty-five miles inland was a fortune in gold, and the field was wide open. That New Guinea was a League of Nations mandate, its administration entrusted to Australia for the sole benefit of its indigenous inhabitants, was a notion entirely lost on Leahy. But he was not alone in regarding the territory as a land of white opportunity. It was the prevailing white view.

In its few short years as a mandate, New Guinea had already come to be dominated by white business interests. They considered the Territory very much as a business proposition, its inhabitants business assets. The Mandated Territory's administration was understaffed, underfinanced, and headed by a succession of retired World War One army generals who knew little about colonial government. In 1924 its District Services section—those assigned to the welfare and supervision of the half-million indigenes then under colonial control—amounted to forty-three. The main task of these Australian patrol officers, of *kiaps*, to use the pidgin term, was to ensure a steady supply of cheap, healthy labourers to serve the needs of the white traders, planters and gold miners.

En route to Salamaua—the mainland embarkation point for the gold field—Leahy's ship had stopped for a time at Rabaul, centre of white colonial rule in New Guinea and its outlying islands for nearly half a century. Here he would pick up something of the entrenched code of conduct that all newcomers were quickly expected to emulate. The civilised *kanakas*, New Guineans under established colonial control, called all white people, regardless of status, *masta* or *misis*. They were expected to stand up when spoken to, obey curfew laws which kept them off the streets at certain times, and to step aside when meeting Europeans on pavements.

There was no social intimacy between the races. New Guineans were prohibited from living in towns or frequenting white areas except when under orders. All facilities were rigidly segregated. *Kanakas*, any New

Guineans, were not supposed to wear clothing above the waist—ostensibly as a health measure, in practice a device to further delineate their low status. The proper term when addressing a New Guinean male, no matter what his age, was *boi* (boy). Beyond the control of the administration were the *bus kanakas*—the "wild natives"—and these were generally regarded as treacherous, bloodthirsty savages.

Fifty years of German and then Australian rule had done little to improve the lives of the New Guineans—materially or spiritually. Large-scale recruitment depleted village populations of their young men, disrupting traditional economic and social life. Christian missionaries eroded traditional belief and custom, while foreign diseases—dysentery, influenza, tuberculosis, veneral disease—undermined their health. There was even a belief in some official circles that New Guinea's indigenous population was doomed to dwindle into insignificance, although the administration pragmatically put the health of the large force of indentured labourers at the top of its priorities.

By and large the Australians were confident their mere presence served to uplift the New Guineans, whom they considered an inferior race in cultural and even evolutionary terms. The notion of an eventual rise to equality was by and large considered fanciful, although some were prepared to put a time scale on it—five hundred to a thousand years. So the whites of those days thought they were in New Guinea forever, destined by birth and culture to rule, and that the black man was destined to serve them forever, and never to rise. The imperial sun, of course, was about to set, and these were twilight notions indeed, but they were nonetheless real in the New Guinea of 1926.

Colonialism turned ordinary people overnight into potentates. Australians enjoyed a huge leap in status merely by stepping ashore. Non-entities at home became *masta* or *misis*, adopted the white cotton uniform, took credit for the achievements of western civilisation and began to complain about the servants. "The natives of this Territory," wrote Salamaua's bank manager J. H. Johns to his parents, "are mean souled, thieving rotters, and education only gives them an added cunning."[2]

Chapter Two

LIFTING THE VEIL

Salamaua was a ramshackle collection of tents, palm thatch huts and wooden shacks when Michael Leahy stepped ashore in August 1926. The town had sprung up overnight to service the Edie Creek goldfield. The field was only thirty-five miles away in a direct line, but Leahy was staggered to learn that this particular thirty-five miles took eight days to walk, so rugged was the terrain. At Salamaua there was a tin shed hotel, an administration office staffed by a mining warden and a patrol officer, a bank, a hospital, a handful of trading stores and a cemetery, whose population already included miners felled by dysentery and malaria's fatal complication, blackwater fever.

In Rabaul, Leahy had been cautioned that no white man ever carried his own pack in New Guinea: that was "native" work. But he and his friends now found themselves cooling their heels in Salamaua for want of carriers. The first wave of miners had gone off with every available one of them. For several days Leahy watched a succession of miners come in from the goldfields—some striding along at the head of a line of *bois*, others on stretchers, wracked with fever and dysentery. In his book *The Land That Time Forgot*, written in 1937 with the American writer Maurice Crain, Leahy wrote, "One of them had a chamois money belt around his middle, so heavy with gold dust that it seemed to impede his movements. He unstrapped it with evident relief and tossed it on the ground. A circle of wide-eyed and open-mouthed newcomers gathered around him. . . . The miner patronisingly opened the money belt and poured out some in his hand. It looked just as we might have expected gold dust to look, ranging all the way from tiny yellow flecks to rough bits the size of a match head."

The sight of all that glittering, instant wealth marked the real onset of Michael Leahy's gold fever. A driving urge to find his own El Dorado would goad him relentlessly for the next eight years. Ignoring the advice about carriers, Leahy and his friends shouldered their own packs and headed off into the jungle. At first the going was easy. Gradually, however, the travelling turned into a agonising daily steeple chase in the drizzling rain as the exhausted men, plagued by mosquitos, dragged their feet up and down an endless progression of steep ridges. Leahy arrived at the goldfields exhausted but managed to win a rich claim in a ballot, a claim that other miners told him was worth at least fifteen thousand pounds. "I dropped off to sleep," he wrote of that first night, "trying to figure out how long it would have taken me, at my old job in the railroad office in Queensland, to save fifteen thousand pounds. It ran into several lifetimes."

The next morning he collapsed with malarial fever, recovering only to realise that without tools and indentured labourers to work his section of the creek and carry in supplies from the coast, he was helpless. Sick and disappointed, Leahy was forced to relinquish a claim he knew would have made him wealthy for life, and returned to Salamaua. A few weeks later he was back at the goldfields, this time better prepared. A veteran miner/prospector named Helmuth Baum, who had come to New Guinea when the Germans ruled there, had taken a liking to Leahy and had offered to split with him a claim at Edie Creek. After three days Leahy had recovered seventy ounces of gold, a fantastic yield. And then he came down with appendicitis and had no choice but to walk away from another fortune.

OPPOSITE: *A group of miners at Edie Creek, taken around 1930. Michael Leahy stands in front at left. His brother Jim is in the third row on the right with his arms crossed.*

Leahy's share of the three days' takings paid for the voyage home to Brisbane, and (the moment he left the hospital some months later) for the voyage straight back to New Guinea. He went ashore at Salamaua without a penny to his name but managed to land a job bartending at the Salamaua hotel. He watched miners get drunk on their takings, he listened to their talk, and he realised that he had now missed his chance at Edie Creek. The easily recoverable gold had been worked out, and the era of the small-time miner was coming to an end. Big companies were now forming to work the gold on a scale beyond the scope of the individual. Leahy cut his losses and turned to prospecting. In occasional partnership with Helmuth Baum, he searched the country in the vicinity of Edie Creek with no great success, but in the process accumulated experience and a "line" (team) of New Guineans—most of them from villages along the Waria River contacted by the Germans thirty years before. These men would prove indispensable to Leahy in the years ahead.

As the 1920s came to a close Leahy was joined by his brothers Patrick and James. With prospecting yielding no results, 1930 found the Leahy brothers under contract to the colonial administration supervising the building of roads on the Edie Creek goldfields, by now a sizeable Australian settlement. This work suited Patrick and James— particularly James, who says he hated strenuous outdoor life—but not Michael. He was merely building up his depleted capital before another stint of prospecting.

Now, after scouring the rugged country in the vicinity of the coast and Edie Creek for more gold, the Australians began to wonder about the towering mountain ranges off in the interior, and what might lie beyond them. Prospectors were spreading far and wide in their search for another Edie Creek, and in 1930, there were rumours of payable gold on the upper reaches of the Ramu. This river rose in the Bismarck Ranges, on the very edge of the unexplored territory: the great blank— 25,000 square miles—that appeared in maps of the day. Leahy decided to check the Ramu reports. He was capable and popular, and as a gesture of goodwill, miners at Edie Creek subscribed several hundred pounds towards the expedition's costs. A new goldfield meant new opportunities for them as well.

What no one knew then was that two German Lutheran missionaries Bergman and Eliere had travelled to the edge of the easternmost highland valleys the year before, glimpsed the big populations they contained, and returned tight-lipped, anxious to keep the news from the Australians.* They mostly hated—the arrogant kiaps, the prospectors, the labour recruiters, the Catholic missionary rivals. The Lutherans vainly hoped to keep their secret and preserve the highland people from the exploitation suffered by the lowlanders and coastal people. But the isolation of New Guinea's one million highlanders was about to end.

In 1930, colonial influence extended as far inland as the tiny Lutheran settlement of Lehona, set in the upper foothills of the Bismarck Ranges. This was to be Leahy's base camp and springboard into the interior. Leahy had teamed up with a fellow prospector named Michael Dwyer, and they intended a series of short prospecting trips to test out the upper tributaries of the Ramu, which rose above them. Lehona was at the edge of the unknown. There were no trails to follow, and Leahy tried to hire a local guide who might have some knowledge of the jungle-covered mountains rearing up ahead. But there were no volunteers. Lehona was staffed by coastal New Guinean evangelists—Lutheran converts sent out by their German missionary mentors to spread the Protestant gospel. They tried to dissuade the prospectors and their line of Waria men from venturing in any further, telling Leahy's Waria *boss-boi* (head man) Ewunga Goiba of impassable mountains ahead, inhabited by wild and bloodthirsty *bus kanakas* who were sure to kill and eat them. It is possible these evangelists were under orders from Lutheran missionaries to discourage men like Leahy and Dwyer from heading inland, but Goiba dismissed their fearsome tales.

At 8:30 A.M. on May 26, 1930, Leahy, Dwyer and their fifteen New Guinean carriers set off from Lehona. They carried with them an Uncontrolled Area Permit, which gave them the right, as the name implies, to enter regions beyond the administration's control. The permit required all expedition members to be inoculated against typhoid and other infectious diseases in order to protect the people they might encounter. It also stipulated that six men be armed and capable of defending the party against "native attack." It was a frontier governed by permits, but a frontier nevertheless.

In comparison with the epic, arduous and interminable journeys of exploration on other continents, lifting the veil from New Guinea's highland valleys was a relatively simple affair. After a day's hard climbing the party had scaled the heights of the Bismarcks and could look

*The Lutherans claim today to have known about the eastern highland valleys as early as the mid-1920s.

Leahy, Dwyer and the line of coastal New Guineans on the eve of their departure into the interior in May 1930. Ewunga Goiba is in the middle row, third from right.

across to the country beyond. Leahy was amazed. Instead of more rugged, forest-clad ranges, he could see grassy open country. Even then he refused to believe his eyes, attributing the grass country to forest fires.

But when darkness fell, Leahy and Dwyer were alarmed to see innumerable pinpricks of light in the distance. The new country was not only open, it was obviously populated. They had not bargained for this, and spent a sleepless night, expecting an attack at any time. Dawn found them awake and waiting with loaded rifles, and a homemade bomb. Fearing a mass attack, Leahy filled a can with gelignite, stones and rifle bullets. It was not necessary. Soon after sunrise, the party made its first contact with the highlanders.

"It was a relief finally when the *kanakas* came in sight," Leahy wrote in his book, "the men . . . in front, armed with bows and arrows, the women behind bringing stalks of sugarcane. When he saw the women, Ewunga told me at once that there would be no fight. We waved to them to come on, which they did cautiously, stopping every few yards to look us over. When a few of them finally got up courage to approach, we could see that they were utterly thunderstruck by our appearance. When I took off my hat, those nearest to me backed away in terror.

"One old chap came forward gingerly with open mouth, and touched me to see if I was real. Then he knelt down, and rubbed his hands over my bare legs, possibly to find if they were painted, and grabbed me around the knees and hugged them, rubbing his bushy head against me. . . . The women and children gradually got up courage to approach also, and presently the camp was swarming with the lot of them, all running about and jabbering at once, pointing to . . . everything that was new to them."

There would be no attack. Far from threatening the newcomers, the people were fearful, then friendly, some of them even crying, so great was their emotion. Before long, Leahy's carriers were "laughing and making friends . . . and sharing the stalks of sugarcane." With growing confidence in his safety, Leahy walked over to a patch of garden and was once again amazed. "I had never seen anything like them elsewhere on the island . . . beans, sweet potatoes and sugarcane were growing in long straight rows. . . . Straight drainage ditches ran beside the rows, and each garden was fenced from the wandering pigs by a hedge . . ." Leahy noticed other things. The people spoke a totally unfamiliar language. The men all carried weapons—bows and arrows, stone axes—and many were battlescarred. They decorated themselves with shells.

As this first day wore on, it became increasingly apparent that they had blundered into a very large population. As they walked through the grassy valley, prospecting the creeks for traces of gold—for that was why they were there—great crowds followed along behind them, obviously in a highly emotional state. As night fell Leahy made camp, still feeling far from secure. Guards were posted around the clock, and at dawn Ewunga Goiba issued trade axes for the unarmed carriers. The expedition moved off again, and the highlanders walked in procession around them. Leahy noticed that at a certain point the crowds would drop away, while individuals pantomimed dire warnings of danger ahead. He guessed they were referring to the proximity of their own enemies. And yet, although the people obviously fought each other, and were obviously territorial, there had been no hint of an attack against the prospecting expedition. Quite the contrary. There were smiles and tears, hugging and stroking, wonderment. Some blew eerie notes of welcome from high-pitched bamboo flutes.

From the response of the people, Leahy knew he was in country

never before penetrated by Europeans, and before long he was wondering if the geographers had got it all wrong with their assumptions
about New Guinea's unpopulated interior. On the morning of June 4,
ten days after leaving Lehona, he was convinced of it. The two prospectors climbed a high rocky knoll and gazed out on a "very big and
apparently level valley." They had entered the Goroka/Asaro—one of
the main valley systems of the highlands. They saw fresh running
streams, a green patchwork of gardens stretching off as far as the eye
could see, while smoke from innumerable cooking fires hazed the air,
rising through the thatched roofs of the circular huts. It was an astounding vista, made all the keener for Leahy by the discovery, in almost every stream he tried, of small traces of gold. Before long, he
could make out through his field glasses hundreds of tiny figures, running towards them. Once again the pattern of contact was repeated—a
tense and nervy time as each side approached the other, incomprehen-
sion, shock, astonishment, high emotion.

"Day after day," wrote Leahy in his book, "we kept on the move
down the river, always anxious because of the numbers of the *kanakas*,
feeling that our only hope of safety lay in getting out of their way before
their astonishment wore off." It was clear by now that the river system
they were following was not, as they had hoped, going to swing around
and lead them back down to the north coast. It was tending to the
south, further into the interior. And then the grassy valleys gave way
to heavily timbered, steeply descending gorge country. They were
hopelessly lost. Both men agreed it was too dangerous to retrace their
steps through the open valleys with their big populations. The supply
of steel axes and knives and the glass beads they had brought with
them as trade to buy food were dwindling. They had not brought any
shells, which the people seemed to value more highly than anything
else. There was nothing for it but to press on down the river they were
following, on the reasonable assumption that somewhere, sometime,
they would come to the sea.

Seven weeks later, after many tribulations, they did arrive at the
coast. It was not the north coast of New Guinea, but the south coast of
Papua. On the heights of the Bismarck Range above Lehona, the streams
flowing into the Ramu rise within a few kilometres of those running
southwest into the great Purari system of Papua. Leahy, Dwyer and the
Waria carriers had unwittingly joined the Purari system and crossed the
entire island of New Guinea by accident. In so doing they had stumbled

"Karmarmentina natives meet us in 1932" is Leahy's description of this photo. The Karmarmentina is another tributary of the Asaro. The bows and arrows the men are carrying are standard weaponry of the eastern highlanders.

upon, and walked straight across, one of the biggest of the populated highland valleys.

The prospectors kept quiet about the traces of gold they had found in nearly every stream in the valley, but the Papuan authorities demanded full reports of Leahy and Dwyer's journey, making further exploration of the highlands inevitable. And for the next four years, Leahy would set the pace. Travelling down the Purari River he had noticed its confluence with a very big stream coming in from the west. Its enormous volume indicated that like the Purari it drained a huge area. The sandy banks where the two rivers met were littered with human bones—remnants of corpses swept downriver. Leahy correctly assumed that this was further evidence of more heavily populated valleys to the west. But he kept quiet about that as well.

Leahy and Dwyer wasted no time in returning to the Mandated Territory, and by October of the same year they were back in the big valley they had first entered the previous May, anxious to have the new country to themselves before rival prospectors came crowding in. Travelling westwards along the valley this time, they were able to determine its full extent. It ran for many miles, and as the two prospectors worked their way along its rivers they moved among thousands and thousands of people who were encountering Europeans for the first time, among them Kirupano Eza'e and his people. Leahy had a camera with him—a German Leica—and he began to photograph the people staring at him from behind the rope line that was now set out to mark the perimeter of the camp.

These newly contacted people in the Goroka and Asaro valleys registered the same stunned amazement Leahy and Dwyer had encountered earlier, but as the days passed Leahy's apprehension gradually faded. He had begun to realise that in these initial encounters the highlanders appeared to have no thoughts of harming the newcomers. "Not once," he wrote in his book, "did we feel ourselves in any real danger of native attack although . . . the numerous wounds and scars, and the occasional burnt out villages we saw attested to the fact that they were constantly fighting among themselves . . . I began to have an entirely erroneous idea of the safety of travel and boasted to Dwyer that a white man could probably go anywhere in New Guinea with no better weapon than a walking stick, if he kept his wits about him."

Surrounded every day by thousands of onlookers, Leahy and Dwyer tested the river gravel, hoping to hit upon a fortune. They were tantalised by small traces in many of the streams—tiny specks of yellow in the bottom of the panning dish—but found nothing substantial, nothing approaching the fabulously rich Edie Creek. Leahy did note in his diary however, that a tributary of the river the local people called the Bena Bena tested moderately well as a dredging proposition. It was a significant observation, because at the end of 1930 the talk of the whole mining community in New Guinea centred around gold dredging and the Bulolo River.

As a small time, free-lance prospector, Leahy's major objective was the discovery of another Edie Creek—a massive concentration of surface

OPPOSITE: *Crowds standing at the roped-off perimeter of the Asaro River camp area. Leahy had dogs trained to bite any highlanders not wearing the* **lap lap** *who ventured inside the line.*

gold, easily recoverable by individual operators and their indentured labourers. If he could find such a lode first, then Leahy could stake the best claim and his fortune would be assured. It was not quite a matter of picking up the nuggets, but it was not far from it. The gold-rich river gravel was sluiced through a long wooden box with a slatted bottom and the gold collected along the slats. The technique was profitable so

Man standing at the perimeter line, Bena Bena camp, 1932. He wears a necklace of white cowrie shells—the most popular variety in the eastern highland valleys.

Man with bow and arrows, Dunantina/Bena Bena region, 1932. Leahy has captioned this photo: " 'Tarzan', intelligent, influential fight leader."

long as the gold remained in reasonable quantity. After several years of intense activity at Edie Creek the good gold had been largely worked out. But the mother lode had been shedding its wealth into the creek for millions of years. Edie Creek was a tributary of the Bulolo River; so

Group of **gunbois** *and carriers look down on the Wahgi River flowing through gorge country southeast of the Chimbu, 1934.*

was Koranga Creek, where more gold had been discovered. For millions of years those creeks had been sweeping their gold down into the Bulolo, and the Bulolo ran through a broad, flat valley. It had changed its course many times over the years, gradually depositing layers of gravel over a wide area, and when the river valley was tested in the late 1920s, tens of thousands of acres were found to be gold bearing. To mine it by hand was impossible—the quantity of gold won for the effort required was ridiculously small. But the British and the Americans had by then perfected the design and operation of huge mechanical dredges—weighing up to three thousand tons—which could scoop up and process thousands of tons of gold-bearing gravel every day.

A syndicate of Australian miners decided to put dredges into the Bulolo Valley. Transporting the machinery by land was impossible—the country was too rugged. So the syndicate hit upon flying the dredges in piece by piece. It was a huge capital outlay, but according to the tests it was worth it. When the dredges were in place in 1932, gold would be recovered not by the ounce, but by the ton. The estimate, accurate as it turned out, was that the Bulolo River valley contained a hundred tons of gold.

The crucial element in this large-scale mining effort was the international price of gold. In 1930, it was still very low at four pounds an ounce. The Bulolo Valley was rich enough to return a dividend at that price, but on the basis of the tests he was able to carry out with his panning dish Leahy judged the valley of the Bena Bena a marginal proposition. Not worth the huge financial outlay involved in establishing a dredging operation, which would also involve flying the machines in, piece by piece. Not with gold at four pounds an ounce. If the price rose, of course, it would be another matter altogether.

But as 1930 turned into 1931 prices did not rise, and Michael Leahy lost interest in the highland valleys he had visited. He had found no deposits rich enough to be worth exploiting himself using small-scale mining techniques, and his estimate of the Bena Bena as dredging potential was not good enough to entice one of the big mining companies to throw its weight behind him. And as prospecting in unknown country was an expensive business, he was running short of money again. Unlike the Lutherans, the presence of large and unknown populations was to him of only passing interest. Leahy was after gold, and as there appeared to be no payable amounts in the valley, he went elsewhere, unaware of the extraordinary and lasting impact his sudden arrival had made upon the tens of thousands of people he had walked among during these first two brief encounters.

Chapter Three

SKYMEN AND THE LIVING DEAD

There is no great difficulty today in finding highlanders who participated in these events of fifty years ago. It is simply a matter of following Michael Leahy's well documented line of march and talking to people along the way. In most cases the villages bear the same or similar names to those listed by Leahy in his diary. Some of them, like Kirupano Eza'e's village, are close to present-day administrative centres, and others lie along paved or dirt roads. Some are more remote, but in all of them, the response to our arrival is much the same. Young children converge from everywhere, and our interpreter sends them into the houses or vegetable gardens to find the old people who remember the *Taim wait man ikamap pastaim long hilans*—the first coming of the Australians. Invariably in each location there are men and women willing to tell their personal history of first contact with the representatives of the outside world. They may not know Leahy or his companions by name, but their descriptions of events invariably coincide, and virtually all use the word *spirit* to describe the strangers and their sudden arrival. The explanation for this is not hard to find. All highlanders

Chuave man wearing a headband of small shells and pig tusks through his septum. Taken February 1933—when Leahy first sighted the Wahgi Valley.

shared their existence with the unseen world of the dead. "We had experienced the presence of dead people before," says Gopie Ataiamelaho of Gama Village near Goroka, "but we'd never actually seen them in their physical form. We knew of their presence, by hearing them whistle, or hearing their voices singing. That's how we knew the dead were present. Other times we would feel the dead around us when someone was sick, and one of the ritual experts was performing cere-monies over him. Sometimes then we would feel the presence of the dead."

And the dead could not be ignored. The spirits could be benevolent and protective, or malevolent and destructive. Human well-being de-pended upon their continued goodwill. Generally speaking, at death a person's soul took its place in the spirit world, and it was to this com-munity of ancestral spirits that the people applied to improve the wel-fare of their lives. There were other spirits as well—gods, giants, ogres, legendary figures, mythological personifications of the sun, the moon, lightning.

The highlanders' universe, then, was made up of themselves, their allies, their enemies and the spirits. And then came the Australians. Obviously not their allies. Enemies perhaps? That assumption was quickly dispelled. The only other explanation was that the strangers were spir-its—either their reincarnated relatives and ancestors, or some other spirit disguised in human form.

Fifty years later the highland people recall these events with a cer-tain wry amusement. But their belief in a spirit world gave them a ready-made framework into which the coming of the Australians and their carriers fitted easily, enabling them to come to terms quickly with an event for which they were otherwise totally unprepared—to make ex-plicable the inexplicable.

On his second journey through the Goroka and Asaro valleys, in November 1930, Michael Leahy passed close by the village of Kirupano Eza'e on November 6 and continued on past the present-day town of Goroka as he travelled west. It was at this time that Sole Sole of Goro-honota Village in the Goroka Valley heard news of the strangers. "We believed that when people died they went in that direction," he said, pointing to the east. "So we immediately thought they were ghosts or dead people." When the strangers were interpreted to be the returning dead, they were greeted with tearful elation—fear of the spirits, joy at the return of loved ones or revered ancestors. It was only a short step for the highlanders to imagine that they recognized particular individ-uals—prominent men, fathers, brothers, sons.

"So we sent messages out in all directions," says Sole Sole, "telling everybody around. And everybody came, and we all gathered to look at them. This was the time when we gave them a pig and also one of our men stole a knife from them. We all gathered around to look, we were pointing at them and we were saying, 'Aah, that one—that must be . . .' and we named one of our people who had died before. 'That must be him.' And we'd point to another one and say that that must be this other dead person we knew had died before . . . and we were naming them.' "

Gopie, from Gama Village near Goroka, heard the calls that strangers were coming and rushed down to where they had camped. He was confused about the identity of the white men but had no doubt who the black carriers were. They were dead clansmen. One was his late cousin Ulaline. The evidence was overwhelming. "My cousin had been killed in a tribal fight. When he came towards me I saw half his finger missing, and I recognised him as my dead cousin. The reason his finger was cut off was that [when alive] he'd had too many children with his wife. His people had punished him by cutting off his little finger. When he came towards me I said to him, 'Cousin!' And he lifted his eyebrows. So I knew it was definitely him. He was the same colour, the very same man. His facial expression, the way he talked, laughed—exactly the same. And it wasn't only me who thought this, everyone

Chuave people at the rope line. Probably February 1933.

did. Today I tell this story to the pastors at the Seventh Day Adventist Church—but they just laugh at me."

At first Michael Leahy did not fully comprehend the underlying nature of his reception by the highlanders. He believed his initial passage was made easier (and safer) by the mere novelty of his arrival. In fact, even his most ordinary everyday activities were being analysed for a deeper meaning. Kize Kize Obaneso of Asariufa Village near Goroka remembers that "after they had built their tents one of them took an axe and went across to an old, dead, dry tree that had been planted long ago by a man who had since died. We thought this old man, whose name was Vojavona, had come back from the dead to cut down his own tree for firewood. We were very pleased that he knew his own tree."

Leahy's companion Michael Dwyer had false teeth, which he utilised on several occasions to disperse the crowd of onlookers. "We were all gathered there watching these strange people," says Sole Sole from Gorohonota, "when one of the white men pulled out his teeth. When we saw this everyone just ran in all directions." This was further incontrovertible evidence. Teeth might fall from a dead man's skull, but surely not from the living.

One man said that when the strangers gestured to their bodies, they interpreted this as the dead person telling of the wounds that had killed him. Any gesture of familiarity was seized upon, but also the reverse. Another man remembers that when the white men looked at them and then looked away, it was assumed to be deliberate: the dead were attempting to move about without being recognised by their living relatives. The dead, after all, did not always have the best interests of the living at heart.

Nor, for that matter, did the nonhuman entities of the spirit world, some of whom were known to be wild and distinctly ill disposed towards mortals. While Leahy's coastal carriers were almost invariably taken as the returning dead, sometimes the white man's appearance and behaviour coincided more closely with one or another of these mythological figures.

Gopie's first interpretation, before other evidence convinced him that the white men were ancestral dead, was that they were sky beings. "I asked myself: who are these people? They must be somebody from the heavens. Have they come to kill us or what? We wondered if this could be the end of us, and it gave us a feeling of sorrow. We said: 'We must not touch them!' We were terribly frightened." Others in the Asaro took the white men to be Hasu Hasu—the mythical being who expressed its power in lightning.

What counted in these situations was the peoples' attitude towards the spirit figure, or rather its attitude towards them. Among the Mikaru people on the southern fringes of the highlands, the arrival of white men heralded a catastrophe—nothing less than the end of their world. The white men of course were Leahy and Dwyer on their anxious trek down the Purari River, but word had reached the Mikaru before their arrival that strangers were coming with large and fierce dogs. Men owning large dogs had status among the Mikaru, and in their feverish excitement they speculated whether what they were facing was the return of the fearsome giant known as Souw, the principal figure in their creation story. Souw was known to be angry with the Mikaru. In the distant past when he lived among them a party of their ancestors had caught him copulating with his daughter, a grave crime. Souw was ashamed and enraged at being caught, and the people still retained the belief that one day he would come back to earth and punish them for shaming him. When Leahy and Dwyer, both tall men, arrived, the Mikaru were full of fear. Their white skin (Souw had white skin) their big dogs, and their clothing (Souw ensured his immortality by changing his skin like a snake) stamped them as reincarnations of Souw. The Mikaru fled in terror, although a few very brave men came back and met the white men.[1]

At this point in their journey, Leahy and Dwyer were worried men themselves—hopelessly lost but committed to going on—and they moved quickly through Mikaru territory. But not before the people saw Leahy's men wielding their steel axes, felling saplings for tent poles. Further terror for the Mikaru. They believed that the sky itself was supported by certain trees growing along the horizon. The strangers were heading quickly and purposefully in that direction. Did Souw intend wreaking his vengeance upon them by cutting down the trees and allowing the sky to fall upon them?

At about the time Leahy was passing through Mikaru territory, he was making diary references to the timidity of the people, unaware of what was really going on. In first contact situations the intruders often made judgements of the people they were meeting in terms of whether they were friendly, timid or hostile, while being unaware of the deeper reasons behind these responses.

When Michael Leahy passed through the Mikaru country in July

1930 survival was uppermost in his mind, not the search for gold. In October and November 1930, back in the Goroka and Asaro valleys, Leahy was much more in control of the situation. The usual practice was to pull up and camp in the early afternoon, before the regular afternoon rain showers made things uncomfortable. The camp was usually sited close to a village and stream. The choice of a campsite involved pantomimed negotiations with the gathered crowd, and once the area was chosen, poles were cut and a rope line stretched around them to mark the boundary. Leahy had trained several ferocious dogs to attack the highlanders if they came into the camp enclosure. The dogs could distinguish them by their scanty clothing—the carriers all wore the skirtlike *lap lap*.

Each of Leahy's Waria men had their assigned jobs in the camp: bartering for food, erecting tents, digging latrine pits, cooking, guard duty. All this was done quickly, and under the intense scrutiny of hundreds, sometimes thousands of onlookers. As the afternoon wore on word would spread through the countryside and newcomers would join the crowds pressing up against the rope boundary.

If there was no prospecting work to be done Leahy might use these afternoons to photograph the scene outside the rope line, often developing the film himself in a nearby stream. In the late afternoon he would take to his tent and write his diary entry for the day. November 1, 1930, reads: "About three hundred men and marys [*meri* if the pidgin word for women] all outside our roped area, gazing at us like prize cattle at a country show." The terse entries in Leahy's diaries suggest he was already becoming aware that he was participating in a singular historical event and that he had an unparalleled opportunity to record it. He later sent away to America for correspondence courses in writing and photography and there was to be a growing sophistication over the years in the quality of his visual and written output.

Meals were eaten before sundown. As there was no necessity to carry any more than emergency food supplies, Leahy travelled comfortably. The white men ate at camp tables, seated on folding chairs and slept on comfortable stretchers. At dusk guards were posted, and it was now time to disperse the dense crowds of onlookers, if necessary, by loosing the savage dogs trained to attack anyone not wearing a *lap lap*.

Today many highland people clearly recall the detail of the camps—the tents, the rope line, the dogs, the impossibility of closer inspection. Kize Kize Obaneso says his people stood outside the rope line looking in at their dead relatives. "Our older people wanted to go and hug and hold them—so they built a fence around with rope to keep us out." Apart from the rope, Kize Kize remembers that the strange smell of the white people had a powerful deterrent effect, as well. It was like nothing they had ever smelled before and it frightened them. The feeling was mutual. "Nigs pong woefully," wrote Leahy in his diary at one point.

Gavey Akamo remembers the white men camping a few hundred yards away from his village in the middle of the Asaro Valley. "They smelt so differently, these strange people. We thought it would kill us, so we covered our noses with the leaves from a special bush that grows near cucumbers. It had a particularly nice smell, and it covered up theirs."

When on the march the strangers would pass quickly through the crowds of highlanders and disappear as mysteriously as they came. The people would be left, as was Kirupano's clan, to "sit down and develop stories." But when they camped for the night, here was an opportunity to examine the strangers more closely and explore initial assumptions. A striking example of this investigative process was told by Gavey Akamo and his wife Sirizo Gavey.

Sirizo recounted a story well known to her people in the precontact times of a beautiful young widow who had decided it was time to look for a new husband. After much travelling the widow reached the top of a distant mountain, and there she saw a young man lying on the grass. He invited her on a journey, and for days the pair travelled through a beautiful region of flowers. Eventually they arrived at the man's village, and the girl joined his other wives. That night they lay down together, but after a time the girl woke up, looked to her husband and saw only his white skeleton lying there. In the morning there was nothing at all. The woman was shocked, and realised that she was in a place where everybody was dead. To join her dead husband she had no choice but to kill herself. Meanwhile her brothers, concerned that she had not returned, followed her trail and came upon her dead body. They carried it back to their village, and buried it in the traditional way.

So it was thought that the dead could take human form by day, and become skeletons by night. Sirizo's husband Gavey says his people thought that when the strangers lay down to sleep at night, the flesh would go from their bones and they would turn back into skeletons. And they set about proving it.

Gavey was a small boy at the time of contact, but he vividly remem-

bers the older people speculating about the skeletons and trying to work out some way of getting in close enough to the camp to see. He says two redoubtable warriors came forward and declared their willingness to take on the mission. "They were very daring," says Gavey, "famous for their night raiding and feared by all our enemies. Death meant nothing to them. For them night was like daytime and they were the ones to dare find out about these white men. Their names were Gapumbarihe and Nigamangule.

"There were guard dogs in the camp during the night, but these two men were very careful. They crept very quietly, so as not to break any twigs. If the dogs approached they would lie quietly until they went away, and then gradually creep closer. They spent the whole night trying to peep inside the tent, as close as they dared go. They watched and watched, and they expected to see bones in there, but they could see none. They saw no changes taking place. The strangers stayed the same. So they said we should stop this belief that they were dead people."

Gavey suggests his people came quite quickly to the conclusion the strangers were not dead people. Often this process took a lot longer, sometimes years. After fifty years it is difficult to be precise. But the notion of white men turning into skeletons at night was recalled by old people from the Asaro right through to Kerowagi in the Chimbu, contacted by Leahy the following year. Most had little opportunity to put the matter to the test. Korul Korul from Oknel Village in the Chimbu recalls that "at night we used to wonder whether their flesh stayed on their bones or departed. But we couldn't get in to see because they had this big rope around their tents, men on guard. We thought they were dead people but we just lived in doubt about this."

The highlanders were anxious to detect any areas of similarity between themselves and the strangers. Did they eat? Drink? Sleep? Defecate? "Because they wore *lap laps* and trousers," says Kirupano Eza'e of Seigu, "the people said, 'We think they have no wastes in them. How could they when they were wrapped up so neatly and completely?' We wondered how the excreta could be passed. We wondered much about that."

On the march, Leahy and Dwyer found it necessary to choose a secluded spot and post a guard when they wanted to relieve themselves. Ideally they waited until the camp was set up in the afternoon.

Sirizo Gavey and Gavey Akamo in their garden at Asaroka Village in the Asaro Valley, 1983.

A screened latrine pit was dug within the roped-off area.* But the high-landers' curiosity could not be left unsatisfied for long. "One of the people hid," recalls Kirupano, "and watched them going to excrete. He came back and said, 'Those men from heaven went to excrete over there.' Once they had left many men went to take a look. When they saw that it smelt bad, they said, 'Their skin might be different, but their shit smells bad like ours.' "

In the Enga district, far to the west, Naia Imulan from Tori Village, contacted by Leahy in 1934, says his people entertained one theory that the strangers were skypeople. If they were, it was reasoned that their excreta should look like that of birds, and when the people subse-quently dug it up they were surprised to discover otherwise. The inter-est in excreta went beyond merely establishing the similarity of human functions, as throughout the highlands, bodily wastes were an impor-tant element in sorcery. A man became very vulnerable, for example, if his enemies got hold of his faeces, semen or saliva.

The strangers' bodies were covered in a strange material. They must have something important to hide. "We had only our traditional dress to cover our private parts," says Gasowe of Makiroka Village in the Asaro. "So when we saw these new strangers, with clothes and belts all over them, we thought they must have a huge penis they were trying to cover up. We thought it must be so long it was wrapped round and round their waists. It was because they were wearing these strange clothes and belts. The thought of that really used to scare us. The women used to be on the lookout and they would run away."

Reinforcing these assumptions were more mythological stories deal-ing with the exploits of men with giant penises. In the past, say the Kafe people for example, Hefioza lived alone on a mountain near the village of Henganofi (now a small settlement around a high school on the road between Kainantu and Goroka), prevented from travelling far by the enormous length of his penis. When he did travel he carried it coiled in a basket slung over his shoulder. One morning, Hefioza looked down from his mountain and saw a woman working her garden in the valley below. His penis slowly uncoiled and slid down the mountain, all the way to the woman. When she felt it between her legs she grabbed a stone axe and chopped it into pieces. The first piece turned into taro, and the others into yams, bananas, tapioca and sugarcane, which later

---

*In point of fact they were specifically obliged by law to dig the pit as a precaution against the introduction of dysentery and other diseases.

Young girl, Mariefuteger River area, February 1933.

became the peoples' staple foods. The woman, however, did not stop at this point, but kept chopping away until poor Hefioza's penis was down to a normal length. But by this time he was dead. So the woman poured a magic potion down his throat, brought him to life, married him, copulated, and brought forth many children who became ancestors of the Kafe people.[2]

Many Eastern Highlands people remember speculating about the size of the strangers' penises. Enlightenment came to some when the white men were observed washing in the river. "When they had their bath," says Gasowe, "we used to peep at them and that's when we found out we were wrong. In fact they were just the same as all us men." But the sight of the strangers washing themselves provoked considerable consternation. "When we saw them using the soap in the river," says Gasowe, "and we saw all the foam that was on their bodies, we thought it was the pus coming from a dead person's skin, like the milky part from the rotten flesh. Our minds were in a turmoil when we saw such things!"

Leahy spent a great deal of his time testing the river and creeks for gold. In the time honoured fashion of prospectors, he would scoop up gravel and water in his pan and repeatedly swirl it round, gradually isolating specks of gold in the bottom, peering intently, of course, at the result. Good prospects would bring excited comments from Leahy and Dwyer and more speculation from their ever-present highland audience. "When the white men first came to the highlands," says Kirupano Eza'e, "they filled their dishes with sand and washed that in the water. They washed and washed, poured it out again, washed, poured off, washed, poured off. They did that on and on. And we watched, and thought like this: in the past, our ancestors, our forefathers and foremothers, when they died their bodies were burnt, and we used to pick up the bones and ashes and throw them in the river. And so we thought those ancestors of ours had come back to collect and wash their ashes and bones.

"Some men thought like that, and others thought, 'Did they want to wash the bones to make them come back to life?' We weren't clear on things then. But we know now. They got money from our ground. Now we think straight—that's how they made money, but before we didn't think like that. We had many wild thoughts."

For the highlanders almost everything the Europeans brought with them was new and mystifying—not only the items themselves, but the very substances with which they were made; the woven canvas of the

Dan Leahy in tent, Karmarmentina River area, 1932.

tent, the cloth of their shirts, trousers and *lap laps*, their leather shoes and steel axes. (Leahy occasionally came across well-worn steel axes, traded up from the coast, but these were very rare.) To people who had never seen these things before, there was great difficulty in even describing them. One man could only liken Leahy's tents to clouds from the sky, because no natural material known to them could approach the canvas in whiteness. The functions and mechanisms of the white man's goods were equally mystifying—their guns, matches, torches, mirrors, watches, binoculars, cameras, writing paper, pens, rucksacks. Kirupano says his people thought the strangers carried their women in the bags strapped to their shoulders, as there appeared to be no women walking in the line. Obviously the women were let out at night, inside the tents. As for the night lanterns, says Kirupano, it seemed these men from heaven had brought the moon with them, or a piece of it.

OVERLEAF: *Dan Leahy dining in camp, seemingly oblivious to his ever-present gallery of curious highlanders. Gai River Valley, Wabag, 1934.*

But of all the wondrous objects possessed by the white man none could compare to their store of shells. Ranging in size and value from the tiny giri giri to the majestic gold-lipped mother-of-pearl shells, these, together with pigs, were the major wealth objects of the highlands. They were used for personal adornment, for ceremonial exchange, as a measure of personal prestige. A man could marry with contributions of pigs and shells to the woman's family. He would surrender them as compensation payments in disputes, or to allies for assistance given in battle. As the Australian penetration of the highlands increased, the area would be flooded by shells used as barter payments, but at the time of first contact they were quite rare, especially those most highly valued by the people—cowries, giant bailers, and gold-lipped pearlshells (*kina* shells in pidgin).

When Leahy first entered the highlands in June 1930 he took with him as trade goods axes and jews harps, large and small knives, glass beads, three bolts of cheap cloth and, on the advice of his friend Helmuth Baum, a bag of dog's teeth. This was the sort of trade that had passed muster in other parts of New Guinea over the years and Leahy thought he had everything he would need. But when he saw the shell decoration worn by the highlanders he realised he had omitted the most sought after item of all. The dogs' teeth were a definite failure. When Leahy offered them as trade for food, the people rounded up all their dogs and presented them for eating.

When Leahy returned to the highlands in late 1930 he was much better prepared, having scoured Salamaua for shells, particularly the cowries and tiny giri giri popular in the Goroka, Bena Bena and Asaro valleys. Each region had its preferred varieties, and Leahy gradually learnt by trial and error which ones were valuable.

Sometimes the initial fear of newly contacted people made them difficult to approach, but a display of shells usually achieved the desired result. "I would pick out someone," says Ewunga Goiba, the man responsible for buying food, "and as he backed away I would tie the shell onto a stick and try to make him take it. When I approached him he would move back further and further, and I'd move backwards! Then the fellow would come forward again, and I would move forward with encouraging gestures for him to take the shell. 'Oh Papa, you come. Get this good thing.'

"Eventually he would swell up with the desire to have the shell, and he would come and feel it with his hands. Then he would hold it,

New Guinea Goldfields' surveyor Charles Marshall and one of the gunbois *panning for gold, with the onlookers perhaps speculating like Kirupano Eza'e's people that the strangers were reincarnated dead sifting the gravel for their own bones. Asaro/Bena Bena region, 1932.*

and then come and hold my hands. Then he would bring us food and I would buy it."

The shells used mostly by Leahy in the Eastern highlands were small giri giri, bought on the coast for six pence a pound, with three hundred to the pound. A few handfuls would buy the prospectors all the daily food they needed. Everyone recalls their amazement when they saw what the white men had with them: "We were all exclaiming and crying out in excitement! We couldn't believe it!" says one man. "They were so precious to us," says another, "and we said, 'Ahhh! Look at these!' " "We held them in our hands so carefully," adds a third, "and then we would wrap them up in leaves and put them in a house. And then we would have to go and have a look at them so we'd unwrap them again and look at them. We couldn't believe how wonderful they were."

Highlanders believed their ancestral spirits exerted control over human well-being—healthy children, good crops, big pigs and shell wealth. The Australians entered the highlands carrying what amounted to a treasure trove of the most highly prized items of wealth. The peoples' realisation that the strangers were enormously wealthy was a profoundly significant one influencing not only their immediate reaction to explorers like the Leahys, but the whole process of European colonization.

Shells were not the only effective trade items. European salt was highly prized everywhere, the highlanders considering it an improvement over their locally produced variety, made by burning vegetable matter and straining the ashes. But then there was steel—axes, tomahawks, long bush knives, smaller knives, even the tiny blades used in wood planes. When first shown them, some highlanders could not immediately comprehend their value, preferring their own familiar stone axes. In June 1930, on his way down the Purari, Leahy wrote testily in his diary: "They all use stone axes and are too stupid to sell a pig for a tomahawk, asking instead for tambu shell for their personal adornment." (He had no shells then.) But the people usually needed only a demonstration before they realised the value of what was being offered.

Isakoa Hepu of Magitu Village in the Bena Bena Valley was a small boy when he first saw the Australians, but he gives a comprehensive account of his people's reaction to the white man's cornucopia of exotic novelties and familiar treasures: "When the white man came here the people were really afraid of him. He put some salt in his hands and put it on their tongues. They tasted it and said, 'This is good,' and jumped about making noises like this, 'Sssss! Sssss!' Then they came forward and held on to the white man's legs, saying, 'This is a good thing.' Our way of making fire was by pulling hard on a strip of bamboo. The white man got a matchbox and stroked it. He gave them the matchbox and they too stroked it, and the fire flared out. They held the box to their hearts and they were filled with joy. Then the white man got the tambu shells and the tomahawks and gave them to the men around, to even old men. He got a piece of wood and he cut it and the men saw that and were crazy about it. One took the tomahawk and held it gently near his heart, and then went off. We thought he had gone for good, but he came back with a huge pig.''

In the initial encounters any scrap or bauble from the Europeans was likely to be highly prized, invested as it was with great spiritual significance. The item's potential as a spiritual source of wealth and strength was often more important to the highlanders than the actual item itself.

Leahy and Dwyer moved quickly, anxious to prospect as much of the country as possible. Most initial encounters were simply fleeting glimpses as the white men and their carrier line strode across the countryside. Rarely would the prospectors camp in one place for more than

Young girl with shell decorations. Mariefuteger/Chuave region, 1932.

Ulka Wena in 1983. Fifty years earlier, in 1933, Ulka Wena's people saw their first white man and took him to be Konia Taglba, an esteemed ancestor, returning from the dead. Leahy camped on Ulka Wena's ground in March 1933 on his way to the Wahgi Valley.

a night, and as Michael Leahy liked to be on the move as soon as there was light enough to see the path, the nearby people would normally still be sleeping when they left, with only the beaten ground of their campsite as evidence of their passing.

Not quite. Ulka Wena of Kundiawa in the Chimbu gives an account of what usually happened when the white men left. In March 1933 on his expedition to the Wahgi Valley, Leahy camped within a few hundred yards of Ulka Wena's home. "The next morning," says Ulka, "the white man packed up and went, and we came back to where he had slept. And we searched. Our old men believed that these were lightning beings from the sky, with special powers, and so they advised us to collect everything they had left behind. We swept the place and collected everything, tea leaves, matches, tin cans. And we went to the place where he had made his toilet and collected the excreta as well.

"Then we put these special things in a *bilum* [string bag]. We knotted the bilum and hung it on a post where everyone could see it. Then we brought pigs and killed them, placing the dead pigs against the white man's things, along with our weapons. The blood was draining from the pig. We cooked it, and cut it up, and everybody had some. Our old men said: 'We'll use these white man's things in the fights.' Now that we had these special powers we decided to go to war against the Kamenaku and the Naredu. We took the spears and gave them to the best warriors and told them to kill our enemies. When we were successful we knew the white man's power was working with us. We held on to this belief for a long time, until more white men came, when we realised these things were nothing special, just ordinary rubbish, so we threw them away."

The heavens may have opened and brought forth skymen or the living dead, but almost immediately the ever pragmatic highlanders were looking for ways in which these momentous events could be turned to their own advantage in everyday life. Mirami Gena, also of the Chimbu, tells how pieces of toilet paper were collected and burnt with pig's blood on the fire. Men then held their bows and arrows and their hands above the rising smoke to gain strength in preparation for going to war. Gena says one man took a razor blade he had found and scraped it along the bamboo strings of the bows, hoping to impart its magic strength into their weapons.

"The useless end of the matchstick," says Kirupano, "which the strangers had thrown away, was taken by the people, who said, 'These men from heaven threw this thing away so we must take it and eat it later, and we will become like them. And when we go to fight our enemies we will win because this thing is going to help us.' That was the useless end of the used matchstick. But the people took it with care."

Chapter Four

FIRST CASUALTIES

The spirits had appeared among them, and then just as mysteriously had gone again, leaving the highlanders to ponder the
meaning of it all. But if the coming of the white man was of extraordinary interest to them, the existence of the heavily populated highland
valleys created no great sensation in the world at large. There were brief
reports of the Leahy/Dwyer journey down the Purari, but no mention
at all of the really big concentrations of people the two prospectors had
encountered on their second trip through the Goroka, Bena Bena and
Asaro valleys.

Neither was there a great urge to publicise the discoveries. The Lutheran missionaries knew, but they feared any announcement would
bring in the labour recruiters, and worse, the Catholics. Leahy and Dwyer
lost interest in the valleys because there was no payable gold there.
And the administration, desperately understaffed, had no desire to increase its area of responsibility. But the highlanders' reprieve would be
a short one—about eighteen months.

Returning from his second journey in November 1930, Leahy took
a brief hand in his brother Jim's roadworking business on the Edie Creek

goldfields, and then went prospecting again in the nearby headwaters of the Watut and Langemar rivers. Lacking capital of his own, he entered into a form of partnership with the New Guinea Goldfields Company. NGG was controlled by the Australian-registered Mining Trust Limited, which in turn was owned by the London-based Russo Asiatic Consolidated. Russo Asiatic had done very nicely in the Ural Mountains and in Siberia, building up an extensive network of extremely profitable gold-mining operations. But in 1917 the Bolsheviks threw Russo Asiatic out, and it had scoured the world for new gold mines to develop in more amenable political climates. The Mandated Territory of New Guinea in 1929 was far more amenable than the Soviet Union. NGG accumulated a number of Edie Creek leases and began a large scale open cut mine below the creek near the airstrip settlement of Wau which had been built to receive the dredge components flown in for reassembly at nearby Bulolo. The open cut mine was profitable, but NGG was looking for another Bulolo Valley. And to find one it needed experienced prospectors. NGG had a million pounds to spend on the search for new dredging grounds, and it invested its hopes and its capital in Michael Leahy.[1]

Leahy, now approaching 32, had been well and truly blooded. In

Dan Leahy in 1932, age twenty.   *Dan Leahy in 1984.*

May 1931 nomadic tribesmen attacked his prospecting camp on the headwaters of the Langemar River at dawn. Leahy's brother Patrick and several of his men were wounded by arrows. Leahy himself was clubbed over the head and very nearly killed. Six of the attacking tribesmen* were shot dead, and the rest driven off. Leahy and his party made a rather desperate retreat back to the coastal town of Lae.

Leahy was visibly scarred by the club blow, and throughout his life would suffer from a ringing sensation in one ear. He was marked in other ways as well. From that moment onwards, a ruthless determination seems to have settled upon him never to allow such a thing to happen again. It was kill or be killed, he told himself, an attitude reinforced when he learned shortly afterwards of the death of Helmuth Baum. Another branch of these same nomadic tribesmen had attacked Baum's camp, killing him and most of his carriers.

The man who now joined forces with New Guinea Goldfields was tough, disciplined, experienced and ruthless. He neither smoked nor drank and could not tolerate self indulgence in others. (His brother Patrick was addicted to whisky, and on one occasion Michael had smashed his entire supply with a hammer.) After years of outdoor activity and abstemiousness he had developed extraordinary physical endurance, and could walk twelve hours without rest. These were suitable qualities for a career on the highland frontier, about to open up again.

Patrick Leahy had returned to Australia after his wounding, and his

*These people had experienced at least a decade of contact with Europeans.

First contact. Michael Leahy, who took this series of photos, entitled them: "1933, first contact with a white man, Chuave area, carriers ignored." Taken on the way to the Wahgi, the first shows a man with axe raised, ready to attack. But his hand on his head reveals ambivalence and confusion. His axe is raised more in shock than aggression, and his stance and facial expression reveal fear and confusion in response to this unprecedented situation. The second photo shows the same man face to face with Dan Leahy. The axe has been lowered, but the stance is still tense, with knees bent. The man is open-mouthed with amazement, but there is also a hint of dawning pleasure. Perhaps he is now identifying Dan as a dead relative. Dan Leahy, no doubt aware that one of the **gunbois** *is probably covering him, makes no move to his weapons. He is relaxed and smiling in welcome. In the third photo the axeman turns to others behind him. Now he is more relaxed and confident. He gestures to them and they smile.*

place was taken up by Daniel, at nineteen the youngest of the Leahy brothers.

"When I left school it was in the middle of the Depression," says Dan Leahy today. "I had a job on a dairy farm in North Queensland milking cows, general farm labourer. My room was adjoining the fowl-house and the harness shed. The farmer was a real tough bloke. I mean there was plenty of room in the house, but I had this rotten old place down near the harness shed. There were no lights—I had a hurricane lamp. I came home one morning after washing the dairy and the farm-er's wife said, 'There's a radio [telegram] for you.'

"It said, 'Make arrangements proceed New Guinea' and it gave the date the boat was leaving. Mick had probably just received one of my letters, saying how much I hated it down there! My mother was very worried. There were lots of stories about cannibals and things like that. I just wanted to do what Mick was doing. It was the adventure more than anything else. The gold excited Mick in those days, but not so much me. It gets into the blood, the gold, and it was in Micky's blood much more than it was in mine."

Dan's first job was driving a truck, in the port of Lae while his brother recuperated from his affray near the Langemar. But this combination of Michael and Dan Leahy and New Guinea Goldfields would soon spear-head the penetration of the western highland valleys.

In 1932, with the Depression now biting hard, the price of gold be-gan to rise. By September it had doubled to eight pounds an ounce. The Bulolo Gold Dredging Company's first floating dredge had clanked into operation in March 1932, with a second one nearing completion, and the initial results justified the capital outlay. Marginal dredging prospects in 1930, like Leahy's Bena Bena River in the highlands, now became real propositions. In October 1932, backed financially by the New Guinea Goldfields Company, the two Leahy brothers assembled supplies and carriers for a major expedition.

By mid-1932 the colonial frontier had advanced from Lehona, Lea-hy's old jumping off point in 1930, to the settlement of Kainantu on the eastern edge of the highlands. Here a small number of Australians had begun working a small gold deposit. This had forced the hand of both the Lutherans and the Administration, and both had established out-posts there. A small airstrip had been laid down by the Administration patrol officer stationed at Kainantu, James Taylor.

The Leahy brothers strode through Kainantu in October 1932 at the

A village in the southeast Chimbu, 1934. Leahy has written: "Note deep dry moat bridged with saplings—a defence precaution on narrow ridges."

head of a very well equipped New Guinea Goldfields party that included NGG's experienced American geologist Hector Kingsbury. The plan was to test out the Bena Bena as a dredging proposition, and to prospect further westward, probing out beyond the limits of the Asaro Valley visited by Leahy eighteen months before.

Michael Leahy's 1930 journeys through the highlands apparently had been unmarred by bloodshed of any kind. The highland people were simply too astonished by the arrival of the white men, and too convinced of their supernatural origin, to do anything but let them pass through. And if safety lay in surprise, it also lay in the brevity of these early encounters. The prospectors had moved quickly, anxious to try out the country as soon as possible. First contact for most highlanders had been a fleeting glimpse of the white men as they strode past.

New Guinea Goldfields' geologist Hector Kingsbury with a group of Dunantina people in 1932. Note that everyone, including the young boy at left, carries weapons.

On a number of occasions in 1930, Michael Leahy had given a demonstration of the power of rifle fire by shooting a pig or through a piece of wood. "I set up three wooden slabs against the hillside . . ." he wrote in his book, "then Dwyer herded the natives out of range and I blazed away, the high-powered bullet tearing through the slabs as if they hadn't been there. . . . The kanakas simply fell over backwards. Some of them ran away, others grovelled on their bellies."

All the highlanders today vividly remember their shock and amazement at what the gun could do. "These rifles," says Kirupano Eza'e, "were thought to be just a piece of wood which they carried around. And some said, 'Let's kill them.' But others said, 'No, these men who

Dan Leahy demonstrates a rifle to onlookers, 1934. In the first shot he is outside the frame as he aims the rifle at a pig or piece of wood. The crowd is interested but calm. The next shot is taken just after the rifle is fired. Arms are raised in shock, shoulders involuntarily hunched in fear. Some have leapt to their feet. Contrast the highlanders with the men of the carrier line standing behind, who are calm and relaxed.

have died and come back, we shouldn't kill them.' Some were afraid but others thought of killing them. They learnt their mistake when the strangers fired their rifles and shot a piece of wood. Our people saw that and were afraid, saying it would be terrible if they shot us like that."

"When the strangers shot the pigs," says Ulka Wena, "we were so frightened we were falling over ourselves and bumping into each other to get away. The shells had been distributed for the pigs, and we were so excited about these. But we were in two minds at the same time . . . frightened of the gun, but hungry for the shells."

Highlander fighting technique involved the ability to dodge something they could see—a spear or arrow. But a rifle? There was a loud noise, a puff of smoke, and a distant piece of wood would disintegrate, a tied-up pig collapse, its head blown apart. For most, the gun demonstration was a frightening experience, producing the effect the Australians intended. But the highlanders' long isolation had given them a great sense of their own strength and fighting prowess. Warfare was a significant part of men's lives. It was the system for settling disputes and administering justice. There was no professional fighting class; every man was his own policeman, every man a soldier "on active duty"[2] for his adult life. Each clan had its traditional major enemies, with whom it always fought, and its minor enemies, with whom it was alternately at peace or at war.

Weapons and fighting techniques varied throughout the highlands, and armed encounters ranged from small-scale raids or ambushes to elaborate engagements, sometimes involving thousands of fighting men meeting on an open battleground agreed upon by both sides. Weapons included bows and arrows, spears and axes. These large-scale battles were highly formal affairs, governed by rules that worked to minimise the number of casualties, and in fact throughout the highlands most deaths occurred in ambushes and raids. Occasionally a clan would be routed, and then the victors would pursue the vanquished, looting and destroying their villages. The survivors might then be forced to take refuge with their allies for a number of years to regroup and restore their depleted numbers before returning to their traditional territory.

There was however an important concept of balance governing relationships between communities—particularly among clans that maintained a variety of trading and marriage alliances. Any excess of violence with such people was to be deplored, as it disrupted all sorts of other

Man with bloodied sling, taken near Kainantu in 1932. Michael Leahy has captioned this: "Patched up." The man had apparently been recently shot in the arm. Leahy and his followers shot dead at least forty-one highlanders between 1930 and 1934 and wounded many more. This is the only existing photograph of an apparent victim. Dan Leahy says he and his brother always endeavoured to dress the wounds of victims of gunfire, but most were too fearful to venture close again after the incident.

relationships and would inevitably be repaid. While fighting men might be valued for their qualities of confidence, aggression and fearlessness, there was even greater value placed on the abilities of the reconciler, the man who could make contact with the enemy and bring about peace. Differences were settled wherever possible by the exchange of compensatory payments, but even when enmity spilled over into open warfare the casualties were usually kept to a minimum. Often the deaths of one or two people were enough to bring a conflict to an end.

Nevertheless, the highland people placed a high value on bravery and daring, and when they saw what the strangers were carrying, some realised that here were valuables for which the risks were worth taking.

Having seen what the gun could do, most say today they did not think of attacking the strangers, despite their treasures. But the responses were never uniform. Many did not see the gun demonstration first-hand. Some did not think of the gun as something that could threaten humans. Pigs, perhaps, and pieces of wood, but not a human being. The Leahy brothers did not provoke violence, but neither did they hesitate to defend themselves if their safety was threatened. At least forty-one highlanders were shot dead by the Leahys and their armed carriers because of their failure to understand the true nature of the white men and their guns. Leahy records forty-one deaths in his diary but there is little doubt the actual figure was higher. And the bloodshed began in November 1932.

Dan Leahy was nineteen when he marched into the Bena Bena Valley that month. Today he lives on his coffee plantation near Mount Hagen in the Wahgi Valley and is the only surviving Leahy brother. Poor eyesight and hearing and a recent stroke severely restrict his activities now (1986) although he still manages a daily stroll around his plantation, leaning on the patient shoulder of an employee. But a great deal of the day is spent in silent isolation. He is unable to read or listen to the radio, and visitors are rare. For these reasons Leahy welcomes the opportunity to reminisce about the early years spent on the highland frontier with his brother. Two-way conversation is difficult because of Dan's severely impaired hearing, but he can talk for hour after hour with little prompting, relating the events of 50 years ago with candour and fine detail.

What comes across most clearly is Dan's certainty of the fundamental legitimacy of his and his brother's activities during these times. There is no shortage of violent detail, but after fifty years Leahy is convinced the violence was unavoidable, that he and his brother had a right to be in the highlands, a right to defend themselves, and that the deaths of the highlanders were entirely their own fault.

"The first time you went in it was easy," says Dan. "They didn't know what we were. It was just like someone from Mars dropped down amongst us now. We wouldn't know what to think or what to do. So the first time the natives would be curious and frightened. Well, the second time you came in they'd be a lot more arrogant than the previous time. They'd say, 'Here's these fellows coming again. They stayed at our place last time, they bought potatoes, pigs, and they gave us all this wonderful pay for it—axes and shells. If they'd been strong they'd have just taken everything they wanted, like we would have done. They must be frightened of us.' You see they thought we weren't powerful, that we didn't know anything about fighting, and couldn't protect ourselves. So they said, 'We won't let all that treasure get through our hands this time.' I wasn't sure of their talk but it looked to me later that this was what they were thinking, because next time you'd come in you'd have a lot of trouble."

The majority of violent incidents between the Leahy brothers and the highlanders took place on their second or third encounter with individual groups, and usually arose from an attempted theft. The shock of first contact had diminished, and the people were more confident. They were very well aware of the strangers' enormous wealth, and they were keen to have some of it themselves. And there were plenty of opportunities: an axe left lying around, a knife sticking out of a carrier's pack as he laboured up a hillside.

So far, the strangers had done them no harm. Perhaps they were incapable of doing so. "We thought the gun was just for shooting pigs, and that it couldn't hurt men," says Kimba Kopol from Oknel Village in the Chimbu. "It never occurred to us that they would use the gun to shoot us," says Gaima Yokumul of the same village.

As for taking from the ancestral dead, surely they had come to distribute their wealth anyway. And the strangers' very identity as ancestral dead was now under question. Their dogs were unfriendly; and they had no evident desire to settle among their living relatives. And if they were not the returning dead but some other form of spirit being, there was no moral imperative against taking their wealth, particularly if they appeared weaker. In many highland legends supernatural beings are pitted against mortal men—usually brave warriors—and sometimes the spirit beings come off second best.

The Leahy brothers were gold prospectors, and very single minded ones at that. Michael Leahy's relationship with the highlanders was determined by his desire to travel and prospect where and when he wanted, in safety. Interruptions were not to be tolerated, and from Leahy's point of view there was only one way to ensure this: the white man had to effectively prove his power and the superiority of his weapons. Any notion the highlanders had that he was weak had to be quickly dispelled. And if that meant killing some of them, then so be it. On colonial frontiers, indigenous human life is seldom held to be of any great value, and the New Guinea highlands in 1932 was no exception.

So far as Leahy was concerned, the crucial element in maintaining the upper hand involved demonstrating at all times that he had total control over his own possessions, and could retrieve anything the people managed to take. Stealing could never be tolerated, because it implied weakness and vulnerability. The intrinsic value of the thing stolen was unimportant. So far as Leahy was concerned then, stealing was synonymous with attack, and therefore, life threatening. Many highlanders were to die in incidents that began over the stealing of items worth a few shillings in a trade store.

"As we marched down the Bena Bena [in November 1932]," wrote Leahy, "through villages we had visited before, we had our first trouble with the natives. At one village where a thousand or more natives were crowded about us, as we broke camp one morning one of the boys called out that a native had stolen a large knife. The kanaka with the knife, yelling at a great rate, ran out through the crowd and headed up the river . . . I began lobbing rifle bullets into the water alongside him. The crowd watching could see the water splash every time a bullet struck, and the thief would jump several feet into the air at each splash. . . . At the third shot the fugitive stopped and held up his hands, and presently the stolen knife came back to us, tied to the end of a bow, and held aloft so that we could see it flashing in the sunlight a long way off."

On the following day the highlanders suffered what were probably their first casualties. "At the very next village," wrote Leahy in his book, "a place where we had camped before, I had a striking illustration of what happens when the kanakas are allowed to get away with a theft. There was a dense mob all around the rope barrier, and one of the boys who had been cutting firewood happened to drop his axe for a moment inside the roped off area.

"A native darted under the rope and grabbed it, and quickly disappeared in the crowd. I would gladly have ignored the incident, but the whole village had noticed it, and was waiting to see what we would do. . . . Women and children began to scatter, and the men to congregate in greater numbers, all plentifully supplied with arrows. Since the camp was badly placed for defence we pulled down the tents and decided to get out of there in a hurry, in order to avoid a fight if possible. I was not worried about the outcome, since all four whites [the Leahys had with them two NGG representatives] and five of our boys were armed with rifles, but wanted to avoid bloodshed. . . .

"Our decision to leave seemed to convince them that we were afraid of them . . . and arrows began to land among us. We ordered the boys not to shoot and fired a number of warning shots over the heads of the attackers. They halted a moment at the report of the guns, but seeing no damage done came surging foward with wild yells. There was now no choice but to show them that the firespears were capable of more than noise. We let them have it, firing deliberately at the legs of those in front, and the battle ended immediately.

"When four or five of the leaders went down the charge halted and we stopped firing. . . . We wasted half an hour trying to get in touch with them again to patch up the wounded but could not get near enough. In camp that night I lined up the boys and read them the riot act on the subject of carelessness with knives, axes and the like, which would place a temptation in the way of the kanakas. I fully believed that if I had promptly nabbed the thief and gotten back that stolen axe we would not have been attacked."

This is Leahy's published account of what happened at the village of Korofeigu on November 20, 1932. In his unpublished diary, Leahy's entry for that day reads: "Wiped off a new Ogofagu [Korofeigu] nigs who pinched an axe and then got too confident and opened up on us." Later on he noted: "Heard there were six nigs killed at Korofaigu in the scrap over the stolen tomahawk." And if, as he stated in his book, Leahy's men did fire over the heads of the attacking warriors, it was not established policy. "One thing we would never do," says Dan Leahy, "was to use the rifle to frighten them. The only time we fired the rifle the battle was absolutely on. It was what the rifle was for—to defend yourself. If someone did get hit, it was meant."

Michael Leahy's surviving Waria men are in no doubt about what they were to do if threatened. Towa Ulta recalls, "*Masta* used to say, 'If the kanakas bring food, we'll be friends with them. But if any of our men are hit with an arrow or spear, you can shoot them. Kill them! Shoot straight! Don't fool round and miss so that the kanakas will think the gun cracks are only the sound of bamboo burning in the fire.' But he didn't want us to shoot for nothing. And we weren't allowed to shoot women or children. That was forbidden. But men we could shoot."

Prospectors on the frontier developed, as a rule, a closer relationship with their *bois* than did their counterparts in the coastal towns and plantations. This was hardly surprising. Leahy depended on the loyalty, skill, and courage of these men for his survival. The Waria men obviously had a professional respect for Michael Leahy. "He was a very tough man," says Ewunga Goiba today. "A hard man in the fights, and on the march. And when he shot a man he never missed. That man would drop on the spot." Ewunga Goiba, *bossboi* to Michael Leahy, had risen as high as any New Guinean could rise in 1932 and like his fellow Warias he served Leahy for many years regularly signing on again when his two-year term of indenture had expired, although he was under no obligation to do so. To men like Ewunga, Towa Ulta and Tupia Osiro, Leahy's three surviving New Guinean employees, the highland *bus kanakas* were foreigners, with different languages, appearance and culture. On the frontier the Warias depended as much upon Leahy as he upon them. This alone would have ensured their loyalty and obedience, which went far beyond their responsibility to him as indentured labourers at five shillings a month.

And what of the Korofeigu? Koritoia Upe for one remembers the fight clearly. He is a prominent man in his community, a director of two large coffee enterprises and part owner of two hundred head of cattle. He no longer lives in his original village where the fight with the Leahys took place. Soon afterwards his people were defeated in war and forced to flee to their present village, about 7 miles along the highway from Goroka.

Koritoia says the white men camped near the river and his people brought them food. A bush knife went missing. "The white men came calling out for the bush knife. We got angry with them, gathered together and tried to attack. But they killed three of our people with their guns. We didn't kill any of them. Their weapons were so much more powerful than ours. I felt inferior. I couldn't retaliate against them."

There was no further thought of attacking the Leahys after this convincing demonstration. Quite the reverse. A month later, a group of Korofeigu men arrived at Leahy's Bena Bena camp a few miles away bearing gifts of food. Leahy wrote in his diary: "Made peace with the Korofeigu."

Once the highlanders had seen firsthand what a gun could do to a man, there was no further thought of confronting the whites. That pattern emerged over and over again. The gunfire was devastating proof of the white man's physical and hence spiritual power and superiority, and so the battles, or rather short-lived skirmishes, were usually followed by a delegation bringing tribute of some sort as an indication of their desire to make peace.

• • •

As 1932 rolled into 1933 the two Leahy brothers kept up a furious pace, establishing their base camp above the Bena Bena River and escorting NGG's geologists around the country as they began the careful task of testing and surveying the potential dredging leases in the surrounding river flats. Under their agreement with the company, any proven, workable proposition would make them both extremely wealthy men, and Michael Leahy's diary during these months, crammed full with the myriad details of prospecting and testing on a large scale, reflects his excitement and optimism. The diary also yields evidence of his modus operandi when trouble flared. "Towa and Barunoma were attacked by Goropa nigs," he wrote on February 4, 1933. "Towa got an arrow in the shoulder—just a flesh wound, but will have to investigate it as the nigs may think we are windy if we leave it go."

LEFT: *Ewunga Goiba, Michael Leahy's* bosboi. *Taken near his home in the Asaro Valley in 1984.*   RIGHT: *Ewunga Goiba in 1932 or thereabouts. Standing with a group of highlanders, he holds an axe and billy can.*

Towa and Barunoma had set off that day to barter for food at Go-ropa, a village several miles from the Bena camp. In particular they wanted a pig. Towa Ulta says today he waited in the village entrance while Barunoma went in with some shells to bargain for a pig. There was an argument over the price, which ended with Barunoma slapping a villager across the face. Weapons were taken up and the two coastal men ran off, followed by a shower of arrows. "I heard the twang of the bow," says Towa, "but before I knew it the arrow had hit my right shoulder. I shifted the gun to my left shoulder and shot and killed the man. After that I ran off because of *masta's* orders about shooting. When we got back, we told Mick the story and he said, 'Jesus! I'll shoot the bastards!' The next day we all went to the area. The natives attacked us. We chased them and chopped up their spears, wrecked their houses, even killed a few of them, maybe twenty or more. Mick told us that was enough fighting. The natives were scared now."

Leahy's version, as recorded in his diary on February 5: "Went over to see what Kropar [Goropa] shot at the boys for and were met on every ridge approaching the village by the nigs all ready for a fight complete with shields and big bundles of extra arrows. Endeavoured to get heard, but they opened up first so our gang just went into action and ran them hell west and crooked . . ."

Today the Leahys' Bena Bena base camp, overlooking the green and beautiful river valley, is a sweet potato field. A dirt road leads out several miles to Goropa, winding through the grassy hillsides where the fighting took place. The old man Seriate agrees it began over a pig. There was a shortage at that time and the villagers did not want to sell any. Seriate says the two strangers began firing with their guns, but didn't hit anyone. The men drove off Towa and Barunoma. "The people chased them and shot one in the ear, because we thought he was only a spirit trying to steal pigs from our house."

Seriate says his people drew first blood in the larger fight the next day, putting an arrow into one of the strangers. "Our man who had fired the arrow let out a war cry to let us know he had hit one of them, but as he was shouting the strangers shot, killing seven of our people. I was a small boy then—one of the village men grabbed me by the hand and pulled me down, but he was too slow and the strangers shot him. He gave me his bow and arrows and I escaped, and hid under a water-fall. What chance did we have with our weapons against their guns?

"We didn't take cover. We thought they were spirits not real peo-

Assistant District Officer James Lindsay Taylor, who accompanied the Leahys into the Wahgi Valley in 1933. Here he is photographed with a group of young camp followers at the Mount Hagen base camp of the 1933 Wahgi Expedition at Kelua.

ple, so we weren't afraid of them. We stood there and they killed our men. Now we saw what power they had and feared them! They killed many of our men and we buried them, putting two or three in the one grave. They killed us but it was our fault. They were people and we thought them to be spirits. Two men gave them pigs, to try to stop them from killing more of our men. In return they gave us an axe and two bush knives."

Seriate's version is coldly verified in Michael Leahy's final diary entry on the matter: "Called the gang off and got some of the nigs to come over to us and explained what the shooting was for, and parted friends. They brought two pigs during the afternoon to cement the peace, as they had seen what the rifles were and were satisfied."

"We made peace," says Seriate, "and that was the end. After that we joined them and went as carriers."

The loss of life at Goropa—fifty years later it is impossible to establish the exact number of killed or wounded—made it a very serious affair. Given the laws that controlled the activities of prospectors in this new country, Leahy could well have been charged on several counts. He broke the Uncontrolled Areas Ordinance by allowing Towa Ulta and Barunoma to travel away from the camp unaccompanied by a European. And it was expressly forbidden under the Ordinance for a prospector or employee to enter a village. But much more serious was Leahy's decision to go to Goropa with an armed party the day after the incident. According to the Ordinance, killing in self-defence was excusable. But killing as a result of a violent encounter brought on by Leahy's decision to "investigate" the matter could hardly be seen as self-defence. Leahy, after all, was merely a private prospector, with no authority whatsoever to mount his own punitive expedition. So according to the letter of the law, he could have faced the serious charge of unlawful killing, in addition to his two breaches of the Uncontrolled Areas Ordinance.

But this was a frontier, and frontier justice prevailed. Leahy reported the incident to James Taylor, the patrol officer stationed at Kainantu, two days' walk from the Bena Bena, and Taylor took him at his word. "Leahy is not a man to shoot unnecessarily," he wrote to his superior at Salamaua, "and if prospectors are given free access to remote parts then the right to shoot when necessary must go with it."[3] The Administration could, and occasionally did, apply the regulations vigorously to get rid of prospectors it considered undesirable. But by this time Leahy was a well-known prospector/explorer in the highlands with the full support of the powerful New Guinea Goldfields Company. He was well regarded by his colleagues and it was assumed by Taylor that whatever Leahy did would have been justified.

The Leahy brothers could not always count on such support, which led occasionally to the exercise of a certain degree of discretion. As Dan Leahy says, "We didn't report some of the things. It would all depend on the fellow who was there. If he was a responsible type he'd say, 'Well, that was bound to happen.' A lot of those things were better left unsaid as far as the government fellow was concerned, because some of them thought they'd have to do something about it. And then, you know, inquiries here, and there and everywhere, and one thing leads to another.

"The only reason we killed people is that if we hadn't killed them they would have killed us and all our carriers. All we were doing was

Bena Bena man, 1932.

protecting ourselves. After you've been in it awhile you make up your mind what you'll do, and that's be a better man than they are, that's all. And quicker.''

The villagers of Goropa, like the Korofeigu before them, accepted the white man's superior weaponry and brought tribute to Michael Leahy's camp. Throughout this early contact period there was to be no extended fighting between highlander and European—just short, sharp encounters, almost inevitably resulting in highlander submission. A handful of white men—a miner, a couple of missionaries, a patrol offi-

cer—were killed in later years, but the retribution was swift and devastating.

There was never an army of occupation in the highlands. There was
no need for it. There was never the slightest chance that the people
would or could have formed alliances on the scale required to seriously
challenge or resist Australian occupation. Everything in their social and
political organisation militated against it. There were leaders—"big men,"
as they were called by the highlanders—of wealth and influence and
prowess in war, but within each tribal and clan grouping the intense
competition between these men ensured that no one managed to gain
overall power, let alone unite other tribes around him into a really significant military force. Nor did news travel rapidly throughout the highlands about the strangers and their fearsome weapons. In their extreme
isolation, each community had to come to terms separately with them.

Despite the killings and the fear they caused, the highlanders remained intensely curious about the Australians, and in particular the
things they had brought with them. They wanted these things. They
could not take them by force, and so they had to find another way. At
the same time, the Leahy brothers (and every European who went there)
wanted things from the highlanders. Food was only a small part of it.
So after the initial contact experience, it was the mutual desire of the
Leahys and the highlanders for what each other had to offer that shaped
their future relationship. For the Leahys that relationship did not develop with the people of the Bena Bena, Goroka and Asaro valleys; the
brothers were to spend only a few months there—from October 1932 to
March 1933. It developed with the people of Mount Hagen in the Wahgi
Valley, one hundred miles to the west, the scene of the next Australian
advance into the New Guinea highlands.

Leahy had correctly guessed the existence of the Wahgi Valley in
1930 during his expedition down the Purari River, when he came across
the big stream flowing into the Purari from the west, its banks littered
with human bones. On his return to the highlands in 1932 he had not
forgotten the river, and its hint of populated valleys farther west. By
the beginning of 1933 the brothers had thoroughly prospected the Eastern Highlands. Eighteen miles of dredging ground in the Bena Bena
Valley had been claimed and pegged on behalf of New Guinea Goldfields and was in the process of being tested. And it looked very promising, perhaps another Bulolo, where two dredges were now hard at

work tearing up the gravel. If there was another big valley farther west then here was the possibility of even more dredging country.

Having pegged out for itself the best potential dredging ground in the highlands so far, NGG was anxious to have first pickings in any new valleys as well. February 1933 saw the Leahy brothers and their Waria men, this time accompanied by NGG surveyor Charles Marshall, hurrying westward. Climbing out of the Asaro Valley they found themselves on a high plateau, and saw in the far distance what appeared to be the beginning of another great, fertile valley, stretching out beyond the horizon.

Excited at the prospect ahead, the Leahys hurried back to their base camp at Bena Bena. Here a small airstrip had been cleared to give NGG officials quick access to their inland operations. Michael Leahy flew out to NGG's headquarters at Wau to get company backing for an immediate and large-scale expedition into the new valley to forestall any competition, and suggested a reconnaissance flight first to see what the prospects might be. G. A. Harrison, general manager of NGG, readily agreed, caught up, like Michael Leahy, in the excitement of what lay ahead.

Chapter Five

==

THE
WAHGI

The fight leader Maasi Pinjinga remembers a fine clear day towards the end of the rainy season. It was in fact March 8, 1933. Maasi and his clan—living not far from Nongamp in the middle of the Wahgi Valley—were caught up in a major tribal war. Maasi, then a man about thirty, had crept with a war party behind enemy lines and was lying concealed in ambush, waiting for his enemies to appear. He recalls that in the middle of the morning (it was ten o'clock) he and his companions heard a low, steady drone.

"We were looking in the bushes," says Maasi, "to see where the noise was coming from, saying, 'Where is it?' Everyone was very excited."

Nopornga Mare, of Ambang near Nongamp, says, "Some people searched the ground while others just left everything and ran for their lives. I ran away with the other people."

Others remember thinking it was some kind of insect or animal making the noise, and searched through bushes or long grass before the enormous volume of the sound sent them running in terror. Most agree it never occurred to them to look up in the air. Maasi and Nopornga both say the first real clue came from watchmen stationed on high ground.

"We were still searching," says Maasi, "when someone called out from the mountain top that a big bird was flying overhead. We thought it some kind of sorcery sent by the enemy tribe. Our friends on the mountain called to us to withdraw our men from behind the enemy lines immediately. Some said it had a lot of plumes in the back and thought it was a huge bird of paradise."

Nopornga says he and his people rushed off to their houses. "We peeped out to see if this thing was going to come back. It did, and then it went off again. We went on with our fighting."

The "bird of paradise" was NGG's chartered Junkers aeroplane carrying Michael, Daniel and James Leahy and their financial backer, NGG's G. A. Harrison, all of them anxious to find out what the Wahgi Valley had to offer. The flight was organised and carried out in total secrecy. The Guinea Airways air charter company pilot, Ian Grabowski, had agreed not to disclose it even to his employers. Grabowski had flown into Bena Bena with a load of testing equipment, explaining later that his delay in returning to the coast was due to engine trouble. The Junkers had taken off from Bena Bena at 9:40 A.M. with enough fuel to remain airborne for about two hours. It carried emergency food supplies, trade goods, arms and ammunition. Michael Leahy sat in the open cockpit to guide the pilot, while the others travelled in the enclosed cabin, sitting on the bare floor.

The plane flew west along the Goroka Valley, climbed to twelve thousand feet to clear the surrounding mountain peaks, flew for twenty anxious minutes through dense cloud, and then dived down through a clear patch. Spread out ahead for a hundred miles between the high mountains was the green, sunlit immensity of the Wahgi. A big river fed by innumerable streams ran through its centre, and oblong houses in homestead groups of four or five dotted across a continuous patchwork of neat, square gardens. The Wahgi, enormous, fertile and heavily populated, greatest of New Guinea's highland valleys, had been "discovered."

For Maasi and Nopornga and the rest of the valley's inhabitants, the flashing object overhead was the vanguard of the twentieth century's belated invasion—a portent of the profound change in store for a culture that would know the aeroplane before it knew the wheel and would see age-old verities turn upside down.

But for the white men circling overhead it was not a time for sober contemplation of what lay in store for the people below. In later years the pilot Grabowski recalled a momentary stunned silence, and then a speculative yell from Michael Leahy: "Gold! gold!"* The three men in the rear cabin rushed from side to side, peering out through the windows. After travelling three-quarters of the way up the valley the plane turned back, its passengers convinced of the pressing need to get into the valley as soon as possible. And while the people of the mid-Wahgi around Nongamp resumed their warfare, the white men made preparations to invade them.

The Leahy brothers would be joined on this trip by the Kainantu patrol officer, James Taylor. In later years the notion would take hold that the administration initiated and planned the trip to make contact with the populations of the new valley and that the Leahys simply accompanied it. That's what Australia's diplomats subsequently reported to the League of Nations Mandates Commission—the watchdog committee exercising a toothless control over Australia's trusteeship. But the reverse was true. The expedition was a secret and frantic race, underwritten by New Guinea Goldfields, with the fixed objective of staking a claim to the Wahgi's gold deposits before anyone else did.

In fact, in January 1933, after five months at Kainantu trying to exercise control on the colonial frontier, Taylor was thoroughly opposed to its further expansion. There had been too many clashes between prospectors and highlanders, and Taylor, the sole government representative, felt powerless to do anything about them. Things were getting out of control. This was no way to extend the "pax australiana." Either back him up with more men and money, he wrote to his superiors, or consolidate the existing frontier by banning all private prospecting west of NGG's Bena Bena base camp. Call it a "super uncontrolled area."[1]

Neither of Taylor's recommendations was accepted. There were no more patrol officers to spare, and the driving ambition of the prospectors to continue pushing into new country could not be stemmed even if the Administration had wanted to, which by 1933 it did not. By then,

*The valley looked as geologically promising as Bulolo but immensely greater in area.

From left to right: Michael, Daniel and James Leahy with coastal employees. Late 1932 or early 1933, most probably on the Bena Bena airstrip. Jim Leahy did not accompany his two brothers on their expeditions but often came out on the light aeroplanes that kept them supplied. Jim says he was also his brother's "eyes and ears" back at Wau, the headquarters of mining exploration in New Guinea at the time.

there were powerful economic disincentives to such a policy. The Administration's primary responsibility under the Mandate was the welfare and the development of the indigenous people. But right from the start it was compromised. Australia still provided no revenue at all to New Guinea, and there was no chance of it doing so now, with the Depression at its height. That made the Administration dependent on white private enterprise—plantations and mining—for its revenue. And with copra prices at rock bottom, mining royalties assumed more and more importance, accounting for 20 percent of total government revenue by 1933. The Administration thus found itself disinclined to prevent New Guinea Goldfields rushing off into the Wahgi Valley before the area had been carefully and systematically opened up and "pacified," which was the recognised procedure.

James Taylor and Michael Leahy had come to New Guinea on the same boat in 1926. While Leahy went prospecting, Taylor spent seven years as an Administration officer in the more settled parts of New

Guinea. Here the racial rigidities and the humiliation of the colonial relationship were most pronounced. Taylor liked New Guineans and developed a concern for their welfare that raised a few eyebrows among Rabaul's white establishment. When he was sent to the frontier outpost of Kainantu, where prospectors were enforcing their own version of the pax Australiana by means of the gun, he was greeted with some suspicion. Taylor was new to the frontier, and when a miner in his district had his Uncontrolled Area Permit cancelled following the shooting of a highlander, Taylor was treated with downright distrust.

Dan Leahy remembers that the word went out to watch him. "He had a bad name, Jim Taylor," says Dan. "We were very skeptical of him." Dan vividly remembers his first brush with Taylor when he and his brother were passing through Kainantu on their way towards Bena Bena in October 1932. "There wasn't much in his tent," he says, "only a table. And on the table there was a book called *The Law of Evidence*." That was enough to make them cautious in their dealings with a new and reputedly conscientious patrol officer. "He was very strict," says Dan, "but when he got more experience then he could judge things more to our way of thinking."

Taylor evidently did harden his attitude towards the killing of high-landers, or at any rate resigned himself to the inevitability of it. Within a few months he was reminding his superiors that if prospectors were given the right to go into new country they had to be given the right to kill as well. The Leahys soon got to know and like Taylor, and Taylor in turn came to greatly admire Michael Leahy. "I was a novice at this time, so far as the highlands were concerned," he said in later years, "and Mick had great experience."

By early 1933, Taylor knew that whatever he might regard as prudent, the pace of westward expansion was unlikely to slacken. The pull of gold was too strong. In February he met Michael Leahy and heard, in strictest confidence, about the new valley and Leahy's planned expedition. He knew that it would almost certainly go ahead, and he wanted to be included. The romantic notion of exploration exerted a powerful pull on Taylor. He became excited at the prospect of entering unknown regions and so he too was caught up in the desire to travel west. "I wrote to the government," he said years afterwards, "and told them we were on the edge of a new sphere of discovery. We must do something, otherwise we will find that we have been left out." The Administration agreed to let Taylor go. Leahy and Taylor became joint leaders—Leahy representing Private Enterprise, Taylor the Administration.

Nopornga Mare of Ambang Village in the mid-Wahgi Valley, with clansmen and women. He remembers, with Maasi Pinjnga of Nongamp, when the first aeroplane flew out over the Wahgi in early 1933.

On March 26, a fortnight after the first flight, another Junkers roared out over the Wahgi Valley, again spreading terror among the inhabitants. On board this time were the European members of the forthcoming expedition—Taylor, Michael and Dan Leahy, and NGG's young surveyor, Ken Spinks. This time they flew right up the valley, looking for suitable areas of flat ground at points along the proposed line of march that could easily be hand graded into rough and ready landing strips for the light aeroplanes which would keep the party resupplied.

Describing the flight in later years, Taylor likened it to flying over the Elysian Fields. "I was elated. It was one of the most exciting times of our lives." Leahy on the other hand, speculated in his diary that night: "There must be fifty miles of dredging ground if there is any gold there." Fifty miles could mean a dozen dredges. Under his agreement with NGG, Leahy was to be paid ten thousand pounds for every dredge committed to the highlands, plus 2½ percent of the eventual profits. In 1933 that represented an enormous fortune.

Exactly one year earlier, in March 1932, Leahy had been among the crowd of Australians on hand to celebrate the opening of dredge number one at Bulolo. The Australians were proud of this achievement, and several short films and newsreels were made of the event. In one, hundreds of whites are shown gathering to watch as the dredge clanks into action after a champagne bottle smashes against its side. The dredge buckets begin scooping up the gold-bearing gravel, and eventually bricks of gold from the smelter are stamped and loaded onto the shoulders of a New Guinean labourer. He takes them out to a waiting plane and hands them to the smiling Australian pilot, who packs them into his cockpit. The pilot waves goodbye and with swelling music the plane takes off, leaving the black man standing empty handed on the airstrip. He too waves goodbye. The plane disappears into the clouds, flying its precious load to distant destinations.

The image is an apt metaphor of prewar Australian colonialism in New Guinea. The smiling man was an indentured labourer, recruited from his distant village, delivered to his white employer for ten pounds, and paid ten shillings a month (enough to support him but not his village family). Under the labour laws he was bound to his employer for three years and was jailed if he absconded. He also could be jailed for refusing to work, or "causing disaffection among his workmates." He was not allowed to drink alcohol, play cards or gamble.

After two or three years in the mines or plantations he went back home with little to show for his efforts. His work was to fetch and carry. He learnt no skills. The apprenticeship training scheme of the Bulolo Gold Dredging Company was not even open to New Guineans until 1958, by which time the gold had gone, the dredges were rusting relics, and the company had diversified to timber milling. When BGD's arch rival New Guinea Goldfields tried to train New Guineans as drivers and machine operators in the early 1930s, opposition from white workers forced the abandonment of the project. In 1929, seven young men from Rabaul were chosen to go to Australia for higher education. They were to become teachers in new government schools. The white Citizens Association protested, flexed its political muscles, and the Administration dropped the plan.

The Australians did not want a skilled or educated work force. Education might produce troublemakers. They wanted manageable, cheap labour. So apart from the basic religious-oriented instruction offered by missionaries, there was no education. With a million people to "civilise," the Administration in the 1930s spent about six thousand pounds annually on education—equivalent to four days' takings from one Bulolo Valley dredge. Ninety-five percent of the gold went straight out of the country. The miners paid 5 percent royalty amounting to about ninety thousand pounds annually by the mid-1930s, but most of this money actually went back into the administration and infrastructure of the mining industry. The biggest "native" budget item was health care, with the emphasis on keeping the labour force healthy.

And so when the people living along the Bena Bena River watched NGG's drilling rigs gouging test holes in the gravel banks in March 1933, the financial stakes were enormous. If Michael Leahy was to be paid ten thousand pounds a dredge, the possible returns to the company could only be guessed at. And the potential consequences to the highlanders were equally enormous. The Bulolo Valley had been lightly populated—only a few thousand people lived there before mining operations began. But the Bena Bena was densely populated, and so was the Wahgi. If there was gold there, then almost overnight there would be massive machines, churning up the fertile river flats to a depth of one hundred feet, destroying all the top soil, leaving behind a morass of boulders and gravel unfit for human habitation.

James Taylor says that on the eve of his departure into the Wahgi Valley he had some misgivings about what they were about to do. He and others within the Administration, a minority, looked on the Australian presence in New Guinea as something of a mixed blessing for the people, weighing the material benefits of colonial occupation against the all-too-obvious psychological trauma and the cultural loss. Taylor and others were actually worried that the entire population might literally be dying out as a consequence of the diseases introduced by the Europeans, to which the people had little immunity. It was happening in other parts of parts of the Pacific. And in occupied New Guinea, Taylor says the population did seem to be declining.

But the highland people contacted so far were largely free of disease. And now there was the Wahgi. To Taylor there was something pristine about this enormous, hidden valley, walled off on all sides by great mountains. In the Depression year of 1933, there was reason enough to ponder the wisdom of ending the Wahgi's long isolation. Taylor did ponder, but it was like trying to prevent the tide from coming in. "If we'd had the power," the old man says today, "we'd have created it as one huge province, not to be entered by anybody, including ourselves. But Chinnery* said you'd need the whole British Army on active duty to prevent people getting in. And that is just what would have happened. As soon as you made the place forbidden, then everyone would want to come in."

*Taylor's ultimate superior, the Director of Administrative Services, who was also a trained anthropologist.

So Taylor bowed to the inevitable. Or rather he embraced the inevitable, his misgivings swept aside in the euphoria of discovery. These were heady days for all the Australians who had energy, ability, ambition and confidence. Exploration was not dead; still in the twentieth century there were veils to be lifted from hidden parts of the globe, and they would be doing the lifting. For the Leahys, the lure of El Dorado, and for Taylor, when it came to the crunch, the benefits of western civilisation, more than outweighed the disadvantages. "I had decided in my mind," he says today, "that ours was a noble task, and that it was our duty to bring the pax Australiana to these people."

Taylor was a humane and sensitive man, a colonial civil servant in the classic British mould, imbued with the imperial tradition of the white man's burden. Actually his inspirations went back even further than Kipling. Taylor once explained his marriage in the 1950s to his wife Yerema, a highlander, in terms of Alexander's dictum to his generals: marry among the people you have conquered.

He was full of contradictions, trying to safeguard the interests of the people while at the same time genuinely believing in the benefit of the colonial advance. He was a romantic imperialist, who could talk forebodingly of Australians as "dark shadows over the Pacific" and yet condone and defend the shooting of people in their own country by prospecting representatives of foreign-owned companies. He could recognise that "we might upset the people in many ways," and yet enthusiastically accompany an enterprise that would measure its success in terms of the number of dredges it could put into the Wahgi and the amount of gold it could profitably take out.

For James Taylor, as for everyone else connected with this enterprise, there was also the driving, dominating personality of Michael Leahy. "He was more than just a prospector," says Taylor. "He had a touch of genius about him, no doubt of it." In 1933, Michael Leahy was in his prime. Thirty-three years old, he was just under six feet tall, with not an ounce of fat on him. Those who knew him then recall his deep, resonant voice, his air of authority and confidence. Men and women, it is said, were straight away drawn to him. He was widely respected. Although capable of great charm, he was a blunt, open man, who said exactly what he thought and hated cant or pretentiousness. He had a fierce temper and a contempt for the establishment. From his diary entries at this time comes the impression of restless energy, sureness of purpose, and a tremendous, suppressed excitement.

Theoretically, this rough-hewn prospector was in the employ of New

James Taylor, 1984.

Michael Leahy carrying his Mauser and his Leica, 1934.

Guinea Goldfields, acting under instructions from Harrison and his team of professional geologists and surveyors. But Leahy made his own rules. In February 1933, irritated by a senior NGG surveyor who he thought had exaggerated ideas of his own importance, Leahy wrote in his diary: "Got away 7 A.M. Charlie objected to us not waiting for him to start kai [breakfast] but was given to understand he is not near as important a person as he imagines he is." Four days later, back at the Bena Bena camp: "Very pleased to see the last of Charles, who is a bloody upstart and has no more idea of running a bush camp as he has of geology." On the eve of their departure for the Wahgi, Leahy made it clear to NGG officials that he did not want the offending surveyor, Charles Marshall, to be part of his team. Marshall did not accompany them.

The company treated its experienced prospector with elaborate deference. After all, he was the key man in the field, and his ten thousand pounds per dredge was a measure of his value. NGG's General Manager Harrison, based at Wau, sent frequent messages to Leahy at Bena Bena. In January 1933, while Leahy was secretly planning his reconnaissance to the west and other NGG personnel were hurrying to complete the pegging of the company's Bena Bena dredging leases before any rivals came on the scene, Harrison wrote soothingly to the man who was carrying all his hopes:

> I think you know me well enough to be sure I won't let you down. . . .
> Just keep me advised as to what you want or would like me to do. . . .
> Look out for the sharks and jackals who will try to benefit by your work
> and initiative. Take my advice and don't be too ready to help any of them.
> You need to keep an eye on [the prospector] Moen particularly. He is up
> for an Adelaide crowd . . . and is now in the Ramu. He told me he would
> probably have a look out your way. Damned impertinence I call it. You've
> got to beat him to it. . . . He's bound to like the look of those [Bena Bena]
> flats and they're nice and handy to your drome. . . . Watch Moen! . . . If
> those river flats are secured before our competitors get them and they prove
> to be paying ground you won't need to do any more prospecting. I'll look
> after your interests, never you fear . . .[2]

During the final days of March 1933 the pilot Grabowski flew into Bena Bena the extra supplies needed for the expedition, which was expected to last six months. Apart from trade goods, prospecting and surveying equipment and cameras (including Leahy's 35-mm Leica and his 16-mm movie camera), the expedition would travel light and rely on buying food along the way along with aerial resupply. Landing grounds would be cleared at the sites already chosen on the reconnaissance flight, and on certain designated days the pilot would fly out over the valley, landing only when he sighted the correct pattern of prearranged smoke signals. Plans were made to clear two airstrips—the first in the middle of the valley, the second at its western extremity—in the vicinity of a large mountain already named by the Germans (who could see it from the coast) as Mount Hagen.

Grabowski had again agreed not to reveal his activities to anyone, and the flights, along with the expedition itself, would be made in complete secrecy. With other prospectors already beginning to suspect from the aerial comings and goings that something new was afoot, Leahy's actions were marked by a sense of urgency. New Guinea Goldfields was determined to get into the valley before anyone else, and there were definitely others in the field against them. Two days before the departure, NGG's young surveyor Ken Spinks, who had Leahy's confidence and would accompany him into the Wahgi, was reporting by letter to his boss Harrison "disconcerting news about the movement of others."[3] It seems that at least two well-equipped parties had left the coast and were heading inland, and, in view of this, reported Spinks, "Mick Leahy proposes to push on as quickly as possible and cover the greatest possible area." It was going to be a race. There was even a plan to have the pilot Grabowski fly out and drop them messages "informing us" wrote Spinks, "of the movements of the 'enemy' to our rear."

At first light on the morning of March 28, 1933 the expedition marched off in single file from the Bena Bena base camp, heading out over the rolling, grass-covered hills to the west. Michael Leahy mounted his 16-mm camera on its tripod and filmed the departure. At the head walks Taylor in his characteristic "Bombay Bloomer" shorts, rifle slung over his shoulder. Following him comes the long line of ninety carriers— Taylor employed sixty, Leahy thirty—while Dan Leahy and Ken Spinks bring up the rear. Spaced at intervals along the line are Taylor's armed

First contact, probably in the vicinity of the Mariefuteger River. Dan Leahy recalls that the people in the Mariefuteger/Chuave region were highly emotional in their greeting, and these photos bear him out.

First contact, April 1933. Taken during the Wahgi expedition's progress through the densely populated Chimbu, where great crowds gathered in a highly emotional state to greet the strangers. Often, as here, the first response was terror; this man moves away as Taylor attempts to greet him. In the background is one of the numerous streams that took up the prospecting attention of Michael Leahy. He was content to leave the business of contact largely up to Taylor.

police in peaked caps and red *lap laps*, and Leahy's armed Warias—among them Ewunga Goiba, Towa Ulta, and Tupia Osiro—each of whom had responsibility for a section of carriers. Some of Leahy's men had married Bena Bena women who also accompanied the expedition. Filming over, Leahy gave his movie camera to a porter and joined Taylor at the head of the column.

Four days later they had passed the westernmost point reached by the Leahy brothers and Charles Marshall on their previous sortie, and were walking through the region known as the Chimbu, making first contact with its dense populations. The diaries of Michael Leahy and James Taylor refer to the extraordinarily emotional response of the Chimbu people, and Dan Leahy backs this up. "Sometimes there were thousands of people following us, yelling and shouting and screaming and singing out. They'd bring up pieces of sweet potato leaves for us to touch, and then wrap them up and put them away in their little bags—or if you spat, there'd be a rush to get it. There'd be hundreds of them following you, and you'd suddenly feel hairs being pulled from the back of your legs and you'd look round and someone would be wrapping them up in a banana leaf. If you took a hair out of your head there'd be a stampede to get it. Sometimes they'd pinch a hair out of the dog's back, or its tail. That would be valuable to them. You could buy things with it if you wanted."

"They regarded us," says Taylor, greatly moved by the pathos of it all, "as people who had been killed in war. At Sina Sina they blocked the road—they put a log across. I said, 'We must go on.' And they said, 'No! You must stay here!' "

Further to the west Taylor remembers that "two children recognised me as their dead father, recently killed. Each took me by the hand and brought their uncles to look into my eyes. And the uncles said, 'Yes! Here is your land, here are your wives and children, here are your pigs and dogs, here is everything! Now all we ask is that you stay.' "

Taylor was making contact with the people, leaving Leahy to concentrate on the prospecting, and the stories told by the Chimbu people

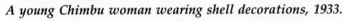

A young Chimbu woman wearing shell decorations, 1933.

today emphasise the arrival of a tall fair man, which Taylor was. To the people of Oknel Village, he was Bare, an important man who had died. "We heard that Bare was coming our way," says Kimba Kopol. "As the white men arrived the old man who was the father of Bare slaughtered all his pigs. We took the meat to the white man and put it in front of him. Everyone was crying. The old man went to the white man and said, 'Bare! You have come back. We are very happy.' We were all standing around crying and waiting to see what would happen. The white man patted the old man on the head and spoke to him, so all of us were then sure that Bare had returned."

Unlike the broad valleys the expedition had left behind, the Chimbu is rugged limestone country—a jumble of ridges and steep gulleys, flanked by sheer limestone walls. It was densely populated. On April 3 they crossed the Chimbu River and camped just above it, about a mile

Chimbu people, some of them wearing "dollar bird" head decorations, react with stunned amazement as the expedition passes through their territory. Note the frightened woman on the right, clutching the arm of the man beside her, while behind her a younger girl holds on to the **bilum** *(bag) she wears on her head; on the left a young boy peers from behind his elders.*

One of a series of five photographs taken by Michael Leahy in the Chimbu during the 1933 Wahgi expedition. The man holding the staff and wearing the embarrassed grin is Michael Leahy's employee Porte. The crying women are convinced Porte is their relative returned from the dead. They clutch onto him in tearful elation and try to prevent him from leaving.

from the present-day town of Kundiawa. To Ulka Wena, who saw them that day, Taylor was the big man Konia Taglba come home from the place of the dead. In life Konia had been tall, solid and pale skinned. At Kerowagi a day later the woman Aglem Ter says her clanspeople thought Taylor was the deceased Kaglnogl, although some doubted it—Kaglnogl's hair was curly, not straight; his eyes dark, not blue; and his nose big and flat, not straight and sharp. But his relatives had convinced themselves, says Aglem, and cried all night.

It was about this time that Michael Leahy took a remarkable series of photographs. "We came to a village," says Dan, "and all the people were standing around, looking at us in amazement. All of a sudden a woman cried out and rushed in, grabbing hold of one of our armed boys [Porte]. Apparently he had a very strong resemblance to one of

Chauve people in the Chimbu, 1933. Taken as they crowd around the camp perimeter.

her sons, killed in a recent war. We couldn't speak to the people, of course, but it was obvious: he was her son; she was the mother. She was weeping and holding him, and then all the relatives came up and did the same, in their turn. It was hard getting away from that village. We tried to make signs saying we'd come back, but in the end we went off, leaving the woman weeping and wailing. They tried to follow us but of course they couldn't go very far. Before long it was enemy country and they had to turn back."

This unknown mother was left, then, in sorrow and confusion, mourning the second passing of her son. Meanwhile, Michael Leahy was soon noting in his diary: "Got the first gold—a couple of very fine colours out of the top layer of wash. . . . It looks good for the country further on."

The following day they left the gorge country of the Chimbu and were moving through the rich, cultivated terraces of the Wahgi Valley. Instead of the houses being concentrated in villages, they were dotted in small groups or hamlets that seemed to form one continuous settlement as far as the eye could see. Each group of houses had its own vegetable gardens and bamboo and casuarina groves, and was decorated with ornamental flowers and shrubs. The people were of a different physical type; they were taller than the eastern highlanders, broad shouldered and muscular. The men were all bearded, impressing the Australians with their ornate stone axes, massive pronged spears and heavy bark belts. As always the expedition's arrival was greeted with amazement, but the Australians noted that the Wahgi people seemed more reserved than the Chimbu.

Near the middle of the valley Leahy took another series of remarkable photographs. The first shows Taylor in the close foreground, and a group of highland men with spears can be seen in the distance.

After initially waving a greeting to the spearmen fifty yards away, Taylor began walking towards them. It was a tense, uncertain moment. He was making contact with Maasi Pinjinga's people of the middle Wahgi, whom Maasi says initially mistook the white men for their enemies. As Taylor approached, Michael Leahy put down his camera and took up his gun, to cover Taylor in case of trouble. There was none: "I went forward," recalls Taylor, "stopped and put my arms out, and made the sounds of an aircraft, and then pointed to the sky. And the leading people said, in their own language of course but I could tell what they meant, 'We know you! We saw you go over the top!' I went and shook hands with the front group, about four or five of them." Back went the camera to Leahy's gimlet eye. The representatives of one culture make first contact with the representatives of another. One of the policemen points skywards, driving home their association with the *balus* (pidgin for bird, or aeroplane) of a fortnight before. The meeting was frozen in time by Michael Leahy's camera.

A few decades earlier, when photography was still a primitive, slow and laborious business of wooden boxes on heavy tripods and glass plates that had to be replaced after each exposure, it would have been impossible for Leahy to capture these events. But by the time he went to New Guinea he could buy a lightweight, reliable German camera and load it with rolls of fast, reliable Kodak film. By 1933, Leahy's camera was as familiar a part of his daily equipment as his gun. Photographs invariably show the Leica strung around his neck and the Mauser slung over his shoulder. In any situation he simply lifted the Leica to his eye, sighted the shot, pressed the button, wound the roll and squeezed off another shot.

Just as the modern camera enabled him to take these photographs, the modern gun allowed him the freedom to do so, a freedom not available to his nineteenth-century counterparts. During the mid-1800s, for example, an occupational hazard of the Australian sandalwood traders working among the Pacific islands was to be overrun by Melanesians armed with no more than clubs and bows and arrows. The whites died

First contact in the mid-Wahgi, April 1933. The first photograph shows Taylor striding forward, just about to remove his hat to give the waiting people a clearer view of his face. In the next Taylor has opened his arms to denote peace, but he is also mimicking the noise and appearance of an aeroplane—for these people the first portent of the coming invasion. The people are very frightened, and at this point Michael Leahy shouldered his Leica and covered Taylor with his rifle. No trouble ensued as the two sides drew near, so Leahy began photographing again. Taylor is walking up and down mimicking the plane, while a policeman points to the sky to denote the passage of the plane a few weeks before. In the final photograph the Wahgi men delightedly shake hands—a highland custom prior to contact.

because their muzzle-loaded pistols and muskets fired single shots and took half a minute to reload.

In the 1930s, Michael Leahy could put his Leica to his eye in all sorts of contact situations, some of them potentially dangerous to him and his companions, because he felt safe to do so. His gun was a superlative killing instrument, and he was an accurate shot. His diary reveals the care he gave to the choice and maintenance of his weaponry. He discusses with himself the type of gun best suited for creating the maximum impression. He prided himself in having the best, whether it be walking boots from America, lightweight tents from Italy, a Mauser rifle from Germany or a Leica camera.

When he first entered the highlands in 1930 he took a camera with him but rarely used it. On that expedition he was essentially a prospector, absorbed in the business of prospecting and then of survival. By 1933, walking into the Wahgi Valley with James Taylor, he obviously saw himself as an explorer as well, and the hobby of photography had become an abiding interest, spurred on by the recognition that here was an unparalleled opportunity to document on film a unique event.

Leahy had earlier worked away on his American correspondence courses in photography and journalism, and by 1933 his desire to improve in these areas was showing obvious results. "The camera was never off his shoulder," says Dan Leahy, a professional approach no doubt responsible for the multitude of photographs of sudden, dramatic events, snapped off in quick succession.

In his later years, Michael Leahy would come to regard this massive collection—more than five thousand 35-mm photographs along with several hours of 16-mm film—as the major record of his own accomplishment. But the photographs are a major accomplishment in their own right. For a man with no professional background in photography just the sheer volume of his work is extraordinary. He was not hesitant to shoot a complete roll of film on one quickly unfolding event. He had a natural eye for composition and an appreciation of the value of spontaneity. Of course his work was made easier, indeed possible, by his subjects' ignorance of the camera.

As a photographer he was most at home in first contact situations. On his many expeditions into new country before and after 1933 he thought it necessary to record anthropological information—his tiny handwritten notes on the contact sheets list in great detail aspects of highland dress, decoration, weaponry and so on. But fortunately his interest in all this was an afterthought. At the moment of photography, he was primarily concerned with capturing the expressions, movements and emotions of highlanders responding to him for the first time.

When not on the march his photographs depict he was also interested in the practical aspects of people's lives—methods of gardening, drainage, the construction of houses, the manufacture of weapons, burial customs and so on. But surprisingly, given the amount of time he would spend among highland people, neither his diary nor photographs show evidence of a curiosity to delve more deeply into their complex social and cultural life. Certainly Leahy photographed spectacular ceremonies, dances and feasts, but there is no sense that he sought to find out what was really going on. And with few exceptions there are no intimate portraits of family life, of the relationships between individuals, or between himself and the highland people amongst whom he would eventually settle. Even those he came to know well are mostly relegated to anonymity in his captions. The language barrier was a formidable one, of course, but more so was the assumption of cultural superiority which in those days shut off so many Europeans from the alien peoples they moved among. There was no interest in attempting to understand a culture that was regarded at best as valueless, and at worst as utterly barbaric. Only the missionaries, by and large, whose task it was to capture the minds and souls of the people, saw the need to become fluent in their languages and conversant with their cultures.

Michael Leahy captured brilliantly the drama, the fear, the elation of first contact, of the highland people responding to *him*. But his photographs and diary show that he lacked the interest to delve deeper than the surface aspects of the highland mind and culture. And that fact, in later life, would have sad consequences for this brave, able and enterprising man.

A week later, the expedition was nearing the head of the Wahgi Valley, where Leahy and Taylor intended establishing their base camp. They had been resupplied with trade goods at an airstrip hurriedly cleared in the middle of the valley, and planned to repeat this procedure at their final destination, Mount Hagen. April 16 saw them travelling through marshy country on the northern side of the Wahgi River near the head of the valley. Leahy had found good traces of gold in the river gravel around Nongamp in the mid Wahgi, but nothing much since then. Heavy rain had caused low-level flooding, obscuring the paths, and Leahy and Taylor were relying on local people to show them the way. It is likely that this was the day they met Yamka Maepkang Miti of Kelua.

Miti told his story at his clan's settlement near Kelua, where Leahy and Taylor would establish their base camp in April 1933, in a windowless hut crowded with men, their faces barely visible in the slight glow of the fire smouldering in the center. Miti explained that at the time he had travelled several miles to the east to attend a funeral. It was here he heard the news. "A Roklaka man yelled out, 'The sun always rises! The river always flows in its banks! And the rocks have always been there! But the makers of all these things are coming up now. Perhaps they are spirits, perhaps they will eat us all, but I'm bringing them.'

"I was an arrogant young man then, I was fierce, like a dog. I ran to look. Mick and Jim were in front. Dan and another man were behind, and there were a lot of people in between. They came towards me. Kiap Taylor came close as though he knew me. I said it was my grandfather. I ran towards him and grabbed his knees. I said, 'Oh! It's you!' And he knew me. It was enough to communicate with our eyes. Who knew their language? We just made signs.

"I heard this white man's word—'papa'—for the first time. Then he gave me a piece of red *lap lap* and put it on my neck, and we sat side-by-side together. The people said, 'This man Miti, why is he going with them? He's going to be eaten!' My elder brother started moaning, shaking his hands in despair, tearing at his beard. But some others said, 'Wait a minute. Let's see what happens before you get too upset.'

"There was a bird that flew from the direction of the river. I thought the thing they carried was nothing, but there was smoke, and the bird went to pieces. The people were really frightened, and scattered in all directions. They disappeared like wild pigs. Taylor wanted me to go with him, but the direction was through my enemies' territory."

At this point Miti left the expedition for a time. Another man, Ndika Komp Nikints, takes up the narrative. Nikints heard in the late afternoon that "spirits" were at Baklaka. "Early next morning," he says, "when the birds first made their noise, I left home. I saw my uncles. They were bringing food and were exclaiming about these strange spirits that ate so much. They had set up tents and we stayed to watch. They told us not to bring our spears near their place. So we left them stuck in the ground a little way from the area. I sat watching Kiap Taylor. I saw him wipe his face with his hand. He came closer towards me. He made signs to go to him and I thought, 'Is he making signs at me, or someone else?' And I looked around me. Kiap Taylor kept pointing at me, and seemed to be saying, 'You come!' The people around said, 'He's looking at you and telling you to go.' I got up and stood behind some other people, to get away from him.

"Kiap Taylor still came after me, pointing. So eventually I went with him inside the fenced area. You see I was a young man then and very curious about this new thing. Kiap Taylor gestured towards me. 'Where do you live?' he seemed to be saying, pointing in various directions. I pointed to Kelua way. He gestured that he was going that way too, and that we would go together. The policeman packed up all of their things and we went. Up the road a bit as we were walking a great crowd of people swarmed around us. I was walking first, showing the

Yamka Maepkang Miti of Kelua (center, wearing a white T-shirt) who guided the expedition the last few miles to Kelua (Mount Hagen); April 16–18, 1933. Shown here in 1983 discussing with another man the arrival of the Australians fifty years earlier. The onlookers are clanspeople and family, members of Miti's Yamka tribe.

road, Taylor was behind me with the dog, and the others followed."

Here Yamka Miti rejoined the procession, and was also a witness to the events about to happen. On this day, Tuesday April 18, Taylor records in his diary that a large number of people had gathered and were following the expedition as it marched with local guides over open grasslands. "There was much calling out," wrote Taylor, "and after about a mile I halted the line, and went to the rear, and endeavoured to quiet the natives and persuade them to discard their weapons. They refused to put down their arms and made a further hostile demonstration."

Yamka Miti remembers that "all these people were ready to have a fight with the strangers. The people were powerful—so many spears and shields! But I thought to myself, 'I've seen them kill two birds. I wonder how you'll go against them.' "

Ndika Nikints, who unlike Miti had not seen the guns fire, continues, "The Yamka and the Kuklika and all the people around us were making a lot of noise, shouting and calling out war cries. They were saying that they wanted to take everything from the white men. Some people snatched things from the carriers, like tins and trade goods. Then Kiap Taylor broke this thing he was carrying and before we knew anything we heard it crack. Everything happened at once. Everyone was pissing and shitting themselves in terror. Mother! Father! I was horrified. I wanted to run away but a carrier held me firmly by the shoulder. the muskets got the people—their stomachs came out, their heads came off. Three men were killed and one was wounded. The dead ones were a Yamka Manamp man, a Kawelka Goimpa, and one Ndika Klimbil. I said, 'Oh, mother!' but that didn't help. I breathed deeply, but that didn't help. I was really desperate. Why did I come here? I should never have come. We thought it was lightning that was eating people up. Was this strange thing something that had come down from the sky to eat us up? What's happening? What's happening?''

Taylor noted in his diary that he had fired several shots over the heads of the crowd, "who then retired, causing no further trouble." Taylor concedes today he did not always record shootings that took place, and this seems to be such an incident. He had come to share Dan Leahy's attitude that such killings were unavoidable and that as the outside world would find these incidents difficult to understand it was best in certain circumstances not to mention them.

Leahy's diary entry that day is concerned with prospecting, and he makes no mention of the shootings. However, when travelling through the same area a few months later he noted: "Passed a couple of tankets [shrubs] planted where a couple had fallen when they got too hostile before."

While the Australians might have downplayed the shootings, they greatly affected the way the newcomers were received by the Yamka and Ndika people among whom they were about to settle. Nikints and Miti, fearing for their lives, led the party the few remaining miles to Kelua, which Leahy and Taylor immediately recognised as an eminently suitable place for an airstrip. Here they set up their base camp and began preparing for the arrival of the aeroplane in ten days' time.

"This area had been burnt before," says Nikints, "and now the ku-nai grass was growing and you could see for miles around. Kiap Taylor said—we'll sleep here. He gestured with his hands and face to show sleeping. The carriers were told to put their things down. The people who had witnessed the killings before had already got here with the news. They told everyone that these spirits had been eating [killing] people along the way and were now coming. People were calling out to each other, 'Don't anyone go close! Go and hide in the bushes. A lot of people have been eaten. Go and hide in the bushes!' This message was passed from one tribe to the next. They yelled out, 'This white spirit is eating all the people, and is coming your way!' ''

Chapter Six

MEN OF ALL
THINGS

Like most highlanders, the people of Mount Hagen took the white men and their carriers to be spirits. But there were no weeping reunions between the living and the returning dead. Yamka Miti's reference to Taylor being his dead grandfather is exceptional, and the family association did not survive the shootings. Today Hageners rarely talk of welcoming back dead relatives, because for most the first news of the strangers was the chilling call that wild spirits were coming, killing people as they went. This spread fear throughout the area because wild spirits were generally thought to cause harm. As the people awaited the arrival of the spirits they cast about, as always, for some explanation.

Nengka Amp Dau* says she heard news that wild spirits were heading to the west of Mount Hagen towards Bul Mountain, home of the wild spirit Aundikla Mugl Timbil. Perhaps these strangers were his relatives, come to join him. But this was very disturbing, because Aun-

*Amp (woman) Dau, from the Nengka tribe.

dikla was a fearsome creature—a giant standing taller than the forest trees, his front like a human, his back covered in a mass of growth like a rain forest. Aundikla was evilly disposed towards humans and would kill them if given the chance. "Our ancestral spirits were friendly, not wild," says Dau, "but this Aundikla, he was the bush spirit. Sometimes he'd shock people by showing himself. We thought the white people were wild spirits at first, come to visit Aundikla on the mountain. They had killed two men and some people said they were spirits coming to eat us. We were shocked. Some ran away. But others were curious and stayed to look."

Ndika Mukuka Wingti's* people at Moika, five miles from Kelua, were not reassured when they thought of some of their legends, which told of giant white beings with fangs who could crack open trees with loud explosions and who hunted men. "We raved about them until daybreak," says Ndika Wingti. "We thought the world ended where the clouds in the sky met the earth, and that they came from somewhere in that direction. But if they were wild spirits, why didn't they eat us all? Why weren't we dead?"

Dan Leahy says there were very few people about when they arrived at Kelua. Men like Nikints, who had attached himself to them, were told to call out for food, but the people were simply too frightened to come close. As the day wore on one or two intrepid souls made tentative approaches, but the impact of the shootings had obviously been shattering. People now recall that there was much speculation. Why was it, if these were wild spirits, that more humans had not been killed? Were the black men ancestral spirits accompanying the wild ones?

On the second day people began to arrive in great numbers. Michael Leahy set up his movie camera and the scenes he took in those early days at Kelua must be considered among the most remarkable visual records of first contact ever taken. "They were all in one long line," says Dan Leahy, and the movie footage bears him out. Moving slowly towards the camera, about eight abreast, is a huge throng of people—men, women and children. The line stretches back for hundreds of yards. As they pass, the camera records the shock on their faces. There is fear, but there is also overwhelming curiosity. The men come with bundles of sugarcane, like tribute bearers in a Roman parade. The women carry net bags of sweet potato. There are no weapons to be seen.

*Wingti, from the Mukuka clan of the Ndika tribe.

Terror kept the Hagen people away at first from the expedition camp at Kelua. And then a great crowd arrived in a long line, bearing gifts of sugarcane and vegetables. Michael Leahy set up his 16-mm motion picture camera, and these scenes are enlarged frames of that footage. These are probably Yamka and Ndika, clanspeople of Yamka Miti and Ndika Nikints.

Dan Leahy remembers that the people were on edge, and this was not simply their response to the newcomers. They were ill at ease with each other. Curiosity had attracted people who would not or could not normally visit this area. The expedition had settled in an area of extraordinary political complexity, like everywhere else in the highlands. Although only two languages are spoken among the majority of the Hagen people—Melpa and Temboka—there are many different tribes, each with its own clans and subclans. Relationships between all these separate groups were in a continual state of flux. Two tribes might be allies, but different clans within each might be enemies. Neither, for that matter, did all the clans in one tribe get on with each other. Warfare could break out between clans or subclans within any one tribe. And none of these friendships or enmities were fixed. Former allies could become enemies and vice versa, and for all sorts of reasons—assassinations, allegations of sorcery, disputes over land, an unpaid debt, insufficient bridewealth (dowry) contributions, lack of proper respect for the dead at a funeral, the theft of pigs. All this was further complicated by extensive intermarriage between the tribes and clans, whether enemies or not. Between the groups then, were networks of individual relationships, each governed by separate obligations and privileges that transcended traditional friendships and hostilities. Certain family members of these marriages could have access to areas normally off limits to their respective clans.

In effect, the movements of every man, woman and child in this heavily populated region were severely restricted. And then came the Australians. They had camped in the territory of the Yamka, not far from the boundary with their neighbours, the Ndika. The majority of clans in each of these two tribes could be said to be allies; they generally enjoyed friendly relations with each other. Among the largest of the Mount Hagen tribes was the Mokei. There were numerous Mokei clans, some of them friendly with the Yamka and Ndika, some not. All these factors had a bearing on who could visit the strangers at Kelua in April 1933 and what kind of experience they would have.

Some had free access. Some had limited access and would be very much on their guard. Some had no access at all. And access determined what sort of information the people could pick up about the strangers. Those unfriendly with the Yamka found it difficult or impossible to get to Kelua, and to make matters worse the information coming to them was often distorted. It had passed through too many mouths or, more likely, was deliberately distorted by enemies keen to capitalise on their privileged situation.

While the Australians remained at Kelua, the Yamka and their allies had freest access to them. They passed on the knowledge they gained to allies and clanspeople living in more distant parts. When these came to visit they were better prepared for what they were going to see. They could ask questions of men like Miti and Nikints, and the white men

Ndika Opramb Rumint (right) and his son, Wai Rumint, at their home at Kog-mul, near Ogelbeng, Mount Hagen, 1984.

were well aware of this. Taylor writes of Yamka Miti "taking the lap lap" (wearing as a loin-covering the skirtlike piece of cloth, in the manner of Leahy's coastal carriers. This came to be regarded as a mark of power by the Hageners). And for their part, the Australians were quick to pick out leaders and acknowledge their status. Obviously it was in their best interests to win over influential men. Before long, Leahy and Taylor were photographing and mentioning in their diaries the "big men" Ndika Powa and Yamka Kaura.*

Ndika Opramb Rumint from Kogmul, about five miles from Kelua, says it was Ndika Nikints who first suggested he visit the camp. Rumint was a big man too, a leader. He had four wives. "I had shells in my nose and feathers all over my head," he says. "I was a big strong young man." Nikints arrived with news of the strangers, and the red *lap lap* to prove it. "When I saw this red thing," says Rumint, "I was amazed and a bit frightened. I said, 'Aahh! I must go and see them.'

"Nikints had said to himself, 'Rumint must be the one to talk to these people.' So I got myself dressed up and I carried my finest axe— the one we normally use for bridewealth. And I went to see what was going on. Nikints carried the *lap lap*. We got closer to the camp where the whites were, and I saw them chopping with their axes, really fast, like I'd never seen before. I was really impressed. Then Kiap Taylor said, 'Bring this man to me.' Two of my clansmen grabbed my hands and tried to stop me. One held my belt and said, 'You mustn't go!' These men were convinced Taylor was going to kill me. But then they said that if I was killed they might as well be killed, too, so they stood by me.

*A "big man" was a man of wealth and power within a tribe. This status was achieved in a process detailed in Chapter 7.

Mokei Nambuka (Sir) Wamp Wan in Mount Hagen township, 1984. An aspiring big man at the time of contact in April 1933, Mokei Wamp braved enemy action to visit the camp of the strangers at Kelua.

"Then Taylor came up and we went into his house-made-of-cloth. He showed me shells and said I could choose one. I took two smaller shells and a big one. One of my uncles had heard that these strange men had taken me, and he had mud all over him [a sign of mourning]. Kiap Taylor came out and asked, 'Why is this man covered in mud?' He was very sorry and gave this man a few small shells. That is what happened."

For enemies of the Yamka and their allies, and for those whose route to Kelua took them through enemy territory, the lack of ready access to the white men created enormous tension and frustration. There was now trading going on at the camp, and the word was beginning to spread that the strangers had wonderful things with them. People were overcome with curiosity and a desire to take part in what was going on. Some now called on marriage connections with enemy groups for safe conduct through hostile territory. Others, like Mokei Nambuka Wamp Wan from Wilya, seven miles from Kelua, joined heavily armed parties determined to see the strangers, come what may, even though it meant taking great risks. For Mokei Wamp it was a particularly dangerous journey. As an aspiring big man he was a prime target for assassination. Among his enemies there would have been great prestige attached to killing him.

Today he is Sir Wamp Wan, knighted by Queen Elizabeth, a leading member of the Roman Catholic Church in Mount Hagen. In 1933 he was about twenty years old, a proven fight leader, and on the way to becoming a big man. His older brother Mokei Nambuka Ninji was already an established leader. Wamp's main danger in visiting the Kelua came not from the Ndika or Yamka but from the Elti and Penambe, or rather the remnants of these two tribes, former neighbours of Mokei clans including Wamp's Nambuka, but defeated and routed by them in a major war ten years earlier, and forced to take refuge among the Ndika near Kelua. The Elti and Penambe were understandably bitter over their disastrous defeat by the Mokei and would have killed Wamp on sight if they could.

Mokei Wamp went with one group of relatives who could ease his passage through Elti-Penambe territory, and with another group to shield him against certain Yamka clans who could have caused him further difficulty. "Quite a group of us went. Whenever a big man travels somewhere normally all the men of the clan go. In this case it was Mokei Ninji, my brother, who was the big man. Almost all the men of my group went on the journey." The party numbered about fifty men, a formidable fighting force.

"My wife and my family said, 'Don't go to the enemy territory because you'll be killed!' [The death of big men was a serious blow, as they were credited with powerful influence over the ancestral dead.] But we decided to make the trip because we had to see these strangers with our own eyes. We couldn't resist it. If these spirits were going to kill and eat us, let them! If our enemies were going to kill us, let them! As we travelled along we carried our arms and looked this way and that, nervously.

"When we saw the whites we said, 'Aahh, so these are the spirits.' We could speak the same language as the Ndika so we could ask them things. The Ndika said, 'Perhaps they are spirits, but look at the things they've given us!' And they showed us some of the shells. Jim Taylor and Mick came and shook hands with Ninji and me. They didn't speak to us, though. Nor did they give us anything. We didn't want to touch any of their things, because we were thinking of the two men who were shot before. I was too afraid of the Elti-Penambe, so I only went once to their camp."

Some men, unwilling to risk their own lives, sent their wives to Kelua instead. Women were often less at risk in foreign parts than their fighting men. And often the wife had family connections to give her a passage not open to her husband. Nevertheless, for these women, it would have been a strange and fearful journey.

Mokei Andagalimp Wak of Koibuga was one of those who sent his womenfolk to the camp. From the list of his enemies it is very clear why he couldn't go himself—his people were then engaged in hostilities with the Elti and Penambe, the Kimi and Kuklika, the Ndika and Yamka. Koibuga was quite close to Kelua, about 5 miles away. Mokei Wak's people were getting odd bits of news of the strange goings on and could see smoke from cooking fires rising above Kelua. "We couldn't go and see," says Wak. "We didn't know what to do! We started climbing trees, trying to have a look. We could see the smoke. We didn't see the people, but we heard about their strange houses. What could you do? We couldn't go there.

"We wondered what type of people are these strangers? We heard that the face was like a human's, but the body kept changing its skin. The skin had holes in it, which they could put things in, and then take them out again. They could put things inside their neck at the front and then take them out again. We just couldn't work that out. The face seemed human enough, but the skin! We told our women to go and get some of the things the others were getting from them. So our women went with food to trade with them. They brought home shells! We men really pushed the women to go and trade. We told them to go one day after another."

The women sent on this quest had to overcome great fear, and today they are proud of the courage they displayed in risking their lives for their husbands' clans. Nor are they reluctant to mention that they left their men perched in trees, helplessly watching them go, desperately curious but too afraid to follow. In 1982, Kentiga Amp Kwimbe walked again the few miles from Koibuga to Kelua, and told her story standing on the site of the camp—a flat plateau of waving *kunai* grass with a commanding view of the surrounding countryside, some six miles from the present-day township of Mount Hagen. She pointed out where the tents had been, and the rope line around the camp perimeter where the women, in uneasy proximity to their enemies, traded their vegetables for beads, small shells and salt.

"We had more food than we could hope to use," says Dan Leahy of the first few days at Kelua, "and they were bringing more and more, you couldn't stop them." His brother and Taylor were also noting in their diaries the friendliness of the people. Within a few days Hageners were flocking to the camp. They had realised that the strangers had things they wanted and that they could get some of them easily by merely supplying vegetables, something they grew in abundance.

For the Hageners this was very strange indeed—to trade vegetables, which they did not value as wealth, for shells, which they most certainly did. It was an unprecedented situation. In the past, big men mainly controlled the flow of shells. Now here was a situation where they were potentially available to anyone who had something the white men wanted, and nearly everyone had a vegetable garden.

But soon, the people around Mount Hagen were to experience another great shock. The first airstrip in the highlands was built by Taylor at Kainantu in late 1932. In November of that year the NGG geologist Hector Kingsbury, whom the Leahys were escorting around the Eastern Highlands, recorded on his own 16-mm movie camera a young man seeing an aeroplane landing for the first time. It is a memorable and touching scene. Narmu Varnu came from Seerupu Village about twenty miles from Kainantu. He had never been this far from his village before. Kingsbury begins his film sequence with Narmu standing next to Michael Leahy on the edge of the airstrip. Leahy and several other white men tower over the short and stocky youth. The film is silent, but it's obvious when the sound of the approaching plane is heard. The white men turn around, point to the sky and gesture for Narmu to look in the same direction. He smiles uncomprehendingly, unable to see anything. Then suddenly he sees the plane and his expression changes from nervous apprehension to utter terror. The plane approaches, Narmu clutches Leahy around the waist. Leahy laughs and keeps pointing to the plane. Narmu shields himself behind Leahy, still clutching him, and then quickly peeks out at the approaching aircraft. Despairingly, as it roars past, he buries his head against the white man, who laughs and forces Narmu to keep looking as the plane taxies to a stop.

Narmu Varnu died in his village in 1982 before his stories of those times could be recorded, but there is no shortage of other informants. Michael Leahy built an airstrip at Bena Bena in December 1932, and Isakoa Hepu, a small boy from the nearby village of Magitu who had joined the camp, remembers his people's responses when the first plane

---

OVERLEAF: *A plane has just landed at the Kelua airstrip, 1933. Crates of shells are unloaded from the cargo door, demonstrating to the watching Hageners the strangers' enormous wealth. The Hageners dub the strangers "men-of-all-things."*

landed there. "All the men and women held each other tightly and cried, 'Today will be the end of us all!' *Masta* Mick patted them on their chests and said it wasn't so, it was only bringing their cargo supplies. But the people lay flat on the ground and then ran off, keeping their heads as close as possible to the earth. Once home they killed their pigs and clung on to their brothers and cried for each other. They made their last feasts. But after that crying and feasting, nothing happened. And the people said, 'That thing has instead brought us good things.' "

Four months later, on March 27, 1933, it was the turn of the Hagen people. Barely ten days after the coming of Aundikla Mugl Timbil's spirit friends, a plane landed at the Kelua camp. The airstrip had been laid out on the site of old garden beds, and as soon as they arrived at Kelua the carriers had been put to work filling in the drainage ditches and smoothing down the surface. Some of the Hagen men helped them. "Of course you couldn't talk to them," says Dan Leahy, "but we'd more or less explain as best we could with sign language that we didn't want to steal their land, we just wanted to straighten it out for this big bird to land. They were quite willing to help us. Anyone who came along and helped, we'd give them some shells and beads."

Michael Leahy filmed this activity—expedition carriers and eager Hageners digging away at the ground with sharpened sticks, and then later filmed scenes of long lines of men, standing forty abreast with their arms linked, stamping up and down the airstrip to pack the earth.

Big crowds began gathering on the cleared strip on April 26, the day before the plane was due. Taylor solemnly announced that it would make its appearance the following day. He could tell them that because the flight time had been prearranged with the pilot. It was one more trick in the Australians' copious bag, like Captain Good in Rider Haggard's *King Solomon's Mines* who saves himself and his companions from death by accurately predicting to the threatening Africans, with the help of a naval almanac, the imminent eclipse of the moon.

Mokei Kominika Kubal Nori and his clan initially thought the plane might be their own Mokei spirits coming to save them from the machinations of their enemies. The Mokei Kominika had had a worrying time since the arrival of the strangers. Barred from access to Kelua, they assumed the whites were the ancestral spirits of their Ndika and Yamka enemies who had decided to settle among their clans' people. "We were really shaken by the whole thing," says Kubal Nori, "and we thought those spirits were going to eat us and we were wondering if our own Mokei spirits would come in time.

"When we heard the noise of the plane, we thought it was our own Mokei spirits returning! We started digging in the graves and looking inside the spirit houses. We dug in the ground—talk about digging! We dug everywhere! We didn't realise the sound was coming from above. We didn't see it, and we didn't see it land at Kelua. We just didn't know what had happened."

Ndika Rumint's people had seen the plane heading in the direction of Kelua and off they went after it. Here, according to the Leahy and Taylor diaries, about a thousand Hageners had gathered to watch as the plan roared into view and circled to make sure four fires were burning, one at each corner of the airstrip—the agreed-on signal that all was well to land. It swept down for a bumpy landing and the watching highlanders flattened themselves on the ground. Kentiga Amp Kwimbe, sent by her Koibuga menfolk to trade at Kelua, was there that day. "We thought it was a great bird," she says. "Suddenly it came. Faster! Louder! When it came closer it looked huge, and we fell to the ground and hid our faces. We wetted and fouled ourselves in fear and confusion."

The aeroplane was the very latest type available—a De Haviland Foxmoth biplane. The pilot sat up front in an open cockpit while his passengers and cargo enjoyed the novel comfort of an enclosed cabin. Dan Leahy says that when the pilot Grabowski jumped down from his cockpit the watching people simply moaned with astonishment. And then a door opened in the fuselage and from the cabin emerged Hector Kingsbury, the NGG geologist, and Ted Taylor, Jim Taylor's administrative superior—come to check on the expedition's progress.

"We got to Kelua," says Ndika Rumint, "and there were crowds of people gathered there to see. People from all over the place. And there it was, waiting for everyone to have a look. You should have seen it! It was a pretty thing, and shiny, like the oil on somebody's skin. We watched, and it started making that noise, brrr. It would stop and then start again. Everyone just about shitted themselves when it started making that noise again.

"We were wondering what was inside, and when we saw people we got even more frightened. I had been to the camp before so I was a bit calmer than the rest. The same people I had seen on my earlier visit were getting friendly with this thing and the people who had come inside. I felt a little better when I saw this. And it came with things— trade goods, axes, shells, to name just a few. Heaps of them! Then we said, 'These men must be men-of-all-things.' "

This change in interpretation from wild spirit to "men-of-all-things" was a major shift in perception. The strangers were not wild spirits or returning dead or some form of deity; they were the "men-of-all-things." Ndika Rumint uses the word *melwuö*—literally, "things men"—but this does not mean that the people thought the strangers were ordinary human beings like themselves or that they weren't associated with the spirit world; quite the contrary. They obviously had a strong and successful relationship with the spirit world, and it was that relationship that gave them access to and control of enormous wealth, "all things." That made them extraordinary beings—human or otherwise.

"At first," says Ndika Wingti, "we used to wonder why they had come. We thought, 'Who are these people?' But when we saw the things they were trading we thought, 'We must befriend them now. They must be our people.' When we saw them giving out things we just knew they must be really close to us, part of our own people."

This shift in perception did not happen immediately, and it did not happen to all Hageners at once. Almost certainly it passed unnoticed by the Australians. Taylor was busy showing his boss around the camp and reporting progress, and the Leahy brothers were hearing disappointing news from Hector Kingsbury. Michael Leahy had set off for the Wahgi confident that NGG's Bena Bena dredging leases would make him a wealthy man even before he knew what treasures the new valley might hold in store. The American geologist now took him aside and broke the news that the Bena Bena gravel terraces, while undoubtedly rich in gold, were technically unsuited to large-scale dredging and that the company was abandoning its operations there.

The Leahy brothers took Kingsbury's news in stride. They had great hopes of the Wahgi, and the indications looked positive. Michael Leahy was an incurable optimist when it came to gold prospecting. Both his brothers talk about the gold fever that spurred him on during these heady months. When Kingsbury had flown with Grabowski to the airstrip in the middle Wahgi three weeks earlier, Leahy was waiting for him with gold samples taken from the nearby river. Leahy wanted to peg out a claim on the spot, obsessed as he was with being beaten to the punch by rival prospectors, in particular the "enemy to our rear" mentioned darkly by NGG surveyor Spinks in his letter to Harrison. Kingsbury soothed Leahy with the news that this particular enemy, who turned out to be the English geologist Nason-Jones, was preoccupied with prospecting the Bena Bena Valley and had no apparent plans to move into the Wahgi, although the news was now out about the Leahy/Taylor expedition. For the time being, at least, the NGG party had the place to themselves.

A man and woman at Kelua, 1933.

Now at Kelua, Kingsbury heard Leahy's news that while they had found no significant traces of gold between the middle of the valley and here at its head, the surrounding country looked geologically promising. Kingsbury agreed that the best option was to establish Kelua as a base camp as intended, from which further prospecting excursions could be launched. After several hours of discussions, under the concentrated gaze of a thousand people, Grabowski climbed back into his cockpit, and Ted Taylor into the cabin. Kingsbury had decided to stay on at Kelua for a few days to examine the immediate country.

The plane took off. "The thousand natives watching," wrote Taylor in his diary, "went on their knees and bowed their heads, like Mahommedans in prayer." Taylor and Leahy busied themselves with their cameras recording these memorable scenes.

The filmic record of those times contains many examples of Australians demonstrating their technological wonders to suitably impressed onlookers. The highlanders watch planes land and cringe in terror; they start at demonstrated rifle fire; stare uncomprehendingly at record players; grin at mirrors. The pathos of their terror and mystification is certainly preserved for posterity, but the movie scenes and photographs reflect as well the Australians' confidence and pride in their own civilisation. It was an easy step for them to assume that the obvious material superiority of their culture was equalled by an intellectual and moral superiority as well.

Chapter Seven

MOKA

The tin lid was lying under some grass, shining in the sun, and I saw it. Quietly I crawled towards it." Kopia Kerika Kubal, who lived seven miles from Kelua, was about twelve years old in April 1933. Kubal acts out for us his adventure of fifty years ago. He has already placed the lid of a common tin can under some dry grass, where it catches the sun. Now he sits down and slides himself carefully across the grass, peering around with wide, mock nervous eyes, until he sits in front of the tin lid. His foot then creeps out, clamps down on the lid and draws it slowly back to his lap. "I hid the lid under my bark belt, and whispered to my friend, 'I've got it.' I thought someone might say, 'Kubal has stolen the tin lid!' But no one did. I was really happy I had it, so I got up, made sure I wasn't going to drop it, felt it with my hands and then I went straight home.

"On the way people asked me to stay overnight because it was getting late, but I wouldn't stop. I was afraid they might see what I'd taken. So I went straight home. There were a lot of people gathered around at my place. My mother and father were both there and they

Kopia Kerika Kubal tells his grandchildren how he stole a tin lid from the strangers' camp at Kelua in 1933.

said, 'Where have you been?' I said, 'I've been to see these new spirits everyone's talking about.' They said, 'You're lying!' I said, 'I'll show you I'm not telling lies!' and I showed them the tin lid.

"When they saw it they yelled out, 'Aahh! Where'd you get that?!' 'Give it to me!' my uncle said. And my father said, 'Why should he? He didn't go and get it to give it to you!' My father said he'd make it into a headdress. Later we would loan it to people when they wanted to wear it in a *sing sing* (dancing) and they would pay us in return for borrowing it. We were very careful to wear it only when the white men couldn't possibly see it and take it back from us."

As had happened everywhere else, the Hagen people were initially very curious about the newcomers' things, even their discarded items of rubbish, endowed as they were with spiritual significance. But the earlier shootings quite obviously made a strong impression on the people. If they did try to take things, it was done with all the care shown by Kubal.

For their own part the Australians wanted things from the Hageners. When it came to vegetables they had more than enough. The beads and small shells were taken eagerly in return for sweet potatoes, greens and sugarcane. But the white men were not so successful buying pigs. The Hageners seemed reluctant to part with them for this small trade. Like all highlanders they placed great value on their pigs. They were far more than a mere food source—they were sacrificial victims and wealth objects at the same time, and, spirits or not, the Hagen people were not prepared to part with them for a handful of small shells. The steel goods were not proving immediately attractive, either. Some time went by before the people fully appreciated their superiority over stone tools.

On his second day at Kelua, Michael Leahy noted in his diary: "Plenty of native foods coming, no pigs so far. If we had mother-of-pearl shell I think we would get all we want." Leahy had noticed that certain men and women were wearing around their necks pearlshells that had been worked into a crescent shape. When the first plane had landed, Taylor and Leahy made arrangements for a bag of pearlshell to come in on the next flight.

Hector Kingsbury had remained behind at Kelua to talk business, but he also played the tourist. Before long he was trying to buy souvenirs to take home—in particular the beautifully carved ceremonial axes and spears the men carried with them. But Kingsbury was having no luck; the people would not accept the usual beads, steel knives and small shells. Kingsbury was not to know that the stone axes he wanted were not mere weapons but wealth objects as well, highly prized by the Hagen people as bridewealth contributions.

On April 28, only a day after its first landing, the plane was back again with another load of equipment and trade goods, including the requested bag of pearlshell. Kingsbury wrote the next day to his wife at Wau: "There was a big crowd here to meet the plane. . . . Hundreds assembled, coming even after the plane had left, from all directions far and near. They were greatly impressed by the plane, but the most spectacular events happened after it had gone.

"There was speech making all afternoon. There would be a clear central ring around which the natives sat or kneeled to hear the address delivered in turn by old men of the different clans. Some of these speeches would last for an hour or more, with real oratorical gestures. Finally this broke up, and the natives walked about, talking and feeding their eyes on the strange sights. During all the day we had been trying to trade with the natives for their stone axes and spears, but nothing seemed to tempt them. They would shake their heads as much as to say 'nothing doing,' although we had offered them knives, axes, steel things of all sorts, tins and even some of the shells that proved to be good trade elsewhere. We finally gave up.

"The plane had brought in a new type of shell for Taylor. These were called gold-lipped shells—large flat shells with a mother-of-pearl centre. We had forgotten about these, mainly because they belonged to Taylor, who was away. When Mick remembered about these the fun began. Mick took one shell, and immediately the crowd thronged about. And then the speeches started all over again. One fellow took the shell, held it up to the mob, who immediately sat down to listen. . . . All the fine points of the shell were told about in detail."[1]

The white men now realised they had something of real value to the people. But they could not imagine just how valuable the *kina** shell was and what a central part it played in the economic, social and political life of the Hagen people. Nor did they realise that their possession of the *kina* shells gave them—in the eyes of the Hageners—a status greater than anything bestowed on them so far.

Impressed with their own technology, particularly their aeroplanes, the Australians assumed the Hageners would be similarly impressed. And the Hageners were impressed, but it is easy to overestimate the impact of western technology upon a people who were interpreting everything that was happening in supernatural terms. Aeroplanes were seen in the Wahgi Valley before motor cars. That might have meant something to the Australians, who considered aeroplanes more technologically advanced than cars. But to the Hageners in these early times all these things were in the realm of the supernatural. Something that flew through the air was not necessarily more amazing than something that drove along the ground. And, paradoxically, this may have reduced the impact of what they were seeing. But when the aeroplanes at Kelua began disgorging from their bellies crate after crate of pearlshell, the amazement of the Hageners knew no bounds. Aundikla Mugl Timbil's spirit friends had become men-of-all-things, or as some called them, the shellmen.

The arrival of the pearlshells produced one immediate result. The Europeans no longer had to worry about fresh meat. They were offered more pigs than they knew what to do with. "He opened a case full of shells," says Ndika Nikints, "and I looked into the case and cried out

*The *kina*, or pearlshell, is now Papua New Guinea's basic unit of currency. Its value is a little higher than the Australian dollar.

with amazement. Aaii! I was shaking my hand in excitement I was so impressed. Then he said, "Pig!" I didn't understand and wondered what he was talking about. He said, 'Pig! Pig!' I still didn't understand. So he made a grunting noise.

"I realised he wanted to give the shell for a pig. Aahh! I really wanted the shell, but my house was far away. Father! What could I do? Then I thought of Ndika Powa. He had a settlement nearby, where the church is now, that's where his temporary home was then. He had a pig tied up there. He and his people had moved away when the strangers came, and someone else was keeping an eye on the pig. So I went there and called out, 'Is anybody there?' An old man came out, and I said, 'Where's Powa?' The old man replied, 'He's scared, and he's gone away.'

"I said to him, 'Bring this pig quickly!' He was afraid, and he hesitated. 'Give it to me! I'll take it!' So I took the pig to the camp and the white man saw it. He picked the big shell up and gave it to me. I took it to the old man and said, 'Take this and give it to Ndika Powa. And tell him the people-eating spirits wanted to eat the pig and gave this shell in return. You all ran off, thinking he was a spirit. Well, what do you think now? He is the shellman! And I'm with him! Go and bring Powa!' When he went and showed the shell to Powa, Powa returned to his temporary place and called out to me. I heard the call and went there and said, 'Powa! This strange man that came, he's not a spirit, he's the shellman! Hurry quickly, there's a lot more shells!' "

Shells of various types were valuable almost everywhere in the highlands as personal adornment and for use in the exchange cycle common to so many Melanesian societies. But in the Hagen area the pearlshell was prized above everything as the fundamental basis of wealth—beautiful, precious, and, above all, rare. At the time of contact, the majority of them were controlled by the big men. With so few available, the arrival of each new pearlshell, traded through countless hands

Gold-lipped pearlshells, called kina *shells, laid out in display during a* moka *exchange.* Kina *shells were the principal object of wealth in the Hagen region at the time of contact, and the Australians were soon distributing vast quantities of them in payment for various goods and services. This* moka *was photographed at Mount Hagen by Dan Leahy in the late 1930s, when the number of pearlshells in circulation had greatly increased in comparison to the situation existing in 1933. The shells seen here are set on a backing of clay covered wood for display purposes and are laid out on a bed of fern leaves. Ropes of smaller shells lie beside them.*

up from the coast, was a great occasion. "Not everyone had a chance of possessing a *kina* shell," says Penambe Wia Tugl from Kunguma. "Most of us never had a chance. I cannot describe in words how valuable they were. If a man wanted to pass on a kina shell to someone he would warn them with a sign that something very special was coming—for example, the leaf of the mara tree—green on top, white underneath and split down the middle. That signalled the receiver could keep the shell to make *moka*. This was all secret, and the big men would whisper about it. The person to receive the shell wouldn't be able to sleep at night for thinking about it. We'd build a man's house, decorate the *sing sing* ground [open area where ceremonies were held] and wait anxiously for the big day with paint ready to decorate the shell. And when we heard it coming—say about two tribes away—we'd get really excited."

In Mount Hagen the pearlshell was used as personal decoration and, along with other valuables, particularly pigs, could be given to cement alliances, signal the end of hostilities or form part of a bridewealth contribution in marriage. But these functions were minor when compared to its use in the system of competitive exchange—gift-giving between men, which in Mount Hagen had been developed to an extraordinary degree. It was known as the *moka*.[2]

The object of the competition was prestige, and the basic rule of the *moka* exchange was that if a person was given a gift by another, he was then put under an obligation to reciprocate. And he was obliged to return even more than the initial gift, or risk losing prestige.

Put very simply, pigs were raised to acquire shells, and both were offered as gifts in the initial phase of the *moka* exchange. A person who could "make *moka*" successfully—return more than he was given—enjoyed a position of temporary superiority over his opponent. He might have more than one opponent at one time and be involved in making *moka* with all of them at varying times or simultaneously. If a man could operate the *moka* system successfully over a number of years, accumulating and giving away great wealth, then this was one sure way of becoming a big man—one who enjoyed great prestige and therefore great influence. It was a long and arduous path to big man status, and once there, there was no guarantee of tenure. The position carried no hereditary title or permanent office. It certainly helped to be the son of a big man, but basically everyone was on his own. Aspirants had to start at the bottom and make their own way up. And great personal qualities were needed. A young man began by working hard to raise

Prominent men display the wealth of their clans at a great religious festival photographed by Dan Leahy in 1937. The two leading men wear bailer shells as decorations, almost as valuable as the kinas *they are holding in front of them. A long procession of men in pairs passes before thousands of spectators.*

pigs, and with these he acquired enough shells to step onto the first rung of the competitive ladder. This was where the hard work began. He needed a strong and commanding personality to attract around him the supporters essential to his long-term success. Supporters—the majority of men, independent landowners, usually married to one wife— contributed the capital the big man needed to engage in large-scale *moka* exchanges with other big men.

The big man's objective was not the physical accumulation of shells—although they were regarded as incredibly beautiful things—but rather the knowledge that he was owed this wealth by others. It was this debt that brought prestige to the big man, his immediate clan, and his network of supporters, some of whom might be drawn from other clans as well. By widening his contacts the big man could extend his web of personal influence and therefore increase the number of his supporters. He could achieve further influence and support for his ventures by the arrangement of strategic marriages or by offering favours like the advancement of bridewealth contributions to impecunious men. Eventually, the big man would come up against the support block of competing big men—intensely jealous of their own power and prestige. And it was this competition that ensured that no one man rose to dominance over all others.

The NGG geologist Hector Kingsbury was observing big men at work on the Kelua airfield in April 1933 when he wrote of the hour-long speeches. Oratorical ability was crucial to success. So was the ability to settle disputes. Often big men were able fight leaders, although they tended to be cool headed and persuasive rather than aggressive and hot blooded.

Big men were wealthy, influential, usually owned extensive gardens and had more than one wife. The more garden areas a big man controlled and the more wives he had to raise vegetables and pigs, the larger became his economic base. The wives of big men usually but not necessarily enjoyed high status, along with the mothers of potential big men. Among women, prestige went to those who worked hard, were good gardeners and pig raisers. All women married, and almost all men. Those who did not were either mentally ill or propertyless men dependent on the big men. "Normally the poor man lived close by the big man," says Mokei Kominika Kwipi Nembil from Kelua, himself a former big man, "and they would do jobs for the big man like cutting firewood or looking after his garden. They'd probably eat food from the big man's garden. The big man would help the poor man in many ways, like helping his son to be married."

It was a society in which everyone had a place, and no one lacked the basic necessities of life. People knew their place within the clan, and ultimately it was to their own clan that all owed their first allegiance. The big man was tied down in a web of obligation—others to him, him to others, and so each person ultimately drew benefit from the competitive exchange society.

The Australian gold prospectors had little trouble establishing themselves among these people. The Hageners, in particular their leaders and spokesmen, were skilful politicians and keen traders. The big men the Leahys won over were men like Yamka Kaura, Ndika Powa, and Ndika Rumint. Dan Leahy remembers his first meeting with Yamka Kaura at Kelua. "He more or less took over the whole situation, and he really was the head man, the man we used to go to when we wanted any decisions made, about what we'd do, to ask where we'd go to get timber for building huts. Kaura would tell us. While we used Kelua as a base he was the main one. He wasn't a real big man [in size] but he was quite an impressive man. He had ten tons of self-confidence. The

Ewunga Goiba offers a bailer shell in exchange for a pig, which the man's wife is holding. Kelua, 1933.

other big men like Powa, they came later on. They never had as much control of the situation as Kaura did. See, it was Yamka land where the airstrip was, and Kaura's line were the people with the say."

There are photographs of some of these men, taken at Kelua during the early weeks of contact. Each wears the *omak*, status symbol of the big man—a string of bamboo sticks hanging from the neck, each stick signifying that eight to ten *kina* shells had been given away by the wearer in *moka* exchange. Kaura and Powa were particularly powerful leaders, with many lesser men at their beck and call, and they monopolised the

LEFT: *Big man Yamka Kaura, photographed at Kelua in early 1933. Around his neck he wears the* omak, *each stick signifying that he has given eight or ten* kina *shells in* moka *exchange. He is also wearing a fine piece of carved shell, highly prized in a society where in the precontact times the arrival of a single piece of pearlshell was a great occasion. Kaura wears an elaborate headdress— the shell headband, a hairnet typical of the region, and a top ornament of cassowary plumes. His clan territory encompassed the Kelua area, and he formed a close association with the Leahys and Taylor in 1933.* CENTER: *A mid-Wahgi man wearing as decoration an empty tin can; most probably it once contained sardines. At first every scrap from the Australians was highly valued for decorative purposes but, more importantly, for its strength-giving potential.* RIGHT: *Wabag man, 1934.*

Shirley Temple comes to Mount Hagen, 1934.

shell wealth—or did until the Australians arrived. With their unlimited supply of pearlshells, the newcomers now held the ultimate trump card.

When Michael Leahy opened up the first sack of shells on the Kelua airstrip on April 29, 1933, the news spread quickly. Penambe Tugl remembers receiving his first *kina* shells from the Australians: "I felt as important as the big man! As I was decorating them* I was thinking, now I'll be able to make *moka*! Get married! I can do anything now I have the ultimate! I had a feeling of excitement, of ownership. I put

---

Kina shells used in *moka* were set into a circular board of painted clay for display.

them near my head at night, and didn't quite go to sleep, thinking about the shells. Sometimes I'd decorate them and hang them up, and then I'd look at them and admire them. Then I'd sit down, and go out, come back and look! And other people would come and admire them. I just can't explain how I felt about them. I really felt important."

Initially the Hagen people were very interested in everything the Australians had, as shown by the poignant photographs of men wearing headdresses featuring the white man's discarded refuse—cereal packages, tin lids, labels. It was not to last. Scraps of cardboard, beads and trinkets were a passing novelty (although the Hageners found them useful for buying traditional valuables from people living further down the valley with no access to Kelua) compared to the growing appreciation of the steel tools, and above all, shells. The demand for pearlshells was insatiable. Some inflation naturally occurred over a period of years, but this did not detract from the desirability of the shells. Before long aeroplanes were flying them in by the crate-load. To a people who in precontact times might have had to wait a year for the appearance of a single shell, the white man's source seemed inexhaustible. It was. The Leahy brothers were buying theirs in bulk from Australian pearling stations and could afford to be choosy.

"It was easy to get the best quality," says Dan Leahy, "because pearlshell was hard to sell in those days. The value put on it in Australia was nothing compared to the value the highlanders put on it. It was like gold to them, and as hard to get. They had to wait and see what was coming their way—they couldn't just go and get it. We were the people who could more or less wave a magic wand and there it was."

With this currency at their disposal the Leahy brothers were in a position to demand from the people virtually anything they required. And the Hageners, those of them with direct access to Kelua, were only too willing to oblige.

Chapter Eight

BRIDEWEALTH

For ten days following the pilot Grabowski's initial landing on April 27, aeroplanes had been arriving almost every day at Kelua, and each time a great crowd gathered to watch. Big men delivered lengthy orations to their followers about the planes and the now-regular loads of pearlshells they delivered. Michael Leahy filmed one of these speeches. The big man Kaura stands in a small open space, surrounded by hundreds of seated men, women and children. James Taylor is seen standing to one side, with a group of his police. Kaura's audience listens attentively as he points to the plane, at the Australians and back at the plane, presumably giving his comments on the extraordinary happenings.

From all accounts now Kaura was probably telling his audience of their great good fortune. So far as these Hageners were concerned, a group of strange beings had dropped down among them and seemed to be the source of great wealth. And furthermore these shellmen had chosen to settle among them exclusively—the Yamka and their allies. It seemed a golden age was about to begin.

And then, three weeks after arriving at Kelua, the shellmen packed up and left. Or so it seemed at first to the people around Kelua early on the morning of May 9 as all four white men and most of their carrier line prepared to take to the road. Michael Leahy's actual intention was to go on several short prospecting excursions into the surrounding countryside. They had tested all the streams in the immediate vicinity, finding only slight traces of gold, and it was time to look further afield.

Leaving a handful of Taylor's police behind to look after the stores, Leahy expected to be away about a fortnight. But the Yamka and Ndika people did not know this, and Leahy records their consternation in his diary. "A couple of the locals arrived before we left, and when they seen [sic] the tents down and us ready to go, threw ashes over their bodies and ran around wailing. One of them grabbed a tomahawk and made as if to cut his finger off—a custom of theirs when one of their near relatives dies. We took the tomahawk off him. . . . He appeared to be more concerned about the plane not coming any more if we went away than the fact that we were going away."

The white men were away eleven days; eleven fruitless days, as it turned out; their panning dishes turned up no traces of gold. But for the Hageners back at Kelua it was a different story. Half a dozen police and carriers had been left behind to guard the stores. And their leader, Sergeant Buassi, had the keys to the cache of pearlshell. The Hageners kept bringing their pigs along for sale, and Buassi, who was very fond of pork, was happy to oblige them. When Leahy returned to Kelua on May 20 he noted: "Got a wonderful reception from the locals. . . . The boy in charge—Buassi—had twelve pigs in a sty and had eaten twelve in the twelve days we were away." At the current rate of exchange, there were as a result of these transactions twenty-four more pearlshells now in circulation—bringing ever-growing prestige to the Ndika/Yamka alliance around Kelua.

But there was tragedy awaiting some of the Hageners living outside this privileged circle who were frustrated by the obvious enrichment of their enemies and rivals and dangerously lacking in first-hand knowledge of what power the strangers had at their disposal. Certainly those Mokei clans with limited or no access to Kelua had heard of the earlier killings, but they had not seen with their own eyes the effect of rifle bullets on human flesh. Their subsequent experience is vividly remembered today in Mount Hagen. It seems to have taken place about a month after the Australians' arrival, and it involved a stolen lap lap. The Mokei were held responsible, and the white men went after them.

Mokei Nambuka Titip and Ndika Komp Amp Kenga Kama, at their home at Kuminga, near Mount Hagen, in 1983. Mokei Titip was shot in the elbow during a skirmish with Leahy and Taylor a few weeks after the arrival of the Australians.

Today the Mokei admit there was some truth in the stealing charge, but they blame the Yamka for sending the whites after them, and they say the whites attacked the wrong Mokei clans, anyway. It seems it was the Mokei Pangamp who stole the *lap lap*. When the Mokei Nambuka heard that the whites were coming in strength to retrieve it, they thought the Mokei in general were under attack, and so it was they who took the field against them and suffered the consequences. The Pangamp, who stole the *lap lap* in the first place, appear to have discreetly withdrawn at this point.

"We really meant business!" says Mokei Nambuka Wamp Wan. "We were jumping up and down and calling out our war cries. At the time we had no idea what the gun could do. We saw the white men arrive, down there where the fish-and-chip shop is now. They were firing guns at us from a really long distance, too far for us to throw our spears. We tried, but we didn't get any of them. Mokei Joea was doing well for a while, jumping around and dodging bullets. When I saw him fall down I took his body and left it in a house near where the courthouse is now, and then I ran to where the Highlander Hotel is. The white men came after us still and it was at this place that Titip was wounded."

Mokei Nambuka Titip's left elbow still bears the scar of that fight. Titip, from Kuminga, had not been to Kelua. Like most of the Mokei he was too frightened of his enemies to approach. "Only the prominent Mokei like Wamp and Ninji had been game to visit," says Titip. "We had sharp spears, and we said, 'Those whites, they haven't brought anything to fight with!' We thought we were going to win. The bullet went in my left elbow and out the other side. I didn't feel it going in but when I looked there was blood everywhere! My spear dropped, one of my brothers came and put me on his shoulder, and carried me to the *sing sing* ground. He called out to the people but nobody except my wife came and she saw me like that."

Titip's wife, Ndika Komp Amp Kenga Kama, remembers: "His blood was draining out! It filled a whole *muu muu* [pig-cooking] hole. He nearly ran out of blood. I was only newly married to him then. I stayed with him in a separate house. The others left, too frightened to stay. Soon after an aeroplane flew very low over our place and we thought—this has come to finish us off! We had to leave Titip by himself in fear."

"My wife used to peek at what was going on," says Titip, "and come and tell me. My father was alive then and my brother too, but none of them would dare come near me. They left me alone when the plane flew over. It was everyone for himself, running away and hiding. We thought the plane was coming to get us Mokei only because we'd had a fight with these spirits."

"Later," continues Kenga Kama, "we travelled a long way to find a bush doctor [ritual expert] for Titip. He didn't get well for about three years. He just lingered on. The bones were in pieces and kept coming out. We put some soft leaves on his wound, and it was a long time before we got the bush doctor to him, and after he'd been treated by this man his wound got better. The doctor just prayed over him. These days there's money, but then we paid him a lot of shells."

"Everyone tried to work out what could have happened to my arm," adds Titip. "We thought it was a magic thing that wounded me. The bush doctor thought so, too."

Kenga Kama explains: "Before we were fearful of magic. If someone displeased us we could wish harm on them and they could die. This is what we thought must have happened to my husband. I was so sorry for him! I was the one with him all the time. Others had taken my baby and were looking after it. We thought he was going to die. Nowadays with doctors people recover quickly but in those days it took such a long time!"

"I don't feel resentful towards the white man for what they did," says Titip today. "We got no compensation for Joea and I think they should have paid some. But white men don't think like us. If I'd known the language I might have gone to Taylor and said, 'You've killed us for no reason, and we'd like compensation.' But he lives somewhere else now."

James Taylor mentions in his diary an affray with the Mokei on May 29—five weeks after the arrival at Kelua. Taylor says his police were surrounded by Mokei men and they retreated, "keeping the natives at a distance by firing over their heads." In his book Leahy relates that after several of Taylor's men were surrounded by the Mokei while gathering wood, a rescue party went to their assistance and "a few shots fired at long range stopped the rush, the Mogai [Mokei] retiring in confusion with their wounded—thunderstruck, doubtless, at weapons which could bring a man down at such a distance." Whatever happened, and neither Leahy nor Taylor mention a stolen *lap lap*, the incident had a powerful effect on the Mokei.

"When we saw Titip's wound," says Mokei Wamp Wan, "we said, 'We'll have to make friends with them or they'll wipe us out. We mustn't touch anything that belongs to them, or steal anything, or even collect up things belonging to them we find lying around.' Someone brought an old tin and we said to him, 'Why'd you do that?' We hid it and were frightened they might come looking for it and kill some more of us."

The day after the incident, Michael Leahy noted that a delegation of Yamka men woke them at Kelua with the news that Mokei clans were combining to rush the camp and wipe everyone out. Leahy says the Yamka even smeared themselves with mud in anticipatory mourning. This was completely outside the usual pattern of behavior, and it is likely the Yamka were playing politics—attempting to stir up more trouble between the Australians and the Mokei. And that is borne out by what took place the following day, when a delegation of Mokei, including those Leahy said had been "looked over" two days earlier, approached the camp leading a big pig. Instead of attacking, Leahy writes, "they want to be friends, which is OK with us. We don't want any trouble while we are away from this base. There would not be enough boys to hold off a determined rush."

Soon after this clash the Australians left on their second prospecting excursion, and accompanying them this time was the big man Yamka

Kaura. Leahy noted that his presence on the trip would probably guarantee the safety of Buassi and his companions, who were once again left to look after the camp. Another big man wanted to come along as well, but one of his wives became so distraught at the prospect of losing him that the Australians left him behind. She had thrown herself on the ground weeping hysterically, apparently convinced that her husband would never return. This event underlined the fact that six weeks after their first contact with the white men the Hagen people were still far from certain of their nature or intentions. "It would have been a good scheme to bring him also," wrote Leahy, "to show him that we were not out to do any killing or eating of kanakas as they appear to imagine."

While they were away an event took place at Kelua which would reveal more to the Hagen people about the true nature of the strangers than anything so far. Sergeant Buassi was once again left with the key to the shell store, and when the white men returned after eighteen days away, Buassi had taken the Hagen woman Nengka Amp Dau as his wife.

Now a sprightly woman in her mid-sixties, Nengka Dau, would have been about fifteen or sixteen in 1933, and therefore approaching marriage age. Had the white men not arrived she could have expected to join the household of a rising big man as his youngest wife, or perhaps have married a less important single man. Dau would have had some say in the choice of husband, but strong influences would have come from her menfolk, who had political considerations in mind.

Marriages were cemented with a series of ceremonies, in which the groom's parents presented bridewealth to the bride's parents—ceremonial axes, pigs, *kina* shells. Once married, the woman then joined her husband's clan but her own clan relatives took a close interest in her welfare, and if they thought she was being mistreated might request compensation or attempt to punish her husband. And since many women came from clans that could turn into future enemies of their husbands' people, everyone had to treat them carefully. If women by and large played a secondary role in the ceremonial and political life of the clan, they could still exert, privately, a powerful influence on their menfolk, playing a key if unsung role in clan affairs. Marriage was very often used for political purposes—healing old enmities, gaining wealth, forging new relationships—and this is what her menfolk most likely had in mind now for Dau. Here was a fine opportunity not only to gain access to more shells as bridewealth but also to strengthen the ties between themselves and the newcomers.

Nengka Amp Dau buying sweet potatoes at the Mount Hagen markets in 1983. Dau was the first woman in the Hagen area to be married to one of the strangers.

It was inevitable that before long the members of the Leahy/Taylor expedition would cast their eyes towards the Hagen women. It's hard now to say who took the initiative, but men from both sides obviously understood each other soon enough. All the Hagen men had to do was persuade the women to go along with their plans. The women could not normally be forced against their will—that could lead to endless trouble later on—but they could be persuaded to marry one of these strangers for the good of the clan. Or they could be tricked into it, in the hope that things would work out satisfactorily. This is what was about to happen to Dau at Kelua in June 1933.

It was the fortnight the main body was again away from camp. Dau's Nengka clan was friendly with both Yamka and Ndika, and, in the company of friends, she had been a regular visitor to Kelua from the start, trading vegetables for small shells and salt. But even after six weeks, she says, the women were still very nervous, wondering if it was safe to go there. On one occasion the strangers were inside their fence, cooking meat. Dau was sitting outside with some other women and her uncle, Ndika Opa. She says that a coastal man gave Opa an axe and some shells and she now suspects that her uncle had been surreptitiously negotiating her bridewealth. The next day there was a big feast at her place, and Ndika Opa suggested they take the leftover food down to Kelua. Dau thinks Opa must have agreed to bring her to the coastal man that day. On their way they passed some other coastal men, washing at the river, and as usual they were disgusted with the "spirit smell" of the soap.

"Opa must have pointed me out to them," says Dau, "and one of them went to take the bag of food I was carrying away from me. I got frightened and ran back to Opa. 'Don't be afraid,' he said, 'he's given us shells and things. Let him have the sugarcane from your bag.' So these men ate the sugarcane. I was wondering if they were going to pay for it. They said they'd give me things once we were at their place. On the way they were looking at me, talking among themselves and laughing.

"When we were at their camp Opa said to me, 'The other girls (who were with us) can go now. We'll go and get paid for the sugarcane.' I

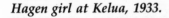

Hagen girl at Kelua, 1933.

thought he was telling the truth, so I went with him to their house inside the fence. The coastal man said, 'Come quickly! Otherwise the dog will bite you people.' I wanted to turn around and leave, but then I was frightened of the dogs. They made us tea, but we didn't like to drink it. But other food, like pork, bananas and sugarcane, we ate with them. By this time it was getting late, and the sun was going down. I was sitting next to Opa and I began nudging him, saying, 'When are we going to leave?' We had been sitting in one place all the time."

At this point a case was broken open, and a collection of trade goods—axes, shells and spades, was brought out to Ndika Opa. Dau was confused and alarmed. "I wondered why they were giving us so many things, and I started to cry. I said to Opa, 'Let's go! We'll take some now and go.' Opa said, 'We'll go soon—just wait a while.' I thought I would go home with him, but then he said he had to go to the toilet. I believed him and let him go. He left, and they unchained the dogs! Then I began crying. I put my face in my hands and I was sobbing, I was so upset. I was crying, not knowing what to do. The coastal men said, 'Don't cry.' And they wiped away my tears with a handkerchief. This made me cry louder!

So Dau found herself deserted by her people, alone and trapped within the strangers' compound, unable to communicate with anyone, not even sure if her captors were human beings. On top of this, Dau had been among those who first interpreted the strangers as spirit beings visiting the wild Aundikla, who was known to be particularly menacing to young and attractive women.

When the unmarried men and women of Mount Hagen came together for their courtship ceremonies, it was believed that Aundikla was sometimes present, disguised as a good-looking young man. All the girls would be attracted to him. If there was someone there who could recognise the signs of spirits, he could avert danger by luring Aundikla away with the promise of a feast. "The man who had recognised Aundikla," says Dau, "might say, 'You must stay here! You've done wrong trying to get so close to humans!'" The man would then go back and find out which girl had been particularly friendly with Aundikla. The girl's parents would give the man a big pig, which he would kill and take to Aundikla, an offering usually sufficient to mollify the wild spirit.

But if Aundikla was unrecognised, then he could kill the girl he fancied and disappear, taking her spirit with him. This was what he always had in mind when he went to the courting ceremonies—to choose a pretty girl, abduct and then kill her. It is no wonder that Nengka Dau now thought her time had come. "I was in such a bad state," she continued, "that they went and got a woman [a Bena Bena woman]. At first I thought she was just another man, and I started to cry again. Then she lifted her blouse and showed me her breasts and said, 'Look! I'm a woman too, so don't be afraid. Stay with us.' "

"When I saw she was a woman I went and hugged her and stayed with her. I lived with this woman for three or four days, while the coastal man who was to become my husband brought me food. That first night they cut up a *lap lap* for me to wear, but I said, 'No!' I didn't want it. I never realised I was there to be married. It was only when they brought Meta, dressed to be married, and said, 'See what good things they have already given for Dau!' Then I realised I was there to be married to one of these coastal men."

Ndika Komp Amp Meta was about the same age as Dau. They were to become close friends during their ordeal at Kelua, and close friends they are today. As the second girl to be given in marriage, Meta experienced nothing like Dau's trauma. "I heard Dau had been given by Ndika Opa to a coastal man," she says. "When my brother heard this he said to me, 'Shells are of great importance, and I like the idea that these men are marrying women from here.' He asked me what I thought about it. I said I didn't want to be married to them because I thought they were spirits! For a couple of days he kept asking me to marry one, and finally I agreed. I was only a young girl. I didn't have big breasts then. When we got married we were just becoming grown women.

"My brother killed a pig," continues Meta, "and dressed me up as a bride. He took me to this coastal man. He was a much older man."

Dau explains: "They married Meta to them after me. Then Meta and I stayed together. We had lots of traditional decorations on us, a belt around our waists, shells around our necks. Our two husbands stripped all our things off and put clothes on us. They said the dog would bite us if we stayed near the camp in our ordinary clothes. 'You must change into a *lap lap* and blouse,' they said.

"It's not like how you have clothes today," adds Meta. "We were part naked. It's true we didn't understand a word of their language."

"Then at night," Dau says, "we thought—they're going to eat us! But they didn't. In fact they were very kind to us."

Meta says, laughing, "We had sex together and then we knew they were men!"

Dau nods in agreement: "Yes, that's right. Then we knew they were men. For about one week the man didn't touch me, I was so scared.

A woman dressed for marriage, Mount Hagen, 1933. She wears part of her bride-wealth in **kina** *shells around her neck. Her skin glows from the special oil rubbed into it, which was thought to greatly enhance her beauty. The oil was a valuable trading commodity in the highlands at the time of contact.*

When Meta came they put clothes on us and our husbands took us to different houses."

Meta says, "We lived with them and saw they were human beings like us. With sex organs like our people. We thought they didn't have any. But they did just the same things we did! [Laughter.] Then we proved they were men."

"Meta's husband was a *kukboi* [cook]," adds Dau, "and mine was a policeman. The people must have been wondering. Day after day they came to see if we were still alive, and each day they saw that we were all right. After that the people brought more women—Ndika, Yamka, to mention only a few. Things were calm after that."

On the night he got back from his second and equally unsuccessful excursion, Michael Leahy noted: "A few of the boys have taken wives. The locals appear to reckon if they can marry them, we will stop." Taylor was displeased with Buassi's actions, but since Dau's clanspeople were satisfied that she and Buassi were married, he felt he had to leave things as they were. But as Dau says, it was only the beginning. As news spread of the marriages, there was a general realisation that here was another way of getting pearlshells and steel implements—now becoming almost as popular as shells. Not all Hagen men had pigs they could afford to part with, but a great many had daughters, nieces, sisters. "The locals are still bringing along wives for our boys," noted Leahy on June 19. "Five gold-lipped shells and a tomahawk is the price. They are a really good-looking lot." Two weeks later Sergeant Buassi was telling Leahy that when the people bring a pig for trading, they bring a young woman as well. And on July 13 Leahy writes: "Locals here appear to be determined to supply all the boys with wives, and keep bringing them along to them. Along the water road which has become a sort of lover's walk, with side tracks into the *pit pit** at frequent intervals, the boys are very frequently seen meandering along in the direction of the water with a *gumu* shell or knife in their hands, and they come back in a short time without them."

According to Leahy's diary, there were marriages and casual sexual encounters in these early months. As Leahy noticed, the normal bridewealth for a marriage was five pearlshells and a tomahawk. But a knife and a few smaller shells would pay for a short visit to the *pit pit*. This was a specific response to the arrival of the strangers. Sex on a casual basis was very much frowned upon in Hagen society, and sex for payment was absolutely unheard of. To the women involved it would have been a strange and possibly humiliating experience, perhaps tempered by the satisfaction of knowing they were bringing wealth to their clans. Men say today the women were not forced to participate, but given their position in society, young girls would have found the pressure very hard to resist. In their desire to get some of the new wealth it seems husbands, uncles and brothers had taken to prostituting their women. In the case of Dau and Meta, though, everyone concerned— the girls, their relatives and their future husbands—considered the relationships formal and legitimate marriages.

A coastal New Guinean who married a Hagen woman at this time was Towa Ulta, one of Michael Leahy's armed Waria. "All the women here," says Towa, who now lives in retirement in Mount Hagen, "were good looking. If we liked the girl we had to 'gris't the parents first. It was up to us to decide which woman we wanted. The first time I saw Marpa she was with her parents and they were trying to sell sugarcane,

---

Pit pit is tall, stiff-stemmed grass growing eight to ten feet high, the stem base of which was used by the highlanders as arrow shafts.

†*Gris* is to persuade (to grease).

and I said to her, 'I like your sugarcane.' Her parents used to like me and I would give them shells and salt. They would cook food and put the salt on it and bring it to me. It was the same with all the other men—the parents of the girls we liked became our family in this new place.

"At that time I thought of her as more of a sister," says Towa, who

Ndika Komp Amp Meta at home in Mount Hagen with clan relatives, 1983.

was then aged about sixteen. "She was a nice attractive young girl and I liked her appearance but I wasn't thinking of marriage. Her parents became my parents and we were very close. After that they killed a pig and they brought it with Marpa to me. She came as a bride to me. Marpa was from the Ndika Kundika clan, not far from Kelua. I wanted them to be my friends—her father my father, her mother my mother, Marpa my sister. I was not ready to marry then, I wasn't shaving. I was much younger than the other Waria men and I would have been ashamed to marry. That is the tradition of our place, that the older men must marry first. A man who shaves, who is strong and can hold a job, that is the sort of man who can marry. I was trying to maintain our tradition.

"One day they killed a pig and brought it to me. It is the normal tradition that when a girl goes to get married a pig is taken to the groom's place. They came to the bush house where I used to sleep at Kelua and waited outside the fence, and Marpa's father beckoned to me to come to him. There was no translator at that time, and the father made signs to me, gesturing to the pig and to Marpa and indicating she should stay with me. 'But I don't want this!' I exclaimed. I was more or less speaking to myself because they didn't understand one word I said and I didn't understand them either. I kept saying to myself, 'I don't want this, I don't want this.'

"I said to them, 'Take the pig and take Marpa and go.' But her father was very strong and said, 'No! You eat it. And you two stay together.' Then *Masta* Mick and *Kiap* Taylor saw me and said, 'You come! What is going on here?' I told them I'd made friends with this family but they were insisting I marry the daughter. *Kiap* Taylor said, 'Why don't you marry her?' I said, '*Kiap*, I don't want to marry her, I haven't even shaved yet.' And then *Kiap* Taylor and *Masta* Mick talked by themselves about this and then Taylor said, 'You take her. This is a new group of people and we want to make friends with them so you take her.' Taylor said if we rejected the local people they would think we were bad, so he told me I must marry her. I asked the two white men what I was to do with the pig they had brought. They said they'd pay for it and I could share it out, and the girl could then come and stay with me. I said that was all right for them, but I was afraid of women then, so I went and stayed in the house on my own."

"She stayed with Meta. Some time later Marpa came to my house and we were sharing this house with other people—she and I had our

Leahy's **gunbois** *Tupia Osiro (left) and Towa Ulta. Originally from the Upper Waria River near the coast, they now live with their highlander wives at Mount Hagen, where this photograph was taken in 1983.*

bed at one side and the others on the other. The bridewealth wasn't given at first, but when they came with the pig we gave them two *kina* shells. Later we gave ten *kina* shells for her, so it was twelve *kina* shells altogether for Marpa. It took us about four weeks of getting used to each other before we lived together as husband and wife."

Dau and Meta were obviously lively and courageous women and, despite their youth and initial terror, were soon turning the situation to their own advantage. Leahy says in his diary that the normal bridewealth was five *kina* shells and an axe, but Dau and Meta claim it was far more than that. Dau's figure of fifty shells could be an exaggeration, but then Leahy was away at the time and Buassi might have been carried away by the occasion. Both women agree that because of their high bridewealth contributions they gained a great deal of status among their people.

"They gave fifty shells for me," says Dau, "but no pigs. All my bridewealth went to Ndika Opa—a relative on my mother's side [in the Ndika line]. Later when I was married I'd give shells out to my own people [the Nengka line]. When they got my bridewealth they were able to get more women for men in their own clan. Later I'd give two or three shells at a time to the Nengka clan and this mounted up to quite a few. They became quite wealthy because of me and made long *omaks* because of all the shells I'd been given for my bridewealth."

By her marriage to Buassi, Dau had temporarily obtained a position denied to even the most powerful of big men. She was close to the men-of-all-things. She could even become involved in the distribution of pearlshells. Other women remember that Dau often handed out shells during trading sessions. She could and did favour those close to her, but there were other advantages to these pioneering women. Living at the camp they soon picked up information, and they could pass it to their people, who in turn came to rely on them. Their names became widely known, and today many Hageners recall that Dau and Meta made things clear to them. It was, of course, revolutionary for young girls in this society to enjoy such fame.

"Afterwards," says Yamka Miti, "people like Dau and Meta translated for us. These women were the ones who told us what the white men were saying. They must have picked up the language, married to coastal men. Through them we could communicate a little and find out more about these strangers."

Dau confirms this: "Meta and I became the intermediaries. We said to our people, 'Look here! We're women! We're from here! They haven't eaten us yet, so don't be frightened.' "

After learning of Buassi's marriage, Michael Leahy observed that the big men seemed to think that if intermarriages took place the strangers might remain living among them permanently. More evidence of the long-term objectives of these shrewd old men comes from Leahy and Taylor again, with both noting that on the afternoon of their return to Kelua, Ndika Powa gave a lengthy speech. By listening carefully and asking for explanations in sign language, Taylor came to the conclusion that Powa believed pearlshells grew on trees in the place the strangers had come from—an inexhaustible source. He suggested that now they were related in marriage, a party of Ndika could go out with them and bring back a few cuttings.

Chapter Nine

EWUNGA CREEK

By the end of June 1933, a more or less harmonious relationship existed at Kelua, oiled by the distribution of pearlshells and by the reassuring presence of women like Dau and Meta. "The locals," wrote Leahy on June 19, "are getting more familiar every day. They come inside the fence now." That was a clear indication that the white men no longer feared a sudden attack. But two days later, on June 21, Leahy was worrying about his food supplies running short. He was very low on shells, and so the people were reluctant to bring food. The day after there was no food at all, and Leahy resorted to threatening that the whole party would leave if none was brought. "The native foods started to come in early. They are frightened that we will go away," he wrote on June 23. The aeroplane duly arrived next day with another load of *kina* shells, and trading returned to normal.

But the Hageners were now becoming choosy. Before the coming of the white men, a scrap of shell was treasured. Three months later they miffed Leahy by refusing a shell marred by marine borer. And there was nothing the Australians could do about it; they had the upper hand in weaponry, but they depended on the Hageners for their food. It could have been flown in, but with a hundred mouths to feed and freight at two shillings a pound, this would have been ruinously expensive. There was more to this trading relationship, of course, than the supply of food. Through it the Hageners had access to their most treasured single item. They had every reason to accept the strangers into their midst and encourage them to stay. Had the Australians been unable to provide these pearlshells, then they would probably not have been anywhere near so welcome, and the penetration of the highlands would have been a far bloodier affair than it was. Pearlshells enabled a handful of invaders to manipulate a far from placid people, and to do virtually what they liked.

There was consternation every time the Australians left on prospecting expeditions out of Kelua, and rejoicing when they returned. On July 9 the Leahys and Taylor came back to camp with several seriously ill carriers, and the rejoicing actually turned to weeping when one young coastal man died the next day. "The locals took charge of the burial of the Markham boy," wrote Leahy on July 10, "and took him down to their cemetery. They rubbed mud on their chests and wailed to beat a brass band. They pointed out to us that two boys died on the trip to the east, one now, and if we went south probably more would die. So [they] suggested that we stop right on the drome and they would give us all the *kai* [food], pigs and *marys* [women] we wanted. And the plane could come in occasionally with shells to buy them with. But we must not go away again."

The passage of time, together with Meta and Dau's sexual experiences, must have brought about a dawning suspicion that these people might possibly be human beings after all. The death and burial of the young coastal carrier could only reinforce this suspicion. But this was a very uneven process. "When Dau got married," says Mokei Kubal Nori, "only the Ndika and Yamka saw that and guessed they must be people like us. When the people over there saw the shells they were giving out they thought perhaps these were people rather than spirits. But we Mokei didn't see anything like that."

For week after week these outside tribes had been avidly listening to reports about the flow of shells from Kelua. Old Hageners often refer today to the intense politicking that went on then over access to these strangers. "The Ndika and Yamka," says Mokei Nembil, "were arguing about whose tribe they should settle in. Everybody wanted them—wanted them to be our friends! We all wanted to have them! We all said they were men-of-all-things."

The big man Yamka Kaura, making a speech in front of the Leahy/Taylor camp at Kelua in 1933. Kaura seems to have lost the attention of at least a part of the crowd, and no doubt the presence of photographer Michael Leahy was a distraction. This was unusual, however. The Australians write that these Hagen big men had the ability to hold large audiences in rapt attention for hours when giving speeches. Oratorical ability was an essential skill for aspiring big men, just as it is for aspiring politicians in the highlands today.

The Mokei heard that the Ndika even wanted to build a fence around Kelua to keep the white men inside. The Mokei eventually concluded that the only hope of gaining access to the strangers' treasure was to entice them away from Kelua, and apparently they put considerable effort into doing this. "The Mokei Nambuka wanted the whites," says Mokei Kominika Korua Kolta, "to come and settle on the Mokei land. They said it was much better where they were, with nice rivers and trees. Out at Kelua there wasn't much, really. So we Mokei argued about it for a while with the Ndika and Yamka. The Mokei wanted so much for the white men to come to their land that they began putting mud all over themselves. One elderly Mokei man covered himself in white ash and went all the way to Kelua. The white man asked him, 'Why have you put that ash all over yourself?' The man said, 'I very much want you to take all your belongings and come and settle with us, on Mokei land.' Ndika Powa had already made friends with these whites

by giving Dau and by giving pigs to them. The Ndika wanted them to
stay where they were, and *Kiap* Taylor said, 'I'll stay here.' But somehow the white man must have thought of our offer—good creeks, plenty
of firewood. So shortly he moved over to our Mokei land.''

Korua Kolta was partly right. Leahy was very attracted by a "good
creek" in Mokei territory. In mid-July, despite the earlier recommendations of the Yamka that he stay put at Kelua, the tireless prospector
headed out to the south on another trip that took him at first through
Mokei country. The Yamka were alarmed at this, and tried to stop him
again, but July 17 saw him moving through the Mokei settlements. "They
were dead anxious to make friends," he wrote that night, "and we never
sighted an axe or spear."

This journey took Leahy many miles out towards the Papuan border, through populated and mountainous country that once again lacked
any significant evidence of gold. Ten days later he was moving back
into Mokei country. On this final day—July 26, only eight miles away
from his Kelua base camp, Dan Leahy tested a small creek by filling his
panning dish with gravel and swirling the wash round until sand and

*A man carves his ceremonial spear with a possum tooth, 1934. The man wears
the traditional half-moon shaped pearlshell around his neck and, tied into his
beard, what appear to be nontraditional spent rifle shells.*

pebbles had been swept away. Within a few minutes the Leahy brothers were bending over a dish with enough gold in its bottom to convince them that after seven years of searching, they had struck it rich
at last. With the eternal optimism of the addicted prospector, Leahy
was immediately dreaming of another Edie Creek, shedding its riches
down into another Bulolo Valley.

Naming the creek after Ewunga Goiba, Leahy sent the NGG surveyor Spinks hurrying back to Kelua to fetch his surveying equipment,
while he and his brother systematically tested the prospect over several
days. It looked very good—so good in fact that Michael Leahy immediately began worrying over the thought of someone else moving in on
the claim before he could register it.

In a twelve-page letter to NGG's Harrison, Leahy painted a glittering picture of Ewunga Creek's potential and urged Harrison to send
Kingsbury out at once. "Got a sample ready," he wrote, "but as it's
fairly bulky Guinea Airways or someone handling it may become in-
quisitive and have a look at it. And once the hawks around the Wau
Pub thought there was a reef about they would connect boxing ground
and dredging ground with it and perhaps get out here before you can
give it a look over, and secure everything worth securing. Taylor is
giving us every assistance, and he is not going to say anything to anybody until we are ready to declare it a gold field."[1]

Michael Leahy was convinced in late July 1933 that in Ewunga Creek
he had finally found his El Dorado. The Mokei were no less pleased.
Having been ignored for three months (apart from being shot at), here
suddenly were all these white men, striding around their country, por-
ing over their creeks, camping among them, buying their food and
looking very pleased with themselves. "The local kanakas," wrote Leahy
at the time, "are very excited about our stopping, and brought plenty
of *kai.*" And the next day: "They sure want us to stop, and I think they
will assist in making the [new] drome for us." So the Mokei could also
look forward to aeroplanes, bringing the white man's treasures. But had
they known this white man's immediate ambitions, they might not have
been quite so enthusiastic. "This locality," continued Leahy's letter to
Harrison, "is remarkably like the Edie Creek basin. There is plenty of
standing timber, and grass, which makes boyhouse building easy. . . .
Their parklike sing sing areas and homesteads, surrounded by ornamental shrubs, would make ideal places to erect camps on. . . . There
are plenty of possible [hydroelectric] power schemes if there was anything proved. . . . I can already visualise about four dredges tearing up

the flats lower down . . . but prospectors always do have rather exaggerated ideas."

Four dredges: Forty thousand pounds to the Leahy brothers right away, and much more to come. But for the Mokei, an invading army, thousands of tons of machinery, ceremonial grounds disappearing under "boyhouses" and company villas, dredges chewing up miles of river flats. But Michael Leahy said himself that prospectors can have exaggerated ideas, and, in this case, the reality turned out to be far short of the dream.

By mid-August the Leahy brothers and Hector Kingsbury were preparing to move across to a camping site closer to Ewunga Creek. There was a great deal of movement at Kelua at this time, as Taylor was also leaving the Hagen base camp. He had to return a number of carriers whose labour contracts had expired to their homes near the coast. Taylor intended leaving most of his police and carrier line at the Kelua camp. He would march back down the Wahgi and through the Chimbu to Bena Bena and then on to the coast, taking with him the surveyor Spinks, two policemen for added protection, and twelve Yamka people—including the big man Kaura, who had volunteered to accompany him for their first look at the world outside Mount Hagen.

Taylor had no doubt his absence would be temporary. Ewunga Creek looked promising, and Taylor was also convinced that the size of the populations they had encountered would compel the administration to move into the Wahgi in force. The Territory's new Administrator—General Thomas Griffiths—had virtually assured him of this during a brief flying visit to Kelua the month before. Taylor had laid on a royal welcome for the general—a thousand Hageners in full ceremonial dress drawn up around the airstrip, with a deputation of big men to greet the Great Man. When Griffiths assured Taylor the Administration would not retire from the area, Taylor wrote in his diary: "This was great news to us, and we were all very pleased the area was not to be abandoned, and all our work go for nothing."

On August 14, he led his line down the valley, and the Leahy brothers headed south towards Mokei country. The white men tried reassuring the Ndika and Yamka, and were partially successful. "All day long," noted Taylor just before leaving, "the people sang and danced on the drome. They say when we return they will put on a big dance festival." But the people seemed to know they were losing the Leahys to the Mokei. "Locals all howled," was Michael Leahy's terse farewell observation. Moving quickly, he established a camp at Wilya, near the home

Dan Leahy shows a mirror to Bena Bena men for the first time.

of Mokei Wamp Wan, a long garden terrace that happened to be the nearest flat land to the gold-bearing sections of Ewunga Creek, about a mile away. Here he and his brother immediately set the people to flattening gardens to make way for a new airstrip.

At the same time, Michael Leahy and Kingsbury began systematically testing Ewunga Creek, and the geologist, a man of vast experience, put an immediate damper on Leahy's optimistic forecast. Ewunga was no Edie. But there was definitely gold to be had, and the Leahy brothers began to prepare their own small-scale mining operation to win a bit for themselves while waiting for Kingsbury to determine what New Guinea Goldfields would finally do.

While this was going on, Taylor was encountering a very different situation to that of the outward journey from Bena Bena the previous March. Populations in the vicinity of Kelua allowed him through un-molested—even volunteered to help the carriers with their loads—but by the third day the mood had changed. Amazement, wrote Taylor, had given away to "truculence." His patrol report gives the official ver-sion of this grim journey. On August 17 shots were fired over the heads of threatening warriors. On August 21, approaching the Chimbu, a knife was stolen from the camp and the following morning a great crowd surrounded the small party. "It appeared," wrote Taylor, "that they were only waiting their opportunity to destroy us and plunder our cargo. One fellow actually brought a rope to tie up his share of the loot." Taylor watched for the first sign of attack, and when a man lifted his spear to throw it, he shot him dead.

After two more days travelling through crowds of hostile people, Taylor reported another incident that ended in bloodshed. A thousand jeering men surrounded his party during a midmorning rest. One drew his bow on Spinks, and Taylor shot him. The following day was no different, with crowds of "prancing bowmen" running up and down the line. "There had been a complete change in atmosphere," says Tay-lor today. "Every spur had a war party coming down—you could see enough to defeat the British Army. We had been discussed, there was no doubt about it. They realised we were holding property."

Taylor recalled that on the way in the previous March he had tried to exchange with a Chimbu man a steel tomahawk for a stone one. It was refused, until Taylor threw in a few shells as well. But on the re-turn journey, "there were a hundred people who came down to get a steel axe. They'd been tried out."

Thumbing through a collection of early photographs in 1982, Taylor picked out one of a Chimbu man whose expression evoked memories of that anxious journey in August 1933. In his right hand the man grips a bow and a half dozen arrows. But the most striking thing is his expression of grinning confidence. Taylor says that day after day he and his small party were surrounded by thousands of men with similar expressions. In his official patrol report he acknowledges killing two men, but today he admits these figures were "pretty well modified. When I had to shoot," he says, "the other people would close in, they wouldn't be affected by the shot. Most people who were out to fight wouldn't think they could be hurt at all."

Put more bluntly, Taylor is saying that when surrounded, it was necessary to shoot more than one to stop a rush. "As he was going towards Moroma," says Gerigl Gande of Kerowagi, "all the tribesmen with their bows and arrows were surrounding him, threatening to attack. They threatened them all day and that night. The following day, they began firing arrows; Taylor was trying to indicate his gun, but they took no notice. The people kept pressing in. Taylor shot five of them. They crossed the Korin River. A man named Dange tried to grab one of the axes, and when he tried to do this they shot more of the people."

"Taylor didn't shoot us straight off," says another man from Kerowagi. "He kept on warning us, making sounds like—boom! But we had

Michael Leahy photographed this man in the Bena Bena Valley soon after the expedition departed for the Wahgi Valley in March 1933. When Jim Taylor saw this photograph in 1983, the man's confident expression reminded him immediately of his return journey from Mount Hagen to Bena Bena in August 1933, when he was continually threatened by armed parties convinced of their superiority over the intruders.

no idea what he was talking about, so we kept going closer until he shot us. He had so many goods, and we wanted to get some from him."

The particular misfortune of the Chimbu people in 1933 was that their country lay between the prospecting areas of Bena Bena and Mount Hagen. On the trip out the Leahys wanted to push through as quickly as possible. With Nason-Jones apparently breathing down their necks the white men strode through the Chimbu, leaving behind them a few steel axes and knives. The Chimbus had five long months to think about them. In Mount Hagen it was different. The Australians camped at Kelua for a lengthy period of time and word of their power spread rapidly, so the casualties were kept to a minimum. The Hagen people—some of them—could also get hold of the desired goods by trading. But the Chimbus had no such opportunity. In most cases they had not seen the gun demonstrated. Their subsequent response in August was inevitable.

On August 28, 1933, Taylor walked into the camp at Bena Bena to discover that the administration post he had established there had been abandoned. It was no coincidence that the New Guinea Goldfields Company was also in the process of quitting the camp, having conclusively established that the area was unsuitable for dredging. "It is in my opinion," noted Taylor in his diary, "a retrograde step." While Taylor was struggling back from the Wahgi Valley, Hector Kingsbury was confirming his early suspicion that Ewunga Creek was not a large-scale mining proposition. On August 28, Kingsbury flew from Mount Hagen down to Salamaua with the news. Four days later, Taylor's superior at Salamaua was telling him that despite earlier assurances, there was no immediate plan to extend Administration influence into the Wahgi Valley and that Taylor was to get back to Kelua as soon as possible, wind up the expedition and abandon the post. "It is very disturbing," wrote Taylor, "considering the amount of work in hand, which has not yet been brought to completion."

So after six heady months, James Taylor and Michael Leahy faced bitter disappointment. Leahy's hopes of becoming a millionaire had been dashed, along with Taylor's dreams of a bold extension of the pax Australiana. Having established the existence of hundreds of thousands of new people, the administration intended doing nothing about them for the time being. It had followed in the footsteps of the gold prospectors, and when the gold prospectors weren't interested in an area, the Administration wasn't, either.

Chapter Ten

THE OUTSIDE WORLD

In the mid-1920s a number of Hagen tribes had combined to bring about the downfall of the Elti and Penambe—a powerful combination that had traditionally threatened the Mokei on their southern borders. In the Hagen area, it was the greatest war in living memory. There was much bloodshed, and when it was over the Elti-Penambe had been defeated and routed. Large tracts of land were permanently lost to them, and most of their people were dispersed, seeking refuge wherever they could. Mokei Wamp Wan's Nambuka played a leading role in the war and emerged with considerable territorial gains. Before the war, the Elti-Penambe land included the hilly country drained by Ewunga Creek—called Kuta by the owners—and stretched right down to the long garden terrace known as Wilya, where the Leahy brothers were to build their second airstrip.

Penambe Wia Tugl from Kunguma says today the trouble began when some of his Elti-Penambe people went to observe a battle between rival Ndika clans. While they were watching, one of the Elti men was killed by enemy Mokei. At the funeral some days later, when pigs were killed and eaten and the dead body finally covered up in its grave, a man named Mokei Kolumbai (who was related to the Elti-Penambe by marriage) committed a fatal indiscretion.

"The Mokei man," says Tugl, "just before he ate his piece of pig meat, spat because the dead man's body smelt. Everyone started whispering to the big men, 'This Mokei is spitting at the dead man. It's disrespectful.' Then all of a sudden the Elti went and killed this Mokei man."

This killing sealed the fate of the Elti-Penambe. The Mokei determined to wipe them out. "Just near Kuta," says Tugl, "we had a big battle—back and forth, back and forth. Many, many people were killed, on both sides." As more clans combined against them, the Elti-Penambe found themselves in the worst of all strategic situations—surrounded by hostile clans, with no avenue of escape. "The Tshona and Kulga went and helped the Mokei and fought against us," says Tugl. "Then too the Kopia and the Nokopa. We wanted to flee a certain way but then the Ulga Ulgupuka joined in against us. Then the Pulka and Paraka. The enemies surrounded us, and we were scattered all over the place."

"My brothers and I, young boys at the time, were with my mother the day she was killed. We were carrying bags of sweet potatoes and when we saw the enemy coming close, we threw the bags away and rushed off in different directions. My mother was all by herself when the Mokei killed her. We don't even know what happened to her body—we just left it there and ran off."

Penambe Tugl and his four brothers—Kuan, Wai, Penapul and Kut—managed to escape the massacre. The five youngsters—the eldest was about thirteen—hid during the day and travelled by night through a sea of enemies before reaching friendly clans about two days' walk away. Although the Elti-Penambe had few allies during this catastrophe, some were prepared to help refugees escape, or even take them in. Ndika Rumint, for example, remembers that "While this fight was on I went and got some of them during the night time and helped them to escape near where I live now. Mokei were blocking the way, waiting. We had a lot of shells and pigs, women and children with us from the Elti-Penambe clans. I somehow managed to escape and the Elti-Penambe got away, too. I helped bring them down to the flat land around Kelua."

It was these Elti-Penambe living with the Ndika near Kelua who so frightened Mokei Wamp Wan during his first visit to the Australian camp ten years later. The refugees had not forgotten their crushing defeat, and Wamp had every reason to be nervous. His people were living then at Wilya on land they had captured from the Elti-Penambe, and it was here on a long garden terrace that Leahy built his new airstrip.

Ewunga Creek and the country it drained—known as Kuta—had remained a no-man's land since that war. This situation suited the Leahy brothers perfectly. Their agreement with NGG gave them the sole right to any gold-bearing country not taken up by the company, and this they now did. Claims covering Ewunga Creek were registered with the Administration's mining warden at Salamaua in the names of M. J. and D. J. Leahy. NGG's decision to pull out of the highlands meant the end of the brothers' employment, and their plan was to mine the creek for two months, holiday in Australia, and then return to Mount Hagen the following year. Leahy hoped to raise finance for further prospecting ventures, using Wilya and Ewunga Creek as his base.

Leahy had always been conscious of the practical advantages of communicating freely with the people he was living among, and now that he was actually about to start mining at Kuta this had become an absolute necessity. Dau and Meta—the first Hageners to learn pidgin and act as intermediaries—were with their husbands at Kelua, waiting for Taylor's return. The interpreting role these young women had assumed was unplanned. But at Kuta—as his mining operation came to be called—Leahy needed interpreters of his own. Before coming into the Wahgi Valley he had relied on young boys to translate for him. Youngsters seemed more adept than their elders at picking up pidgin, and Leahy made a practice of encouraging them to join his camp. He had done this at Bena Bena, and some of these boys were still with him. One of them was Isakoa Hepu of Magitu Village.

Recently Isakoa was shown a photograph of three young boys taken fifty years earlier on the airstrip at Bena Bena by Michael Leahy. Surrounded by friends and relatives, he held up the photograph and pointed to the boy on the right. "That's me! The big-nosed one right there! All of you, look! I told you—the white man took me when I was just a kid." Pointing to the one on the left, Isakoa announced: "This one— he's Jokuri—he could speak Kafe."

Jokuri is dead. Isakoa, now in his sixties, joined the Leahy brothers in 1932. He travelled with them on prospecting expeditions hundreds of miles to the west, went out to the coast to see the outside world, took part in the second world war, fighting with Australians against the Japanese, and eventually returned to his own village, about one mile from the old Bena Bena base camp of New Guinea Goldfields.

Three young boys recruited to Michael Leahy's expedition, photographed at Bena Bena camp late in 1932. At left is Jokuri Hari and at right Isakoa Hepu. The boy in the middle is unknown. Jokuri seems more confident than the other two, probably because he was one of the first boys in the Bena Bena Valley to join up with the Leahys and so would by this time be familiar with his surroundings. Isakoa, on the other hand, had only just been recruited, having left his mother in rather distressing circumstances.

When Isakoa joined the Leahys, his father—a village big man and fight leader—had been "poisoned" by his enemies, and his mother had married again. "My mother had told me about my father dying," says Isakoa. "We'd never seen white men before—that's why we thought they must be our own returning dead—and my mother thought Mick Leahy was the spirit of my dead father, who had come to take me. I was very young, with no thoughts of my own.

"One day we were digging for earthworms—well out of sight of the white man's camp. Mick was down at the river, looking for gold, when he saw us. He came up to us and took me. My mother began to cry and said, 'Don't go away!' Mick took me, telling my mother, 'I will look after him, and he'll grow big, and then come back and talk to you people.' Mick held me by the hand. My mother wasn't sure if Mick was my dead father, and she hesitated to let me go in case they killed me. But our village was some distance away, and she had to go. But she said she would come back next morning and find out what they'd done to me."

Isakoa says he was then led back to the camp by Leahy, who handed him over to the care of a Waria man named Lowai. "Lowai gave me food and then we went to sleep in a tent. We couldn't communicate— he used sign language when he wanted us to sleep. *Masta* Mick cut the rope holding up my bark *tapa* [traditional dress] and threw it away. Then he cut a piece of white *lap lap* and gave it to me. Next day my mother and the others all came with mourning mud on their faces, crying. They had no idea what could have happened to me. I was a big man's son, and my father's replacement, and they feared the strangers might have killed me.

"There were two camp dogs, Snowy and Spark. The camp was fenced in with a long rope line and my people stood outside it, afraid of the dogs. I was inside and could see my mother crying. I was afraid of the dogs, too! They were on long chains and could move around and attack

Isakoa Hepu in 1983 sees himself again as a boy in 1932.

the people if the white men wanted them. When *Masta* Mick saw them
crying he gave them axes, knives and shells and told them not to cry.
They saw I'd washed and was wearing a piece of *lap lap*. They realised
I was all right, so they took these things and went away."

Jokuri Hari, the boy on the left of the photograph—was "recruited"
by the Leahy brothers shortly before Isakoa. Jokuri died in 1980 before
his version of events could be recorded, and Dan Leahy is one of the
few men left who was there at the time. He and his brother were prospecting in the Bena Bena Valley and had pulled up near the village of
Mohovetu to buy some sugarcane from the local people and have a cup
of tea. As they headed off again, a man rushed up and grabbed a bush
knife from one of the carrier's packs. He ran off with it and Michael
Leahy began shooting around him until he stopped and began running
back, holding the stolen knife above him. While Michael Leahy was
demonstrating the carrying power of his rifle, Dan Leahy had run into
Mohovetu looking for hostages.

"Most of the natives had disappeared," says Dan, "but we rushed
into the nearest house. I looked up and on the centre pole, right up in
the apex of the roof, was this little kid. He was as high as he could get.
Our boys grabbed him and brought him out. There was an old man
and they brought him as well."

The Leahys made it clear to their hostages that they wanted the
knife back, and the small boy screamed out in fear. "I don't know what
he was telling them," says Dan, "that he was being roasted, I suppose,
or about to have his head cut off." Michael Leahy wrote that it was the
effect of the bullets splashing around the man with the knife that led
him to return, but Dan emphasises the screams of the boy. Whatever
the case, the knife came back, and the Leahys marched off.

Within a month they were back, setting up their Bena Bena base
camp, and among their first visitors was a delegation bringing food from
Mohovetu. Among them were the old man and the small boy, Jokuri
Hari—or Joe Curry, as Dan Leahy says the Australians soon dubbed
him. "Joe was there every day, and after a week or so he attached himself to the camp. We kept him there and thought it would be a good
idea to teach him pidgin, which he picked up very quickly. Within a
few months he was very good, and he became our first interpreter."

Jokuri was doubly valuable to the Leahys at this time because in
addition to pidgin he could speak two highland languages—his native
Kafe, and Bena. Jokuri was an orphan and refugee at Mohovetu and

this probably had something to do with his readiness to join the Leahy camp. Two of Leahy's Waria men—Towa Ulta and Tupia Osiro—took Jokuri under their wing, and these three worked together for many years, eventually sharing a house in their retirement at Mount Hagen. The partnership was broken with Jokuri's death in 1981. Towa and Tupia talk of being both "mother and father" to the young Jokuri, and say they came to think of him as a Waria.

And then there was Narmu Varnu, who also died in 1981. He first met Michael Leahy in 1930, when Leahy and Dwyer passed through Narmu's village of Seerupu on their first expedition into the eastern highland valleys. On their second journey a few months later the two white men went by Seerupu again and were warmly greeted by the young man, who made signs that they had met before.

And then two years later, Leahy was back in Seerupu prospecting for NGG, and this time Narmu insisted on going with him. Leahy agreed. But after a few miles it dawned on Leahy that they could now be among people hostile to Seerupu. Should the boy attempt to run back, he might be killed.

So Narmu found himself tied by a length of rope to one of the Waria, which did nothing for his confidence. He grew very frightened, and soon the people along the track were pointing him out and shaking their heads. Enemies or not, they were upset. Eventually a war party gathered to rescue Narmu, which Leahy dispersed with a volley, causing, he says, no casualties. The Leahys now force marched their way out of this tense situation, and arrived twelve hours later at the new Administration outpost of Kainantu.

Narmu was untied, but his adventures had only just begun. The next day an aeroplane landed at the Kainantu strip, and this is the same Narmu that Hector Kingsbury filmed reacting in terror to the appearance of the plane. Leahy then decided to send the boy on a flight to the coast to give him a quick glimpse of the outside world. The pilot, Bob Gurney, was to fly him to the coastal port of Lae, look after him for a day, and then bring him back. Three days, then, after entrusting himself to these white spirits, the young highlander now found himself strapped into an aeroplane and flying through the air. Sadly, Narmu died at Seerupu Village before recording his own thoughts about this experience—what it was like to glimpse, suddenly, with no preparation at all, an outside world whose existence he had not even imagined. He flew down to Lae on a Tuesday in November 1932 and came back the following day. The pilot put him up at his house, mindful of Michael Leahy's instructions that he sleep under a net at night to ward off malarial mosquitos. Here is Leahy's version of events, as recorded in his book *The Land That Time Forgot*:

> Gurney took him on a shopping expedition and bought him a great collection of coloured gimcracks and baubles, as well as a red lap lap, a mouth organ, a couple of small mirrors, a leather belt, a white cotton singlet, a pound or so of glass beads, and a few knives. He was taken inside a refrigeration chamber in one of the stores, and given a small piece of ice. He had a look at the sea, and saw a fortune in shells lying unclaimed on the beach. He listened to a phonograph, and saw an electric light, and wore out the switch turning the light on and off again. Gurney said that next to the electric light the thing that seemed to interest Narmu most was the heap of tin cans and empty bottles.

On his travels Narmu had also seen a horse. "He kept pointing to the horse," wrote Leahy, "exclaiming *luci fura, luci fura* which means 'big pig.' There are no large animals in New Guinea and he must have known he wouldn't be believed when he got home, and told about seeing a horse, for he insisted on having a few of the long hairs out of the horse's tail to take back with him."

Michael Leahy says that on his return after a day at Lae, Narmu looked "thoroughly pleased with himself. . . . He had a bottle of seawater, and a big box full of his other treasures." The Leahy brothers

Kopia Kerika Rebia, one of the first young translators in Mount Hagen soon after contact in 1933, at his home in the mid-Wahgi, 1983.

Mokei Nambuka Puri, a young Hagen boy, about Kopia Rebia's age when he first met the Leahys. Mokei Puri was among Father William Ross's first school class of thirty Hagen children. Photo about 1936.

then escorted Narmu back to his village and "Narmu spread out his treasures and launched into a great oration, telling, doubtless, about the horse, the phonograph, the airplane and the sea. I could see that some of the hearers were sceptical, but Narmu hauled out his bottle of sea-water, let them taste it, and showed them the long hairs from the horse's tail."

Narmu was among the first highlanders to visit the outside world, but he was not the last. Leahy could see the public relations value in this exercise and was to repeat it many times. Early in 1933, it was Isakoa Hepu's turn. He was flown from Bena Bena to Wau three days after being taken from his mother to the white man's camp.

"*Masta* hung onto my hand until the plane came to a stop," says Isakoa. "When they had loaded the cargo he went to put me in with the pilot. When he was trying to take me to the plane I ran away and hid in the grass. He abused and kicked his men around and sent them out after me. They found me and brought me out. *Masta* patted my chest, and made the sound of the plane and said, 'You are going!' My relatives said, 'Oh, he's being taken by the spirits of his ancestors who died long ago.'

"When I was to go they turned their faces away and said to me, 'You must not eat their rice! You must not eat their meat! You must not eat anything they give you, because if you do, it will send you wild!' They would not look at me when speaking, fearing the *masta* would

Michael Leahy introduces a Hagen big man—possibly Ndika Powa—to the cockpit of a Junkers transport plane. The Australian on the wing is pilot Bob Gurney. Kelua, 1933.

beat them. They would turn their faces away. Mick was a peculiarly harsh man. He had shot some people before [the Korofeigu and Goropa killings], so the people were frightened about this. They felt if they weren't careful he would shoot them. That's why they only let me hear their words, without facing me.

"Mick didn't hit the villagers, but when his labourers did not work well or did something wrong, he would whip them with a big piece of rubber. The people were frightened because they had seen him hit others before." (Dan Leahy says the "rubber" was an aeroplane wing strut. Leahy's men were stripped, stretched out and flogged with this, his most severe form of punishment. Any physical violence against indentured labourers was against the law, but it was customary in New Guinea before the war as a way of maintaining discipline.)

"*Masta* Mick put me in the aeroplane," says Isakoa, "and told the other man there, 'He might try and jump out, so the two of you sit together.' So I sat next to him—just the two of us. When the plane took off and when it went up and down I cried! And that *masta* held me and said, 'You must not cry!' But I kept on until we landed at Wau. If I'd been big I could have looked out, but I was small, so the *masta* put me under his arm and held me there as we went. Just the two of us.

"After landing at Wau, *Masta* Bill drove down in a car towards me. When I saw it I was afraid. He wanted me to go with him in it but I thought that thing would kill me, so I held tightly onto the plane and cried in fear. The *masta* patted me on the chest and put me in the car. I saw houses—green houses, red houses, white houses. I thought I had come to the devil's place, and maybe I would go wild. And then I thought of my mother, and I cried a little.

"I saw cattle, and I was really afraid of them. I saw donkeys. I pissed with fear when I saw them. But I used to go and buy meat from the freezer at Wau and then I realised those animals were food after all. At Wau I stayed with *Masta* Bill. He could take his eye out and pull out his teeth. I used to be afraid of him, too." (Bill Tracy worked for Jim Leahy at Wau. He had a glass eye and false teeth.)

"The idea of sending them out," says Dan Leahy, "was to give them a look at the outside world, how we lived, to show them there were all the motor cars, and all the different machinery and the modern equipment. They had nothing at all! They'd never seen a wheel, much less something pulling it! They only carried things on their backs. It was primitive man to modern civilisation. To show them all that."

When young highlanders like Narmu and Isakoa visited the outside world, they were something of a novelty to the white population. They were fussed over, like zoological curiosities. Michael Leahy told the Lae storekeeper to let Narmu buy anything he wanted, and to debit his account. "He just went and took things off the shelf," says Jim Leahy. "He didn't know anything about paying, or buying." These young travellers were only too eager to spread their information about what they had seen—in whatever form they had digested it. And their fellow highlanders listened avidly to their stories.

According to Michael Leahy the policy of sending children out to the coast was unquestionably a valuable exercise. "Two kanakas," he wrote in his diary at the time, "who were sent to Wau about a week before came back . . . to impress their friends that we were OK, and meant no harm. . . . Got a great reception for bringing [them] back, and immediate applications from about a further thirty natives who wanted to go and see what the outside world was like."

One week later, Leahy wrote to Major Harrison: "The natives here [at Bena Bena] are now OK and appear to be very friendly since their people went in the plane to Wau, Lae and Salamaua. Today they brought three pigs and also some cuttings from shrubs to plant inside our camp area, as peace offerings. Their general behaviour is much friendlier than before."[1]

Narmu remained at Seerupu the rest of his life. Even now it is a very isolated place. He never learnt pidgin and had nothing more to do with the Leahy brothers. The prospectors had different plans for Isakoa, however. He remained at Wau throughout 1933, living with Bill Tracy and becoming a fluent pidgin speaker. Leahy planned to use him as an interpreter at the end of his training.

In August 1933, while Isakoa was making good progress with pidgin and working as a *kukboi* in Tracy's kitchen, the Leahy brothers were mining gold at Kuta and recruiting another group of young trainee translators from the surrounding Hagen clans, the first of whom was Kopia Kerika Rebia from Korabug. Rebia was a young boy living not far from Wilya, the site of the Leahy's second airstrip. Once again Towa Ulta was to be the mentor. "Coastal men—like Towa," says Rebia, "would talk to me in their language, and say '*yu kisim wara*' [pidgin for "go and fetch some water"]. I used to follow him, saying over and again '*yu kisim wara, yu kisim wara.*' Then they'd say to me, '*yu kam bek*' [come back], and I'd go around repeating that—'*yu kam bek, yu kam bek.*' The white man said to the coastal men, 'Don't get cross with him because he keeps repeating the words. If he keeps doing that he'll learn, so just let him go.' "

Two Hagen men photographed inside a transport plane, Kelua, 1933.

"The piece of *lap lap* they gave me to wear—I used to wipe my hands on it after I'd been eating pig and it soon got very dirty. I was given soap and told to go to the river and wash myself. I took my *lap lap* off to bathe and when I'd had my wash I had no idea how to put it back on again! I had to lie the *lap lap* flat on the grass, and then lie down on top of it and tie it round me as I was lying on it. The way I did it you could see my private parts—I didn't have any underclothes then—but the people didn't seem to mind very much."

Despite these early difficulties, Kopia Rebia learnt quickly and at some point in August or September 1933 he too flew out to his first encounter with the world beyond Mount Hagen. "My mother held me by the hand and tried to pull me back, saying, 'Don't take my son away!' She nearly hit the white man! But a Hagen man held her down and they started the plane and we went up into the air. I think I was away one week.

"When we got near, the white man pointed. 'That's the sea, look! That's the sea.' I couldn't believe it! It looked like the sky, never ending. It was enormous. I walked to the sea and I saw great crabs, crawling on posts in the water. I went to pick them up, but as I did the water came at me! I thought the water was trying to get me because I was trying to grab the crab! And on the ground I saw shells. I went to pick them up, but they moved away from me! I couldn't understand it. Now I know they must have been live shells.

"When we were coming back they told me we were getting close to where I lived. I yelled out with all my might to let the people know I was coming back. When I arrived, I said, 'Did you hear me?' They said they heard nothing.

"The first thing I remember about that day was how impressed everyone was that I'd returned. Our people said, 'These whites must have human feelings after all, to bring you back to us.' The people said how happy they were to see me back, and they hugged me. They thought I might be eaten.

"I told them, 'The white people don't eat people! Name anything you can think of—they've got it. They've got good houses, meat, everything! These people have so much wealth, and they want to share it with us. That's why they came here. They didn't come to eat us!' I told our people we had to look after these white people."

If Rebia's memory serves him well, and this is what he said to his people fifty years ago, then Leahy had cause to be grateful to him and well satisfied with his policy of giving selected children a glimpse of the outside world.

As their visits were primarily intended to cement relations, great care was taken to keep them in good health. The Leahys were well aware how damaging it would have been to bring a boy back from the outside world only to have him die a lingering and mysterious death from malaria. Jim Leahy, based at Wau, who looked after many of these young people, put it bluntly: "You had to get them back whole, or it could have been very nasty."

In point of fact the risk these children ran of catching malaria was considerable. The malarial mosquito was uncommon in the highlands above three thousand feet, and the highlanders therefore had very little resistance to the disease. This was an argument used by the German Lutheran missionaries in their campaign against any large-scale movement of highlanders to the coast to ease the ever-present labour shortages on the mining fields and plantations. The coastal New Guineans tended not to sign up again after one stint of indentured labour, particularly those sent to the mines. As a result, the labour recruiters were charging up to twenty pounds per recruit as they were forced further and further outwards to villages where the tainted nature of the mining work was unknown.

When news of the highland populations began to filter out in 1930, despite the best efforts of the Lutherans to prevent it, the labour recruiters turned hungry eyes towards these new human pastures. ". . . if the missions could possibly be kept out," exulted C. J. Levien, a prominent white miner, "it would be possible to take out five thousand good boys from an area twenty by twenty miles, and they would not be missed."[2] Fortunately for the highland people, this suggestion was not taken up. To its credit the prewar Australian administration resisted pressure from miners and planters and imposed a total ban on recruiting in the highland valleys above an altitude of three thousand feet. James Taylor believes that as a result, thousands of lives were saved. The death rate among coastal mining workers was already twice the average.

Very few highlanders in these early years managed to venture out to the coast. But both Taylor and Michael Leahy made a point of including them on their travels within the highlands. There were positive advantages for the white men here, too. The volunteers were eager carriers,

Clansmen tearfully welcome back a Hagen man upon his return from travelling to the coast with the Leahys.

and, again, their safe return home helped promote good relations. A group of Bena Bena people had accompanied the expedition into the Wahgi as carriers. The unknown wife of one of them obviously played a key role in soothing the terrified Dau during her first few days at Kelua. And Taylor took with him twelve men from around Kelua when he walked back out to Bena Bena in September. Bena Bena people travelling to the end of the Wahgi—Hagen people visiting Bena Bena—inconceivable in the time before contact.

The highlanders' extreme curiosity continually overcame their fear of the unknown. These were revolutionary times. Men, women and children set off with the strangers, sometimes on the very first day they encountered them, leaving behind familiar surroundings and loved ones who feared they were going to a certain death. It represented extraordinary bravery. Taylor tells of one highland man who lashed himself to the outside of an aeroplane and announced calmly that whatever his fate, he had to see where it had come from.

Some of these people—Isakoa Hepu and Jokuri Hari among them—

threw in their lot with the Australians, maintaining associations which lasted many years. Others like Narmu Varnu were caught up in a brief and intense experience. And countless others fetched and carried in anonymous obscurity, often not even sure of the very human identity of these remote *mastas*. The Chimbu man Kimba Kopol joined an expedition as a carrier in 1933 because he was convinced that one of the coastal men in the line was his dead uncle. He slept each night with this man in his shelter and each night awoke, silently lit a small fire, and peered intently at his sleeping companion. "I was expecting he would be just bones there because he was a dead person. I used to check him to see if the flesh had parted from the bones. He always looked the same, and I began to think he was an ordinary man. But I wasn't really sure."

And when Kimba Kopol returned from months away, "Everyone was painted in mud and crying. They believed we had returned from the dead. We had to tell them to stop mourning. We were real people, living with real people. The white men were not dead but real. We had been working for them and now we had returned."

What is striking about the accounts of these earliest carriers is the sense of powerlessness they reveal. No private soldier in any army, caught up in some vast campaign, could have been so far removed from the seat of decision making as these, so ignorant of what they were doing and where they were going. They could communicate only in signs. Once outside their own territory, their fate was entirely in the white man's hands. Ndika Nikints was one of the Kelua twelve who marched down to Bena Bena with Taylor in August 1933. After this fearful journey, menaced on all sides by thousands of strange and hostile people, Nikints found himself cooling his heels at the Bena Bena base camp while Taylor, called urgently away to Salamaua, was arguing with his superior over future policy in the Wahgi. After two weeks in this strange place, unimaginably far from home, Nikints says he wept and wept, wondering how he would ever get home again. He was greatly relieved when Taylor returned and the party set off again for Kelua, this time making a much more peaceful journey.

A more plaintive story is told by Penambe Tugl's younger brother Penambe Wai, whose mother had been killed in the big war. In 1938, James Taylor led a very large Administration patrol on an expedition towards the Dutch border. Wai carried his load of expedition supplies in unknown country for thirteen long months. "We travelled and travelled," says Penambe Wai, "we camped at many different places. Once we camped near a river. This area was mountainous and there was no food. We lived on bush ferns and leaves, we ran out of rice. What could we do? We kept on going. We went to a place where the men wear penis gourds and the women were naked.

"When I got to one place I saw a woman who was wearing pig's teeth around her neck. She made signs and said, 'You must be hungry. Come to my place and have some taro.' I said yes. We stayed for a while here. My job was to fetch water. The girl used to follow me. Then she went on a visiting trip, away with her people. Her family had become like a family to me. The day after she left I was told we were going back to Kelua. I waited that night hoping she would come back so I could tell her I was leaving. I waited—and they didn't come back. So I began to cry, and I sang this song:

> *Tina must come—I have to see her before I go*
> *I've long ago forgotten my own people*
> *Tina is my friend and my family*
> *Tina has to come, Tina has to come*
> *Before I go*
> *Tina left a couple of days ago*
> *Tina has to come back before I go.*

"And then I began crying again. I cried a lot about not seeing her. But it took us a few days to pack, and she came back in this time. Her parents said she could go with me, but I wasn't allowed to take her. I talked to them, and gave them all the things I had. 'Perhaps I will see you again,' I said, 'perhaps I'll come back here.' Tina's mother was very upset—she nearly committed suicide by hanging herself. For two days they followed me. I said, 'Go back! One day I'll return!' " Wai never did see her again, but he later married and named one of his daughters after her.

October 1933 marked the end of the first phase of contact in the Wahgi Valley. After five and a half months at Mount Hagen the Leahy brothers began preparations for their departure. They had parted company with New Guinea Goldfields, they wanted a holiday, and they needed to drum up new financial backing in Australia for their further prospecting ventures.

James Taylor had lost his argument with the Administration over an

A raider at Mount Hagen, caught and killed by multiple axe blows.

immediate and permanent government presence in the valley. He was ordered back to Kelua to close the base camp down and late September saw him once more on the track towards the Wahgi (with a greatly relieved Ndika Nikints) noting this time the extreme friendliness of the Chimbu and Wahgi people, in stark contrast to their attitude a month earlier. Approaching Kelua, Taylor says they received a great welcome all along the track. "The returning volunteers who were with us marched with great ceremony, singing native songs. We reached the landing ground at 10 A.M. [on September 29] and at 11 A.M. Mr. Leahy arrived from Mogai [Mokei]."

The Leahys and Taylor spent the next week preparing for their final departure, and every day crowds of up to two thousand gathered around the camp, realising that the strangers were finally all leaving. Both white men recorded that there was much singing and dancing, and on one day twenty pigs were killed as part of a farewell festival.

During this time, rumours reached the Australians that a number of neighbouring Minembi people had been killed after visiting the camp. The Minembi were enemies of the Yamka and Ndika, and on their previous two visits to Kelua had been escorted in and out by Leahy's men. Growing confident, they had ventured in a third time without escort. Returning home, eight of them, two men and six women, had been axed to death.

One of the Administration's first priorities in newly contacted areas was to try to put an end to fighting and killing, gradually introducing instead the western system of impartial justice transcending clan obligation. It was a revolutionary notion, and the highlanders would resist it for years. The law under which they lived required that groups of individuals themselves had the responsibility for correcting wrongs committed against them. But Taylor decided that this was an opportune time to demonstrate the new concept.

Learning the identity of the killers from a local informant, Taylor marched his police over to their village. He called out their names—Yamka Obi, Yamka Maba, Yamka Wager and Yamka Kubarl. Obi and Kubarl came forward to see what the white man wanted and were promptly "arrested." There was no trouble at all, Taylor wrote, in doing this. "In fact the offenders were told to hurry up and not keep us waiting by their friends." The men then learned that by killing the Minembi they had broken the white man's law and would be taken out to "jail" in Salamaua. Taylor recorded that no one seemed disturbed by the arrests, "as they cannot believe we mean them any harm." The killers were going to see the outside world, which a great many other highlanders wanted to do. And in any case, what had they done wrong? The Minembi were arch enemies.

Taylor makes no mention of any motive behind the killing of the Minembi people, but no doubt there were complex underlying reasons—a payback for recent offences, or perhaps revenge for Yamka deaths by Minembi sorcery. But the Assistant District Officer, whose colonial powers included those of policeman, judge and jailer, thought he had to begin somewhere, and the killings gave him a chance to demonstrate one of the reasons why he had come. He was not so much concerned with punishment at this stage—that would have been meaningless—but with introducing some notion of the system of law and order that he represented. Reflecting Administration policy, Taylor believed that the best way to begin was to take these men to the coast, teach them pidgin, and let them see there were ways different to their own. The normal penalty for murder in the Territory was death by hanging, but the long-established practice was to take into account the accused person's familiarity with the Territory Code and the extent to which the killing was dictated by tribal custom. This policy, of course, applied to New Guineans killing New Guineans. When New Guinea highlanders killed white men, as would soon happen, then other white men, miners

and Administration officials found no difficulty in adopting the highland custom of payback.

The "murderers" were duly escorted back to Kelua wearing handcuffs, and kept under guard as final preparations were made to abandon the base camp. Taylor had no idea what the future held, but Michael
Leahy fully intended returning to Mount Hagen within six months, and
he decided to leave a cache of unused supplies on the airstrip, mainly
tinned food. On the eve of their departure he noted in his diary that he
had "asked a couple of locals [in particular the big man Kaura] to look
after it until we get back. They will do anything as long as we come
back. It's going to be difficult to get away."

A week-long display of emotion, feasting and ceremonial dancing
on the Kelua airstrip reached its climax next morning. It was Saturday,
October 7, 1933. At eight-thirty the long line formed up. Taking their
places in it were the handcuffed Yamka prisoners and seven young Hagen
women who had married members of the expedition—Meta, Dau and
Towa's wife Marpa among them. A great crowd had gathered to see
the strangers and the loved ones go, "wailing and crying," according to Taylor. The big man Ndika Powa was a "picture of dignified sorrow" but Yamka Kaura threw himself on the ground, literally tore
his hair, and ran alongside the "men-of-all-things" weeping in anguish.
Michael Leahy was busy with his Leica, so there are photographs to
document it.

For the highland women this was the beginning of a great adventure, as they fought back their terror and headed east along the Wahgi
Valley, soon reaching the outer limits of the territory familiar to them.
The first hurdle came as they approached the Wahgi River, which the
women had never crossed in their lives. "You know this Wahgi," says
Dau, "nowadays it's not flowing as fast or rough as it used to, but then
the river was very high. The tracks weren't any good. They tied us to
the policemen to get us across the river. We were then heading towards
Banz and Minj [lower down the valley]. We went through the bush by
foot. There were no roads. When we were sick they used to carry us
on stretchers, on their shoulders, too. We used to cry, 'Mother! Father!'
we were so exhausted. As we passed through villages, those people
living there would carry us on the stretcher as well. Our men weren't
any good—it was us women who got close to the whites!"

Every day these women travelled among and met first-hand new
peoples, broadly similar in appearance but speaking different languages, wearing different clothing and decorations, living in different

Taken by Michael Leahy on October 7, 1933, as the expedition finally leaves Kelua on the home journey after a stay of nearly six months. Yamka Kaura runs along the carrier line, dismayed that the "men-of-all-things" are actually leaving. Taylor says Kaura literally tore his hair in sorrow and anguish and threw himself upon the ground.

houses. For three weeks the journey took them east through the populated highland valleys—down the Wahgi, across the Chimbu, down into the Asaro, Goroka and Bena Bena with their newly established Lutheran mission outposts, past Kainantu and so right down to the Kassam Pass—the very edge of the massive highland plateau, overlooking the Markham Valley thousands of feet below, a flat dry immensity stretching a hundred miles down to the sea.

Descending from the heights of the Kassam to the Markham, which lies at sea level, the highland women felt the first breath of the equatorial heat. The last 100 miles down the Markham were always the hardest for travellers on foot in those days, and for these women the journey was especially arduous. The climate they knew was the crisp clarity of the highland valleys—five and six thousand feet above sea level, with dry season temperatures rarely rising above 85 degrees. Now they found themselves trudging down the Markham. Behind, purple and shimmering in the heat haze, the enormous mountain ramparts of the highlands rose sheer from the flat valley floor. Occasional clumps of unfamiliar coconut palms gave temporary shelter from the heat.

Several more walking days would have seen them in the rain forest, where the heavy humid air itself seems coloured green, and as they drew near the coast, ordered rows of plantation coconut groves. The odour of mangrove swamps mixed with salt sea air. A scattering of houses, woven palm or wooden and tin roofed, muddy streets lined with more buildings, throngs of people—New Guineans wearing *lap laps*, white men decked out in colonial whites, white women in dresses and wide hats, warehouses, dockyards with their cranes unloading moored freighters, and beyond all this, the blue expanse of the sea.

"We tried to explain to our people [when she returned to Mount Hagen] what we saw," says Dau today. "There were two cars, one bicycle, a motorbike and houses. The bicycle, we told them was like a bush tree that grows around Hagen. You can bend it and make hoops and round shapes. We told them that people would sit on something like this and it would move along. We said it was like how we make the fire—when we did that we put a stick under our foot and with our arms pulled a bush rope backwards and forwards so it rubbed against the wood. We said with the bicycle you do this movement with your legs. The motorbike was like an insect or spider, but much bigger, carrying a person on its back, and it could run along really fast. The car was like the insect that lives in the taro—it carries people and runs along so fast it almost flies! We called it '*möi mbur mel*'—'a ground flying thing.'

"We told our people there were nice houses there, although we didn't see many. And they ate good food. They lead a good life down there. Now many people go to Lae, but then it was a big thing. When we returned the people were happy to see us. They said, 'As far as we were concerned we had received bridewealth for you and we thought you might never come back, that we'd never see you again.' "

"The Hagen . . . people who are with us," wrote Michael Leahy later in his diary, "are thrilled to bits over the sea but I am afraid it will be beyond them to adequately describe it to their people in the bush." Nonetheless it seems Dau made a fair fist of it. "We tried to explain that the saltwater was really huge. It filled up all the space there was. We told them all the rivers from here went into this big area, and it all stayed in the one place. Sometimes the water overflowed onto the land, and then went back, and overflowed again."

When questioned today, old Hageners who made these pioneering journeys invariably agree that what impressed them above all else was the sea. This can be partly explained by the fact that the water was salty, and salt was a scarce and valued commodity. And the people were undoubtedly impressed by the sight of shells lying along the shore. But there was perhaps another explanation behind their fascination with the tropic waters of the Huon Gulf which washed up on the coral beaches of Lae amd Salamaua.

Part of the Hagen cosmology was the belief that where the sky and the earth met, the heavens were connected to the earth by skylegs. It was a concept central to their belief in the inhabited afterworld, with its legions of spirits, human and otherwise. A journey to the east, they believed, would bring them eventually to the place where the heaven met the earth.

The Lutheran missionary Georg Vicedom, who worked in Mount Hagen during the early years of contact, developed a sombre view of these early visits to the coast after talking to the people. ". . . the Europeans," wrote Vicedom in the late thirties, "who took the natives along with them to the coast destroyed this belief, as indeed they shook the whole cosmology altogether. The natives who travelled with the Europeans have never discovered the spirits abroad which they thought to encounter and particularly did not find the sky legs and the land of the sun and the moon in the east, but the sea. With this the main support of their beliefs has collapsed . . ."[3]

Vicedom was writing in the late 1930s, from the gloomy perspective of a German Lutheran missionary in a foreign-dominated colony. He was deeply pessimistic about the future of the highlands, predicting for the people growing confusion and loss of confidence, leading to hopelessness and disintegration. Much of this he blamed on the Australians. He did not like what they were doing in the rest of New Guinea where after twenty-five years of Australian rule there was evidence that what Vicedom predicted for the highlands was already becoming a reality.

Of course it could be argued that his own fellow missionaries were themselves hastening the cultural erosion of the New Guineans with their determined and sophisticated assault upon the religious beliefs of the people. The Australians at this time thought as little of the Lutherans as the Lutherans did of them, and those who were concerned about such matters considered the overall impact of the Lutherans upon the New Guineans to be highly destructive. Furthermore, the presence of these austere, well-educated Germans was a constant reminder to the Australians that they had taken New Guinea as a prize of war. Each side then blamed the other for what was happening, neither side aware that both were part of the same process.

Inescapably, however, these visits to the outside world must have led the highlanders to question their initial assumption that the white men in their midst were extensions of their own society, spirits or otherwise. These visits would reinforce the dawning realisation that completely different human societies existed, that the Leahy brothers, for example, were not clansmen or skybeings or men-of-all-things but strangers indeed—foreigners from another culture.

But what they could not even begin to understand on these fleeting visits was the true meaning of this new world, and the basis on which it operated—its totally different values, concepts and institutions, which the Australians were fully determined to impose upon their newly acquired class of colonial subjects. Taylor's obliging, handcuffed prisoners could hardly have fathomed then the reason behind the handcuffs—an alien rule of law transcending clan obligations and the moral and legal imperative of revenge. Narmu Varnu, let loose in Lae's trade store, buying trinkets on Mr. Leahy's personal account, had no notion of the power of cash—money—which offered the possibility of limitless material wealth, and encouraged the individual accumulation of property—the very antithesis of Narmu's heritage of reciprocity and kinship and the collective good of the clan. And Dau's understanding of the motor car— the "taro beetle"—did not extend to Henry Ford's burgeoning assembly lines and all that lay behind them.

By welcoming the Australians, the highlanders were unknowingly embracing the instruments of their own society's ultimate transformation, and if they followed in the footsteps of their coastal counterparts, drawn into the European orbit four or five decades before, they could expect to take their place on the lowest rung of the new society's hierarchical order.

On the coast, nobody went around with guns. There was no need. In the highlands the Australians were never without them. Highland men were shot when they attacked, and there was a certain bizarre status in this. The warrior was an opponent, and so in some ways an equal. But when the coastal indentured labourer displeased his *masta*, he was stripped and flogged, by his own kind. Lae's white population made a great fuss of Narmu during his brief visit in 1932, dressed in his exotic highland garb. But around Lae, Salamaua, Rabaul and the other centres of white colonial rule in 1932, the nearby tribesmen had long since been turned into labourers and houseboys wearing *lap laps*.

The Australians brought into the highlands and distributed in trade precious items of wealth, and steel tools that drastically reduced manual labour. The highlanders had welcomed them with open arms because their presence seemed to enhance their own society. They were taking advantage of the opportunities offered without realising that they came with strings attached.

Chapter Eleven

DOI

STONE AGE NATIVES DISCOVERED IN NEW GUINEA, announced the *Sydney Morning Herald* on November 16, 1933. "Four white men returned to civilisation last month after an exploring trip through the wilds of New Guinea, during which they traversed an area of 4500 square miles and came into contact with 200,000 natives whose existence had previously been unknown."

Michael and Dan Leahy had sailed south to Australia in the company of James Taylor, and the *Herald*'s reporter had met their ship. He spent most of his time with Taylor, and Taylor made a point of extolling the virtues of the highlanders, who had, in fact, greatly impressed him. They were a "peaceable race," said Taylor, a "most intelligent people" whose agricultural methods would not be out of place in a civilised community.

The passage of years and his long association with the highland people has done nothing to diminish Taylor's affection for them, and there was much in the highland society he could admire. "They had a deep, magical life," he would say in later years, "which I couldn't judge

Women dancing on Leahy's airstrip at Wilya in Mokei territory, 1934. The women link arms to form a circle and with both feet make small jumps to the left or right, rotating the circle—a dance still seen today in the Hagen area.

in those [early] times. It was a rich, primitive life, with certain severe limitations to it. They were on active service perpetually. Not within each group—groups had a pleasant and charming life—marriage ceremonies, funeral feasts, entertainments. But there were few people who travelled more than five miles from their homes. It was fear, yes, but also a way of life. Only an eccentric person would want to go a long way away—there would be something wrong with them.

"Each community had the feeling they were superb—the centre of the universe. I remember the alertness, the alacrity with which they moved, their flashing eyes. They had fine torsos, clean skins, and they were very impressive. To those of us who had worked in other parts of New Guinea, where the life was much harder, and the people of rougher caste, we felt [in the highlands] we were among a medieval society. Perhaps that's going a little too far. But we did not feel we were among savages, the term commonly used about New Guinea people. They were savages, of course, if one defines savages as those who have no legal system in which there are established penalties that are enforceable, fixed to crime. In that respect they were savages. In other ways they were not.

"Their social order was in many ways more rigid than our own. I remember later on at Mount Hagen telling some young women that my sister had been married. They said, 'That's excellent for you—you should do very well out of that.' I said, 'Oh, no, I don't get any benefits at all. She arranged it herself.' They were absolutely horrified that such a barbarous custom could exist.

"We were out seven months, we met thousands of people. Most of our journey was through a green and pleasant land—tracks and hamlets and copses of timber, with meals beside cold streams and flowers. Ours was a happy association. We liked the people and we liked the country. Some time later Mick said to me, 'Jim—good country, good climate, good kanakas. Too good to find gold in.' "

Taylor made those latter observations in the 1960s. But in November 1933, Michael Leahy had by no means finished with gold prospecting. The article in the *Sydney Morning Herald* went on to report that Mr. Leahy was "anxious to go further into the hinterland, and if possible reach the Dutch border. He intended to return next year and proposed to float a company to finance his prospecting." True to his word, Leahy drove down from Sydney to Melbourne—Australia's financial centre— and set about drumming up money for more prospecting. Despite the financial uncertainties of the Depression, despite his own lack of success after eight years of prospecting, Leahy managed to put together a syndicate of backers, led by the former Administrator of the Territory, General Evan Wisdom.

Michael Leahy was, from all reports, a persuasive man. "We would be depressed and down at the mouth," says his brother Jim, "and Mick would come along, and after five minutes of him you'd be up in the air and wanting to climb over the next hill with him. He was a born optimist. He just had a way with him. I remember when Mick and I went to London, Major Harrison was retired from NGG then. He was a man who had been around in his time, he was an old man, but when he introduced Mick at a luncheon he said, 'Here is a man who has given me more thrills than anyone else, and what's more, he kept me churning out the money.' It must have been his charm. I can't put it any other way. Mick had a way with him. He believed in everything he said. I reckoned you didn't have a million pounds until you actually had it, but Mick always had it long before."

"He was always confident," says Dan Leahy, "that he would find El Dorado before he finished his travels. He had the gold fever and there was no doubt about it. It was so marvellous to be in new country . . . it was like chasing the rainbow, to get to that El Dorado we were looking for. You'd get colours of gold in most of the streams, and that was the thing that gave us the heart to go on, that it could be over the next hill."

Leahy's intention was to prospect the country west of Mount Hagen, but there were still many untested streams in the Chimbu and Wahgi that might yet yield their millions. He was about to make his way back to his hometown of Toowoomba for a holiday, when on January 9 of the new year he picked up (as he wrote in his diary) "some very disturbing rumours that a Melbourne crowd have already gone into the Hagen area . . . I will go right back and in, as that Wahgi is too good a possibility to miss."

Leahy caught a train to Sydney that night, another one to Brisbane the next day, drove to Toowoomba to pick up Dan, got his "teeth fixed and a hundred quid out of the bank," caught the first boat to Salamaua, and by January 22, 1934, was walking down the valley of the Waria, "collecting the boys" as he went.

"Another tearful, hopeless sort of a goodbye again at Payela," he wrote in his diary on January 26. "Some bonzer-looking young marys bidding a tearful farewell to very young husbands, but I am afraid . . . their sorrow is short-lived and that like most of our girls the parting is just a preliminary to a good time. . . . Such is the world we live in."

From 1930 to the end of 1934 Michael Leahy kept a daily record of his activities. It was an Invicta–One-Day a Page diary, costing eight shillings and sixpence, and most of the pages of five such diaries are dense with tiny, neat handwriting. In 1934 the blank pages at the beginning give the odd recipe—how to pickle pork, the makings for Swiss rollettes. Names and addresses are interspersed with lists of his men, recording their paydays and terms of indenture. There are detailed lists of supplies, in alphabetical order: custard powder, currants, curry powder, chlorodyne, dynamite, dishes. There are lists of film roll numbers, together with descriptions and catalogues of every photograph: "XXIV– 7,6,8,21 . . . all in Wahgi Valley: Tupia with an axe, Dan looking through

Michael Leahy, Wabag, 1934.

binoculars; C11–11C 1,6,3. Dead man at Hagen, Speech making, marys crying."

In the four diaries covering the years 1930 to 1933 there is little pattern to his writing. He records what he considers the important events of each day—life around the camp, the arrival of an aeroplane, dealings with his financial backers and with the surrounding communities. On the road there are descriptions of the people encountered, unusual incidents, and always, descriptions of the geological terrain and the results of each day's prospecting.

The diary for 1934 is different from the earlier ones. His writing is more personal, with frequent admissions of his fears, hopes, misgivings, guilt. He philosophises about civilisation, missionaries, the white man's burden. But the diary also reveals a rising anger, frustration and disappointment that was not there before.

By early February, Leahy had collected his old stalwarts—Ewunga Goiba, Tupia Osiro, Gesupo, Baranoma, and Towa Ulta with his Hagen wife Marpa. He also had with him the young boy Isakoa Hepu, fresh from his year in Wau. Leahy was in a fever to get back into the Wahgi Valley, and he was furious to find one morning that one of his carriers had had second thoughts about another two years in the highlands and had left, apparently to return to his village. "Owa," wrote Leahy, "was one of my favourites. Either he has a girlfriend in his place, or my familiarity and care for them has reacted the wrong way. . . . They have not the least idea of a fair go. . . . It's a bit disheartening to come to the conclusion that they only appreciate the hard things of life."

He would return to this theme again and again in 1934—the ingratitude of his men, their unreliability, the conviction that kindness was weakness. Rarely a week went past without one of them being beaten for one misdemeanour or another. It is almost as though a weariness of spirit had begun to stalk them all—black servants and white master. On the march back to the Wahgi, camped several miles to the west of Kainantu, Leahy awoke on February 15 to find that two of his most trusted men, Gesupo and Towa Ulta, together with their Hagen wives, had disappeared during the night. Leahy strode back to Kainantu and found them there. Towa was nostalgic for his home on the Waria and, forlorn hope, had imagined he might be somehow able to get back there. But indentured labourers were among the least emancipated of colonial subjects. According to Leahy's diary, the patrol officer in Kainantu—nineteen-year-old Tom Aitchison—gave both men a flogging, and Leahy marched them back to his camp carrying fifty-pound sacks of rice. "They are a most ungrateful mob," he wrote that night. "I think the harder they are treated the better they are."

Leahy had a reputation among his peers as a hard but fair and even kindly taskmaster, and he thought this of himself. "Dealing with civilised natives," he wrote, "is just the same as dealing with uncivilised ones. They must be made to realise that the boss is always right, and is always ready to back his arguments by force if necessary. It's a bit of an effort being always right with some of the shrewd boys who make up my line, but they know I mean well, and am always amenable to reason. In fact I am afraid I leave them go too far in the familiarity line at times."

It was illegal for any nonofficial white man to strike a New Guinean in 1934, and there were some patrol officers who were quite prepared to enforce the law. In practice the custom was universal and unofficially condoned. Leahy's discipline ranged from an open-handed slap across the face, to punching, and, finally, a flogging with the airplane strut. Like most of his peers, he was convinced that only by the exercise of unquestioned authority could the white man maintain his position in New Guinea, where so few held sway over so many. The white man must never appear weak or fallible, and woe betide the black man who discovered otherwise and took advantage of it. Later in 1934 Leahy caught a coastal man threatening his Catholic missionary employer with violence. "I grabbed the boy and Brother Eugene gave him a few with the stick, and then I am afraid I done my block because that boy is now quite satisfied it's no good getting a big head out here in the bush and damaging the prestige of the white man in the eyes of the locals."

To strike a white man invited a thrashing. To kill one risked a massacre. A day after Towa and Gesupo got their flogging, a miner named McGrath was killed by villagers at Finintegu, a day's walk west of Kainantu. McGrath had been working a small gold deposit there, and on February 16 he and his four coastal labourers were rushed by a group of villagers. It was later reported by an investigating patrol officer that McGrath had carelessly left his stores and tools around his camp where they could easily be taken. After continual pilfering, McGrath forced a confrontation by demanding his goods back. Finintegu men and some of their allies began firing arrows at his camp. McGrath shot a man dead, ran for his life, and the Finintegu brought him down in a shower of arrows. By an extraordinary coincidence, the Leahy brothers—on the march towards the Wahgi Valley—arrived on the scene shortly after the killing. McGrath's body was still warm when the Leahys pulled out the arrows. What followed was one of the more brutal episodes of the Australian penetration of the highlands.

The Finintegu people had been under government influence for a year or so. The Australians were determined to make an example of them. Michael Leahy sent his brother hurrying back to Kainantu to report the killing, while "a couple of boys and myself put in the rest of the day sniping at the murderers, and bagged a couple." That afternoon two more miners, alerted by McGrath's escaping men, arrived with their own labour lines and by nightfall a considerable force had assembled at the Leahys' camp. There were half a dozen white men—all seasoned, tough-minded miners and prospectors except for the nineteen-year-old cadet Patrol Officer Tom Aitchison—and a large force of armed coastal men. "We will give the kanakas," wrote Leahy that night, "a hurry up in the morning."

At sunrise Leahy had himself photographed as the Australians prepared for their punitive raid on McGrath's killers. Lined up in front of his camera are the white men and their New Guinean offsiders, who wore white strips of cloth around their heads to distinguish them from those about to be punished. Leahy's diary account of the ensuing battle is stark and brief: "Went up and gave the Ekanofe [people of that area]

The forces of revenge gather together at Michael Leahy's camp near Finintegu in February 1934 following the death the day before of the miner Bernard McGrath. From left to right: Michael Leahy, Bob Dugan, Dan Leahy, Ted Ubank and Cadet Patrol Officer Tom Aitchison. Behind them are the gunbois—wearing white headbands to distinguish them from the Finintegu villagers they are about to attack.

an idea of what a crime it is to shoot a white man." It is hard now to establish the exact casualties of this semiofficial act of retribution, but the bloodshed did not end there. The Leahys resumed their march, but a few days later another government patrol—this time led by Aitchison's senior, John Black—arrived to arrest McGrath's killers, who had, apparently, still not been accounted for. Cornered and made desperate by what had already happened to them, the Finintegu men defied the guns and resisted. According to the official report, it was "one of the most desperate affairs in the history of New Guinea."[1] It was certainly desperate for the Finintegu, armed only with their bows and arrows. They say today they lost twenty-eight of their people, not nineteen, the official tally, after being trapped in a narrow valley and surrounded by men with guns who shot down on them. (McGrath was buried where he fell, and his grave can be seen today, on a hill overlooking Finintegu Village. The Finintegu dead were buried in an unmarked mass grave.)

Five days later, on February 21, Leahy led his line into the old camp at Bena Bena, to collect a cache of stores he'd left there. "Isakoa," he wrote in his tent that night, "who has been at Wau for some months with Jim [Leahy] is very sad. His father was shot to death by kanakas while he was away, his body being then cut to pieces and thrown to the four points of the compass. His mother came along this morning in her widow's weeds, which consist of lots of cane grass seeds similar to large white beads strung all over her, and her whole body thick with mud. She wailed to some purpose, but death, or at least murder, is an everyday occurrence with these people, and they forget it quick."

Very few Australians in New Guinea at that time entertained the notion that every culture, no matter how alien it might seem to outsiders, had its own validity, and Michael Leahy's diaries are not the documents to read for a cool and perceptive view of the complexities of highland society. He was appalled by the manifestations of violence, a violence he considered anarchistic, mindless, without purpose. In fact indiscriminate, uncontrolled killing was uncommon. The level and frequency of violence was governed by all sorts of codes and checks and balances, and the death rate seems to have been nowhere near as high as Leahy's accounts suggest. But this intricate balance was largely hidden from western eyes, just as western violence, compartmentalised and in the main carried out by professionals—the police and the military—was also largely hidden from western eyes. The Australians had been bled white by their participation in one great war this century, and they were about to endure another. But this was 1934. Europeans were still convinced that only they could lay claim to be civilised. They had not, as yet, looked hard in the mirror, or had that mirror thrust at them by others. "When I look at Europe," wrote Frantz Fanon a few decisive decades later, "all I see is one long avalanche of murder."

These Australians in New Guinea were blinded to the level of violence in their own society and to the violence Europeans had exported to other societies during five centuries of colonial expansion. Men like Michael Leahy were equally blinded to the more complex reality of life in the New Guinea highlands by the extreme immediacy and visibility of violence and death there, a violence that certainly reached out to touch every member of the community.

Michael Leahy would gradually come to see violence among the highlanders as their major preoccupation, their drug. His diary in 1934 reveals the mounting moral outrage of the "civilised" man confronting on a day-to-day basis a "primitive" culture whose moral standards he was incapable of recognising, much less tolerating. So the killer of the second husband of Isakoa's mother becomes a murderer, and as murder is deemed commonplace, Isakoa's mother is denied a common humanity. It is assumed she will "forget it quick."

At Bena Bena later that day Leahy learns of another killing—of a woman who had previously befriended one of his carriers. "I wish," he writes, revealing a dull, mounting rage, "I wish we had a free hand here to do some murdering of the murdering bastards."

The Leahy brothers and their carrier line marched out of Bena Bena following the route taken almost one year before, when the marchers had been keyed up with such high expectations. A week later they were camped for the night in the Chimbu. Travelling through this region in 1933, Michael Leahy's diary was full of description—the changing nature of the country, the dress and decorations of the people crowding in around their rope perimeter, whose expressions he immortalised on film. And now in 1934 at the same place, he writes on February 28: "During the evening a tomahawk was pinched out of the tents, and [there followed] a mad chase after it. . . . Tupia bumped off one of the thieves, and Baranoma cleaned up a pig."

On the road again the following morning, Leahy led the party along a high and commanding ridge, "thinly veiled in the morning mist, with spirals of smoke rising from the innumerable native houses scattered all over the grass terraces, the dark gullies gashed by the mountain streams tearing through them, and the high Bismarcks, every small ridge and ravine thrown into relief by the early morning sun . . . [it] made me feel that prospecting, with all its worries and sleepless nights, was almost worthwhile."

Perhaps the beauty of the countryside produced a weariness of killing. March 3, Leahy wrote: "Again, one of the local kanakas pinched a tomahawk and off with it up to his village . . . but instead of going up and getting it back I gave the boy who lost it a good hiding. It's the wrong thing to do . . . but I don't like to have the responsibility of killing more natives than absolutely necessary on our shoulders."

The following day Leahy wrote: "The local kanakas again reached the highest point of hospitality by bringing along the . . . feminine beauty of the district to entertain the boys, or collect some shells. I am afraid it was the trade that really mattered. . . . The natives in every locality where we slept have all done good business. Before daylight this morning we were waked by the noises of fornicating parties."

By the second week in March the Leahy brothers were prospecting their way up the Wahgi Valley, checking streams they had missed the year before in the company of Taylor. But with the Melbourne businessmen wanting quick results, a different atmosphere pervaded the encounters with the valley's inhabitants. "It's a hell of a job," wrote

Leahy, "trying to get anywhere, for the kanakas . . . seem to imagine that we have come along for the express purpose of visiting their relations, and reckon we have no fixed ideas at all on where we want to go." The previous day Leahy had tested a section of the Wahgi River that had looked promising the year before. "Some dishes could not raise a colour," he sadly noted now, ". . . and [I] got very disappointed. I really expected a good prospect."

There was more anger and disappointment when the Leahys walked into Kelua on March 15. They had travelled light, counting on the cache of supplies left at the camp the previous year. They now discovered the camp and its cache ransacked and destroyed.

The explanation was not long in coming. While the Leahy brothers had been in Australia, warfare had erupted around Kelua between the Yamka and their enemies the Minembi. The Minembi had been stung into action by the killings Taylor had chosen to act upon, but there was more to it than that. For a start, the Leahys' ally Yamka Kaura was dead.

"There was a lot of jealousy over who should have the white man," says Mokei Wamp Wan today, "and this caused fights. Kaura didn't want anyone else to come and trade with the white people. He wanted to keep them for himself, and as a result he had a fight with a man and was killed. Because of this there was a fight between the Minembi and the Yamka."

"The locals [Kelua Yamka] were strong in their denunciation of the Benembe [Minembi] tribe," wrote Leahy that night, "whom they reckoned stole all the gear we left. But . . . we eventually heard that the Yamga [Yamka] mob who are really the drome mob, after their big man Kowra [Kaura] got killed sort of made his killing an excuse to pinch all the gear."

Dan Leahy today is more understanding, recalling that Kaura's clansmen blamed the white men for his death and in their anger and sorrow ransacked the camp. The brothers now used this incident to their advantage. Always intending to move straight across to their new camp in Mokei land, they told the Yamka they were leaving Kelua in retaliation for the vandalism. And this is the story that persists today among some of the old Yamka and Mokei.

The Yamka loss was the Mokei gain, according to Mokei Kominika Kwipi Nembil of Kolua, who says the Leahys came back at a particularly opportune time. "We were thinking of the next moka we would have, and wondering where we'd get the shells to give away. It was

First contact to the southwest of Mount Hagen, 1934. Gai River people encountering Dan Leahy.

this time that the white men came back, and we got it all from them. Because the Ndika and Yamka fought over having him, the white man left them and came to our Mokei land."

On his march inland Leahy had picked up rumours of another prospector who had preceded him into the Wahgi Valley, a man of dubious reputation named Ludwig Schmidt. On his arrival at Kelua, Leahy encountered the remnants of Schmidt's line of Bena Bena carriers. Schmidt decided to travel down the Sepik to the north coast by canoe, and as there was no room or need for his carriers he simply abandoned them in the headwaters of the Sepik River to the northwest of Mount Hagen. (Schmidt was executed for atrocities committed against some of the inhabitants of the Sepik headwaters. He was the only white man executed for crimes against New Guineans during the period of the Australian mandate.) The carriers had been told to make their own way back to Bena Bena, at least 125 miles away, and were given neither food, firearms nor trade goods. Most were slaughtered as they tried to make their way home. The few who had managed to struggle through to the deserted post at Kelua had been taken in by the local people. When Leahy met them, all had spear or axe wounds.

Leahy was appalled. "A thing like this," he noted, "will make the name of white men stink . . . for years to come. It's a frightful thing for anyone to take kanakas who absolutely trust a white man, over one hundred miles from their homes through thousands of uncivilised natives . . . and then hunt them back without any defence or food." Schmidt had broken one of Leahy's most fundamental rules—that great care should be taken to protect the lives of a white man's carriers.

When a Waria man died of fever on a side trip out of Kelua with Taylor the year before, Leahy was genuinely upset. "Poor Eiow passed away on Sunday morning," he wrote at the time, "after a wonderful battle with his illness. I feel very bad about it, as he sure was a good boy." It was the concern of the conscientious master for his servant. Leahy was fiercely protective of New Guineans who became allies in his enterprise. He developed a liking and compassion for certain individuals that cut across his general attitude towards New Guineans.

Nevertheless, his response to the violence he saw around him was slipping inexorably into obsession. In stark contrast to the excitement, curiosity and expectation of the halcyon earlier days, he was now fixated upon this violence. Leahy had begun to dehumanise the highlanders, to convince himself that they were without compassion, pity, scruple, remorse; that they were incapable of even the most fleeting sorrow in response to death.

Each night, after long days spent reestablishing his base camp at Wilya among the Mokei, Leahy filled the pages of his diary with observations like the following: "The crowd who went past the camp on Sunday (on March 23) went back to their villages yesterday singing as they went. The reason for their good spirits being that they killed one of their enemies or perhaps backed [avenged] a killing of one of their own mob because that is all their tribal differences amount to . . . just an age-old feud, handed down from generation to generation."

And then, the very next day the frustration, the bitterness, the corrosive anger is swept aside by Michael Leahy's compassion for those who have thrown in their lot with him.

He begins to note down the sad story of Lik Lik, who was "pretty sick with a pain in the region of the solar plexus." Lik Lik (pidgin for "little") was a young Hagen girl who had married another of Leahy's Waria men named Korpore the previous year. Korpore had taken her out to the coast with him, as Towa Ulta had done with Marpa, and Lik Lik had obviously contracted malaria. On March 24 she fell seriously ill. Leahy recorded her struggle for life over the next ten days.

On March 24 he wrote: "An old codger came along today and offered to cure her for a fee of one small shell. He said that while on the coast, she got some foreign matter into her stomach, and it would have to be roused out before she could get well. In fact . . . [he said that] being let into quite a few of the mysteries of the white-skinned people was quite sufficient to make a female . . . very sick. And he proposed to sort of relieve her of some of the burden of her knowledge gleaned in strange and new places, which he said had the form of several different kinds of devils which had taken their abode in her belly."

The man—obviously a ritual expert—then performed various rituals over the girl that he believed would cure her. But by March 29, "Korpore's mary Lik Lik is very sick and we don't like her chances . . . her temperature is 105 . . . she goes raving every night and keeps the whole camp awake. Her father and mother we have now got looking after her, but it don't look too good to me . . . I would like to see her get right as she is the best of the bunch we took out, and was beginning to be of some assistance in turning the talk."

On April 3, Lik Lik died. "Her father and mother," wrote Leahy, "a very nice old couple, . . . were crying very quietly for native mourners. Korpore her husband . . . wailed the loudest. If ever a native experienced the thrill or ordeal of falling in love I think he did, and he is genuinely cut up over her death. He fed, watched and washed her since the day she got ill . . . getting very little sleep at night. . . . However she is gone. . . . The boys carried her to her home, the old folks trailing along in heartbroken silence behind the corpse.

"After a good cry at the house the boys carried her to the family cemetery where the old people decided to leave my boys bury her their way. Their [highland] fashion is to double up the legs, breaking them if the body is already stiff, and place them in a sitting position in a round hole. . . . So finishes poor little Lik Lik, undoubtedly the best-natured poor little mary whom we have seen up to date."

Next day he wrote: "Poor Korpore had another big cry during the evening. I called him up and tried to tell him how sorry I was, and he promptly told me that as I never cried I could not have been very sorry. I wish to heavens I could forget all my troubles and worries by a good cry. Tried to explain to him that we felt sorry but we did not always cry when we had sorrow but Korpore is still almost as primitive as these people and he wants to see outward evidence of any emotions." The two men had no common meeting ground, not even in tragedy.

It was now April 1934. The Leahy brothers had completed the work on their airstrip at Wilya but had moved their camp a mile away to Kuta, the site of their mining operations the year before on Ewunga Creek. This was still their backstop if all else failed, and they worked the mine at every opportunity as they gradually built up their supplies again in readiness for the long-awaited trip to the west. Leahy was still buoyed up with the prospect of another Edie Creek, but he was aware as well that time was now running out on him. There were reports of several other prospecting expeditions in the offing.

Mid-April saw him preparing to move. His diary entry for April 16 is indicative of his mood at this time. "They murder each other with as much compunction as they kill their favourite pig . . . there is only one law they understand and that is the only way to treat them until they learn to adhere to our principles of civilisation, and that is to never let any incident, however trivial, pass over . . . a person must never make any threat or move unless he is prepared to see it right through to the bitter end, and kill or be killed."

The first journey began peacefully enough. Leahy could even privately let slip the fleeting notion that he was trespassing. Camped to the southwest of Mount Hagen, he wrote in his diary on April 21: "There are hundreds of stone age natives . . . around our fence, selling native foods and pigs to Ewunga, the bossboy, who do not realise how fortunate they are in their possession of as much food as they want and unsurpassed . . . land to live and die in, free from all the worries and the troubles of our much overboomed civilisation, which as far as I am concerned is exemplified by a persistent urge to go go go and an insatiable curiosity to see what's over the next ridge and what stones are in the next creek."

But seventeen days into this first of his two expeditions west, it was the same grim story. "Had a bit of a misunderstanding with the kanakas last night." It was more bloodshed. The Leahys had tried to trade for food, and when this was unsuccessful, they commandeered some from the gardens. As a result, ". . . two of them got bowled over, I think, and the whole camp were up all through the night of torrential rain and watching for a rush . . . hell of a night."

This first venture to the southwest—again fruitless—occupied nearly a month. The Leahys spent four weeks back at Mount Hagen preparing a second expedition, and this time they planned to prospect due west as far as the Dutch border, three hundred and seventy-five miles away. Leahy spent his time organising stores, which came in by air, and testing his weaponry. He wrote in his diary: "Got the new Walther on the last plane. It's a good rifle and dead accurate, with high-power bullets it has a great kick . . . and will automate ten, one after another, in great style. Had a couple of shots with my Mauser, and got a bull at two hundred, but got very erratic after. It's a game a person has to keep at to be consistently good. . . . If none are killed the natives reckon that the guns are no good. They can't understand a white man's horror of taking human life. . . . So when we have to kill I like to see a few go over, and then pull up to see how the shrewd men of the village take it, and a few deaths generally finishes that particular village's desire for any further argument with white men."

Leahy's horror of killing fought a losing battle with his prospecting zeal in 1934 and a losing battle with his sense of moral outrage. He lists the growing death toll in his diary with an air of grim satisfaction. Despite his occasional misgivings, it is hard to escape a feeling of inevitability, as though each death is unavoidable and just, an object lesson for recalcitrant savages who get what they deserve. On June 11 the Leahy brothers marched out of Kuta with their line of Waria and Hagen carriers on their long-planned expedition to the Dutch border. This great block of country represented the last major, unexplored region then left in the Mandated Territory, and Leahy knew this was most likely his final crack at the El Dorado.

It was a grim and bloodstained journey. Travelling through the Enga country to the west of Mount Hagen, with its uncontacted populations, proved far more difficult than anything the Leahys had experienced in the past. The country was poorer, food was scarcer, and this made the people reluctant to supply the newcomers. But more importantly, the Enga people did not appear to welcome the new arrivals as returning ancestors or as powerful spirit beings to be feared. This response in the past had eased the Leahy brothers' initial passage. In fact their technique of contact had developed around this assumption. But in the Enga it was different. The people generally thought the strangers were spirits who had come from the sky, but spirits who were not necessarily either feared or respected. The response was neither tearful welcome of the returning dead nor abject terror, but confusion. This made the first en-

counters unpredictable, and therefore much more difficult and dangerous for everyone concerned, black and white.

The Leahy brothers, unaware of the basis of the Enga people's response to them, decided they were among a people more greedy, violent and treacherous than those in the other regions. "They wouldn't
bring any food," recalls Dan Leahy, "they'd bring us nothing at all.
They wanted everything for nothing, if they could. They weren't reasonable like the Hagen people."

The worst day came on June 25, a fortnight after leaving Mount
Hagen. Dan Leahy was suffering from stomach pains, marking the onset of what his brother feared might be a severe form of malaria. By
midday he could hardly walk. The prospectors and their carriers were
now just west of the present-day town of Wabag, administrative capital
of Enga Province, sixty miles west of Mount Hagen. "A thousand or
more kanakas were strung out along our column," Leahy would later
write in his book, "singing in unison, the chant rising to a certain note,
then breaking in a distinct pause, after which the whole chorus would
join in a crashing finish. The roar of the singing alarmed the whole
valley, and all along our line of march new groups of natives gathered
to stare at us, then joined the singing multitude behind. The monotonous song or chant, kept up for hours without a break in its slow cad-
ence, became almost maddening."

The party began to climb a steep ridge—today it is an hour-long trip
from Wabag by four-wheel-drive vehicle—and made camp just below
the village of Doi. The tents were placed in the middle of a flat ceremonial ground. Immediately a dense crowd packed in around the roped-
off camp perimeter. Michael Leahy strolled up the hill about fifty yards
and turned to photograph the scene below him. Then he walked back
down through the crowd, sat down in his tent, rifle beside him, and
wrote up his diary for the day, finishing up with the words "there are
a few loud-mouthed bastards amongst the thousand or more at present
around the roped off area who badly want a lesson."

What happened next was written up the following day. ". . . [I]
was sitting back watching one particularly bigheaded native parading
up and down outside the fence in front of the assembled hundreds,
haranging them in tones which did not seem too complimentary or favourable to us. Of a sudden he dashed off to a prominent knoll overlooking the camp and its crowd of onlookers, and stood on the top of
it holding up a *tanket* [branch]—the native sign of peace. He bawled a
few words to the mob below and threw it away from him as he bounded

down the steep side of the ridge, to a house some hundred feet or so below, reappearing a few minutes later full of what we now saw was "fight," holding in his right hand a long spear ready to throw, and two spare ones in his left hand.

"Before he got to our rope fence I had picked my rifle off the bed and was outside the tent as he got to the rope and poised himself to throw the spear at one of the boys. I put a soft-nosed bullet through his guts and the boys, who had also been watching his earlier attempts to stir up the mob around us, knew that the first spear thrown would be the signal for the hundreds around to rush us and wipe out the camp with their [stone] axes, were waiting for a lead, and immediately opened fire into the mob on four sides.

"The crash of the firearms and the havoc they wrought—a second

The camp at Doi, June 25, 1934. Shortly after this photograph was taken, some fifteen of these villagers were shot dead and an equal number wounded.

Petro Pisine, a witness to the shootings at Doi in June, 1934.

shot had torn out the brains of the big mouth and splattered the ground in the vicinity with blood and the utterly unexpected turning of the tables, completely demoralised them, and instead of what . . . was going to be an easy murder and looting, they carted away at least ten to fifteen corpses and assisted as many more who were wounded to their houses. This morning all quiet, all savvy firearms."

Dan Leahy steadfastly maintains today that the motive behind the spearman's attack was straightforward plunder and murder. He says they had a man with them who could speak the languages of both Hagen and Enga, and that later on this interpreter related what he was overhearing. "The interpreter told us the whole story," says Dan. "He [the spearman] said to them, 'They've got these wonderful things that we need—axes and knives and shell! Look at the shell! Look at the things they have! They can't fight like we can. Now when I kill the white man, you rush in and grab the people, kill them, and this will all be ours and we'll divide it up.' "

Standing today near the spot where Michael Leahy took his photograph, the flat, open ceremonial ground looks very much as it did when the prospecting party camped there. Perhaps the surrounding trees are taller, obscuring the valleys below. The location is striking—atop a great ridge, rearing two thousand feet up from the river valleys on either side, yet hardly more than fifty yards across at its apex. The village occupies the same position as it did then, the houses straggling down each side of the narrow ridge; a wooden picket fence crosses the path the spearman took running down the hill towards Leahy. A group of old people gathered at the ceremonial ground to give their version of the event, pointing out where the spearman had been shot, where they were standing when the volley crashed out. Their version of events tallies with that of the Leahy brothers, but not their version of motive.

The spearman Leahy shot was Pinketa, an influential leader, driven, the Doi people say, not by desire for the strangers' treasure but by the conviction that they should somehow be sent on their way. In the few hours the strangers had been there, the people had formed no firm idea of their nature or origin, and they had had no forewarning about them except for the calls announcing their imminent arrival. One survivor, Petro Pisine, says he thought they were spirits or ghosts, but emphasises his confusion—he had no idea whether they were good or bad spirits. It never occurred to him or to any of them that they might be ancestral dead. Gabriel Kane Miok says they heard calls announcing something from the sky was coming. All the informants say Pinketa wanted to get the men together and discuss what to do with the strangers and grew angry when they ignored him. His anger had prompted the fatal charge.

Petro Pisine says: "We didn't know Pinketa was going to attack; he was trying to get us together for a discussion. We were fascinated by the new things, and we didn't respond quickly to his demands. When we paid no attention to him he got his spear to kill the white men. If we'd paid attention to him he wouldn't have done this."

"We didn't think of attacking the white man to get his things," said another old man. "We didn't want to take his *lap laps*, or other property. What we said is the truth. These white men we'd never known had come, and Pinketa wanted us to give pigs to them, so they'd go away. We'd never seen white men, and we were confused."

"This white man," continued Petro Pisine, "we had never seen such a thing. Did he come from the ground? Did he come from the sky? The water? We were confused. If we'd had any ideas of him we'd have known why he came. We were confused. We wanted to send him away . . . that's why Pinketa made a sign to attack him. So the white man shot him."

Moments after Michael Leahy fired, as he himself wrote, so did all his men, simultaneously, straight into the packed mass surrounding them. Men and women went down together. Towa Ulta, who was there, says some of the bullets went through two or three people. "When he shot in this direction," says Petro Pisine, pointing around him, "Teatakan was killed. Ambom was killed. Nambom was killed. Loo's mother was also killed. In this direction Kiakoa was killed, and over that way Pinketa was killed. This is not counting those who were injured. There were many of them."

Whatever the motive, there is something pathetic about the utterly misplaced, confident bravery of this highland man Pinketa, a metaphor for all the anonymous, futile charges against all the irresistible forces that litter the annals of colonial conquest. Veteran of acts of daring against comprehensible enemies, spear arm poised back, Pinketa ran down the long slope towards the uninvited white man, waiting for him on his own ceremonial ground: Michael Leahy, with his prior knowledge, cool head, dull rage, keen and practiced eye, repeating rifle with soft-nosed bullets that spill out a man's guts and smash his head to pieces.

"The white man asked the people to come and take Pinketa away," says another old Doi witness. "We put him under a nearby tree. He had no head, and we buried him without it. All his head was gone. So we just buried his body. This was a terrible way of killing."

Some time later a single shot rang out. According to Ewunga Goiba, one of the wounded men from Doi was still in the vicinity of the camp. "I went and got my gun," he says, "and I put it to the fellow's head and pulled the trigger. He fell down." Goiba says the gunfire brought Michael Leahy running from his tent still clutching a cup of tea he'd just been drinking. Bitter words were exchanged. "He slapped me," says Goiba, "so I told him that because of my strength only was he able to come and discover these places. If not for me he wouldn't be here. We nearly fought. I told him I'd take my *wantoks* [companions] and leave him here, to be killed by these wild kanakas."

Michael Leahy never mentioned this incident in any form, and his brother denies any knowledge of it, as do Goiba's fellow Waria Tupia Osiro and Towa Ulta. But Goiba has told the story in public several times in recent years, each time repeating it in exact detail. Perhaps Leahy swore everyone to silence at the time, because of what Goiba had done. Goiba says he and Leahy quarrelled into the night before the two men were reconciled. But he still cannot understand, in the light of

Dan Leahy, stricken with malaria, is carried on a stretcher by Engan people during the Leahys' enforced return to Mount Hagen in July 1934.

all the bloodshed, why his employer became so enraged, or why Leahy thought what he had done differed from what had just happened.

The killings did not stop at Doi. The following morning Leahy led his party out of the village. He says the path was lined on either side by the shocked and silent villagers of Doi, who had put aside their weapons. Two hours later they were among people who had not heard of the previous events, and two men menaced them with spears. "Dan put two shots into one and I stonkered the other." A few days later, with Dan too ill to travel, Michael Leahy writes he was again threatened by the nearby villagers, "so had to bump a couple off to show we mean business if they so much as appear to be hostile. They are an impossible mob in this valley . . . tonight we expect a big yike [fight]."

Next day he writes that the night attack did not eventuate. "I think that yesterday's shooting made them realise that we can kill at a distance and are prepared to keep on killing until they get enough bloody sense to realise that their lives count as nothing compared with the lives of the natives . . . who place their services and lives in our keeping by accompanying us and carrying our cargo. . . . One of yesterday's corpses still decorates the main track to our camp and this also gives them something to think about when approaching our camp."

By this stage Leahy was picking up rumours that other white men had come into the area and been driven off, and was wondering whether here lay an explanation for the aggressive behaviour of the people. Ludwig Schmidt had passed through Mount Hagen on his way northwest while the Leahys were still in Australia, and others might have come in from the north coast. But like so many prospectors in those days, they left scant record of their journeys. The Doi people are quite definite that the Leahys were the first white men they had ever seen or heard of.

On July 1, with his brother's condition worsening, Michael Leahy made the painful decision to abandon the expedition and return to Mount Hagen. "It's back in the morning and the Good Lord only knows when we will be privileged to again look into this end of the country, our Melbourne crowd not having had any very hopeful reports from me up to date, cannot be expected to carry on indefinitely."

A stretcher was made up for Dan, and now, writes his brother, the people along their retraced path were offering to carry him back through their territory and show them the way. They travelled through the village of Doi. "It's really remarkable, the difference it has made. Today as we came along not a weapon was to be seen, and we were met by groups of up to fifty of the men who very meekly gave sugarcane or offered *kau kau* [sweet potato] to the boys."

There was one more casualty on the return journey. "A few of the wise men of one of the places passed through, deciding that on appearances our backstops Ewunga and a few of his Waria friends did not look so hot . . . started in to wipe the line out, beginning with Ewunga and Co. However two of their wisest will not in future figure in any *sing sings* or boast of their prowess as murder merchants, a .32 bullet and the contents of a shotgun cartridge cutting short their existences."

It had been a futile journey, and at least twenty men and women were dead in its wake. Returning to Mount Hagen, Leahy sent his young brother down to Salamaua by air for medical treatment. Dan took with him a written report of the shootings for the authorities, more or less accurately repeating the diary account. District Officer Melrose in Salamaua sent the report on to his superior, Acting Director of District Services Eric Taylor, noting: "I am convinced the prospectors could not have acted differently. I therefore propose taking no further action." Taylor sent it along to the Administrator in Rabaul, adding: "I agree . . . I feel certain that drastic action was not taken without justification."[2] The killing of so many people by prospectors should have been fully investigated, of course, but the authorities were content to accept Leahy's version of events, and that ended the matter. Or so the Australians thought.

Chapter Twelve

THE WHITE MAN'S
BURDEN

Twelve months after Australian colonial authorities had relegated these shootings to their files, details of them surfaced in London and Geneva, to the acute embarrassment of the Australian government. And the person responsible for this was not some ferretting journalist but Michael Leahy himself, anxious to secure his place in history. To the day he died, Michael Leahy was a fierce promoter of his record as an explorer. Right from the start he resisted any attempt by the colonial administration to downplay his role in the 1933 Wahgi expedition, which he saw as the pinnacle of his exploring career. "Got a copy of Jim Taylor's map," he wrote in his diary in May 1934, "and he has had the damn cheek to describe our party as accompanying his patrol, so he has at last definitely come out into the open with his views

OVERLEAF: *A spear park near the expedition camp, mid-Wahgi, 1933. The Australians, as they marched westwards along the Wahgi Valley, grew increasingly wary of the spears carried by the highland men. At each campsite they insisted that visitors deposit them a distance away and come on unarmed. The white at the right is James Taylor.*

on the trip. Will drop him a line and tell him a few things." (Mollification came later, when the Administration named a mountain after him in the Goroka Valley.)

Leahy was determined not to let the Administration or anyone else hog the glory. In 1935, en route to England for a holiday, publicity reached him about the travels of the Papuan Patrol Officer Jack Hides earlier that year, during official exploratory patrols into the Papuan interior. To Leahy's fury, Hides claimed first entry into populated regions south of Mount Hagen prospected by Leahy in 1933. Leahy fired off a stream of letters to the Australian newspapers refuting Hides' claims. An acrimonious exchange followed, a twentieth-century version of the celebrated nineteenth-century row between Speke and Burton over the discovery of the Nile's source.

Like those two Victorians, Leahy decided to set his claims before the members of the Royal Geographic Society. It was not easy. Jim Leahy, who accompanied his brother to London, says his first request to address the Society was refused. The Society recognised "official" explorers, or wealthy and educated gentlemen adventurers of the nineteenth century like Speke and Grant and Burton and the Bakers, but not, says Jim Leahy, a couple of Australian prospectors. "Mick exploded. He got his bog Irish up and called them all phonies."

Eventually Leahy was introduced to Admiral Sir William Goodenough, a former president of the Society, who agreed to chair a meeting. Imperial condescension—the British in 1935 still regarded the Australians themselves as colonial subjects—laced the admiral's introductory remarks to the small gathering in the Society rooms on November 21, 1935. "When Michael Leahy left school he became a railway clerk, but the stool on which he sat became shiny with the impatience of his movements. The open air, manual work, adventure claimed him, and it is in New Guinea that most of his years have since been spent. We are anxious to hear what you have to say, Mr. Leahy. You may be frank with us."[1]

Leahy took the admiral at his word. In the tedious, colourless language he evidently thought appropriate for such an occasion, he detailed each of his eleven separate journeys between 1930 and 1934. Discovery took precedence over prospecting, but it was all there—exact descriptions of dress, weapons, landscape, housing, camp locations, their height above sea level, descriptions of various skirmishes with highlanders, casualties. Thirty-one dead, an unknown number of wounded. The toll was well short of the diary total but it was a grim tally, nonetheless.

Leahy saw nothing untoward about these victims of his private prospecting activities. He had by now begun to think of himself primarily as an explorer, and were there not always casualties when white men ventured into alien lands? (It is also worth mentioning that during the Hides expedition many people had been killed, and Hides had been lauded by the public and his superiors in the Papuan administration, who had suppressed the actual numbers of casualties.)

But in London, Leahy's published lecture provoked an uproar in some circles. This was not official exploration, nor was it done in the name of scientific or geographic enlightenment. It was adventurism for private gain, and those who concerned themselves in these matters— particularly the well-being of the world's "native" races, were appalled.

To the Australian High Commissioner in London came a letter from the influential Lord Lamington, former colonial governor of Queensland and of Bombay, expressing outrage at the deaths at the hands of prospectors looking for gold. "It seems to be a terrible lapse from the precautions taken . . . to prevent clashes with the primitive inhabitants," wrote Lamington. "Perhaps you would let me know whether public attention has been called to the matter."[2] By then it had been. To the Permanent Mandates Commission of the League of Nations went a petition from the august Anti Slavery and Aborigines Protection League in London for a formal inquiry into the killings. The league's Secretary John Harris furiously challenged the Australian government:

> Will action be taken against Leahy? I beg to point out that not only does Leahy refer in no less than eight places to the number of natives he had shot, but it seems clear from the text of his lecture that a substantial number of other natives must have been killed. . . . The journeys during which these shootings took place cover a period of four and a half years, their number was ten, and their object the search for gold. . . . It seems to my Committee that if Mr. Leahy had made any report of the shootings, any Administrative official would have been lacking in his duty had he not refused to issue another permit, pending inquiry. . . . Was he [Leahy] in fact engaged in acts of war, and in this connection we draw your attention to his own statement that his methods were those of 'breaking in' the natives from the start. We can find no trace of any authority being given to him for "breaking in" the natives. . . . If the shootings to which he himself has drawn public attention were not acts of war, then were they homicide? If they were homicide, then the seriousness of these acts cannot be exaggerated.[3]

Back and forth went the cables and letters between London and

Canberra, Geneva and Canberra, Canberra and Rabaul. The Australian Prime Minister of the day, under pressure from both the British and the League, ordered a full investigation. A senior Administration official was to inquire into Leahy's activities and report back as soon as possible. The Territory Administrator complied by sending to Mount Hagen Assistant District Officer James Taylor. (The Royal Geographic Society was not unduly perturbed by the furore over the Leahy shootings, and conferred on Leahy its Murchison Grant in recognition of his exploration.)

Despite Leahy's lingering distrust of Taylor (in late 1934 he was still grumbling in his diary about Taylor hogging the glory, and calling him "oily"), the two men greatly respected each other. Taylor opened his inquiry at Kuta and took statements from Michael Leahy and his Waria employees concerning certain fatal incidents between 1930 and 1934. All gave identical versions of events: that the "natives" wanted the party's trade goods, and to this end attacked with the object of killing them all, and would have done so on each occasion had not force been used against them. "As to the actual number of natives killed," Leahy formally told Taylor, "I cannot say definitely. I did not count them. I only know what my boys tell me. They counted them I think. There would not be more than thirty. The boys may have exaggerated as they are prone to do, and the number may be less."[4] Taylor officially concluded that on the occasions examined, Leahy's party was attacked, and fired in self-defence. As a result a total of between eighteen and twenty-five natives were killed, all killings justified in terms of self-defence.

Taylor inquired into five separate incidents, but there are thirteen fatal shooting incidents listed in Leahy's diary between 1930 and 1934, with a total of forty-one deaths. Perhaps Leahy concealed the others from Taylor, but there is no question Taylor was a sympathetic investigator. He admits now to falsifying casualty figures himself, and in any case believed that if prospectors were allowed into uncontrolled territory, "the right to shoot when necessary must go with it." The Territory Administrator agreed. His letter to the Prime Minister, which can be read in the Australian Archives in Canberra, was to have concluded with the following ringing declaration: "These clashes between Europeans and natives can be expected as long as there is new country to be examined and adventurous Europeans to examine it." But discretion got the better of him or his advisers. The defiant paragraph was crossed out, and the more sobre substitution inserted: "It is the policy of the Commonwealth Government to open up and develop as rapidly as

Dan Leahy surveying the country ahead, the valley of the Bena Bena, 1932.

circumstances permit the whole of the Territory held under Mandate. This action is considered essential both for the advancement and welfare of the native population and the economic development of the Territory. . . ."[5]

But that was not at all how the Anti Slavery League saw things, and at the Permanent Mandates Commission in Geneva later in 1936, Commission Chairman Lord Lugard took a somewhat different line when Australian delegates duly discussed their government's findings on Leahy's activities. "What the Commission has just heard was not calculated to make a favourable impression on persons familiar with the ordinary practice of colonial administration," said Lord Lugard in reply. "A primary rule was that no economic activities should be allowed—and prospecting was a form of economic activity—in an area of which the Administration was not in effective control. [I know] of no case similar to that under discussion. On the other hand there were 'closed districts' in British colonies and territories where no activities or penetration were permitted until the control exercised by the authorities was sufficient. It was generally recognised that the Administration entered an area first, and only when it was in a position to ensure respect for the law was the district opened up to private enterprise."[6]

In effect the Australians were rapped on the knuckles. The Commission had no direct control over Australia's stewardship in New Guinea, but the Australians, relatively recent graduates from colonial status themselves, were certainly concerned that their administration be favourably regarded. Of course in hindsight Australia's chagrin could well have been tempered by the League's inaction over Mussolini's brutal invasion of Ethiopia. And Lord Lugard was a retired British colonial administrator whose innovative use of machine guns against cavalry had hastened the imposition of British imperial rule over Nigeria's rebellious northerners earlier in the century. Of course, that had been "official."

The international criticism in 1936 over Leahy's activities in 1934 prompted Michael Leahy, according to his brother, Dan, to give modified versions of his activities when he and the American writer Maurice Crain published *The Land That Time Forgot* in New York and London in 1937. His readers were spared the carnage of Doi; only the spearman running down the hill was killed. Leahy says in the book that immediately he himself fired, there was a burst of gunfire from his men, and "for a horrible moment I thought the boys had lost their heads and were firing into the packed mass of unarmed natives in front of our tent."

According to his diary that is exactly what did take place. "But," says Leahy in his book, "I saw immediately that none of the shots were taking effect. Natives were stampeding in all directions but I saw none fall."

The adjustments were not limited to the Doi massacre. Fatal incidents are omitted, and where they are mentioned, are often modified into woundings. Of course Michael Leahy was not the first colonial adventurer—official or unofficial—to launder his exploits for public consumption or to justify them in the context of the white man's burden.

"I was unable to sleep that night [after Doi] and spent the long hours debating whether the exploration of this cruel country was worth the cost. . . . I could not blame myself for the shooting that had occurred, knowing well that if we had not been able to defend ourselves, all of us would have been wiped out . . .

"Such clashes could be avoided only if white men stayed out of the country altogether—in which case the natives would go right ahead killing each other off anyhow. . . . I decided finally that exploration and the establishment of white authority were worth whatever they might cost . . ."

A view of the Wahgi Valley, taken by Michael Leahy as he marched westwards in April 1933.

Leahy could censor the killings in his book but feel quite at ease in the prevailing climate about publishing the following:

"Dwyer thought it would be a good idea to show them how the rifles worked.

" 'Come on you baboons!' he shouted. 'Pipe down and give attention.'

"The chatter stopped immediately.

" 'That's right, folks, gather round,' he continued. 'Now I want you to get this. It's going to scare the life out of you but it's for your own good. My young friend here,' he waved to me, 'is going to show you something that has your lousy bows and arrows beat all hollow. Hey— you over there—you big-mouthed ape with the shield . . . this is mainly for your benefit.'

"He was grinning at them all the time in his most ingratiating manner, and from his tone the natives probably thought he was saying something extra polite."

Kankas, coons, niggers, apes, monkeys . . . all are sprinkled liberally through Leahy's diary, along with thieving, murdering, sneaky, cruel, godless, merciless, disgusting, wicked, lazy, immoral, shiftless. "For the colonist," wrote Frantz Fanon in *The Wretched of the Earth*, "the native is declared insensitive to ethics: he represents not only the absence of values but also the negation of values. He is, let us dare to admit, the enemy of values, and in this sense he is the absolute evil. He is the corrosive element, destroying all that comes near him; he is the deforming element, disfiguring all that has to do with beauty or morality: he is the depository of maleficent powers, the unconscious and irretrievable instrument of blind forces."[7]

First contact, Chimbu, 1933. An Australian hand reaches out in greeting. The Chimbu man is nervous, but tentatively holds out his hand, watched by the man beside him, who carries a stone axe. A third is more interested in Michael Leahy, taking the photo. Or is he looking at the shiny steel axe, held, along with a rifle, by one of the coastal carriers?

• • •

The people of New Guinea were not only denied a culture of their own, they represented the very antithesis of it. All the more necessary then was the presence of the white man and his civilising influence; all the more justified his actions, whatever they might be. So Michael Leahy, backed by his Melbourne businessmen, could seek his El Dorado among the highlanders and justify the ensuing bloodshed because he saw himself a part of this civilising process. And so did his peers.

The debasing of the people and their culture reinforced in the colonist his right to rule, and it led to actions and comments on those actions by otherwise decent and honourable men which in different circumstances would no doubt horrify them. In October 1934, when Leahy was prospecting back in the Chimbu after his retreat from the Enga, an axe was stolen from a group of Leahy's men. "Lowai stopped him [the thief] with a shot," he wrote in his diary, "and there is one thieving kanaka less." It was the dull rage again, the colonist's occupational disease.

Michael Leahy's retreat from the Enga in June 1934 marked the end of his exploring. He tried out the lower Wahgi and Chimbu again, later in the year, but once more drew a blank. In December 1934 he and Dan made preparations for another expedition west but on December 15 his dreams of an El Dorado finally evaporated. Two prospectors walked into Mount Hagen after travelling right to the Dutch border. They called on Leahy and reported their failure to find enough gold even to "fill a tooth," as he sadly confided in his diary. "That buggers this country for another Edie Creek . . . I don't see now what good Dan and I would do going over the same ground and prospecting . . . I feel as though we have been robbed of our principal interest in life. . . . Looks like we will have to try and settle down to some kind of occupation and try and forget about the gold, which evidently does not exist in the heart of New Guinea."

He was wrong. A master deposit is being developed at Porgera, in the Enga, while at Ok Tedi, in the Star Mountains region of Papua New Guinea's border with Irian Jaya Guinea—the Papua New Guinea national government, with international partners, is mining a gigantic deposit of gold and copper discovered in the 1960s.

Prospecting for gold in uncontacted country had indeed been Leahy's principal interest in life. "I have a very depressed feeling . . ." he wrote five days before Christmas. "It's a bugger, no where more to go, and I don't know how I will settle down to a steady job."

The occupation the two Leahy brothers rather reluctantly settled upon was gold mining. For the rest of the 1930s they worked their claim at Kuta, taking it in turns as one or the other went travelling overseas or worked other gold claims near the coast. From 1934 to 1938 their only permanent European neighbours at Mount Hagen were Catholic and Lutheran missionaries. The highlands had brought scant rewards to gold prospectors, but right from the start these heavily populated valleys had attracted the missionaries. From 1932 onwards both the Lutherans and Catholics had spread westward in the wake of the prospectors. By 1934 both denominations had mission outposts in the Chimbu and the Wahgi.

Like the prospectors, the missionaries moved ahead of the Administration. At the end of 1934 the patrol post at Kainantu, 150 miles to the east of Mount Hagen, was still the only government presence in the highlands. Missionaries and prospectors with Uncontrolled Area Permits could still move freely throughout the valleys, and the understaffed Administration had no chance of adequately monitoring their activities. But at the end of the year a series of events combined to force the Administration into clamping down on the entry of any nonofficial outsiders at all. Just before Christmas 1934, a solitary Catholic missionary in a remote corner of the Chimbu was killed by villagers. They burnt down his grass mission hut. He shot one of their pigs, so they shot him.

Several weeks later another Catholic missionary was killed nearby. In each case the Administration was soundly criticised by the white community of the territory and the Australian mainland press for its failure to protect its white citizens. The Administration responded in early 1935 by deciding to issue no more permits to enter uncontrolled areas. It also stipulated that miners and missionaries already established in declared uncontrolled areas could stay on, but that their movements were restricted to the immediate vicinity of their camps. Even had there been other places to look for gold, the Leahy brothers now were officially forbidden to do so. Unofficial exploring by private individuals or companies, for whatever purpose, was at an end. The highlands had been effectively closed off again to the outside world.

James Taylor photographs a settlement in the Wahgi Valley. A small number of houses are grouped around a cleared ceremonial ground, bordered with casuarina trees. In the middle ground are the garden plots of sugarcane and vegetables, with a banana grove to the right. These hamlets were typical of the Wahgi, unlike the larger villages to the east, and round houses have given way to square or oblong ones.

Only the absence of any major gold discoveries made such an edict enforceable, or, from the Administration's point of view desirable. During the 1926 Edie Creek gold rush the uncontrolled area legislation had broken down completely—the Administration had been powerless to prevent prospectors and miners from flooding in. The decision to close the highlands now was motivated by a concern to protect Europeans from highlanders rather than the other way round. But whatever the motive, it effectively delayed significant white occupation for the next twenty years.

In 1935, there were tens of thousands of people—like those in the Southern Highlands—who would not set eyes on the representatives of the outside world for another twenty years. Hundreds of thousands in that time would see little more than the occasional patrol passing through their territory. These highlanders would live a very different existence to those who found themselves within the immediate influence of a mining, missionary or government outpost. At Doi in 1935 the villagers were still recovering in shocked isolation from their massacre the year before, and four more years would go by before the next outsiders penetrated their region, while at Mount Hagen, Catholic and Lutheran missionaries were putting up churches, and the Leahy brothers were gathering at Kuta a large force to help them work their gold. And while Michael Leahy's horizons might have been closing in on him, those of the Hagen people and their equivalents around the other scattered outposts (where the outside world had gained a foothold) were just beginning to open up.

Chapter Thirteen

WHY HAD THEY COME?

One of the most persistent questions in the minds of the high-landers when the Europeans first arrived was, why had they come? What did they want? "At first we thought they were spirits," says Mokei Wamp Wan, "but when they showed us the shells and gave them to us we thought they must be the shellmen. Then we saw them looking in the streams . . . and we wondered what they were going to do in our place. We had no idea what they were looking for. The big stones we thought they would have taken they didn't seem to be inter-ested in. They used to have a dish and put things in it, shake it, look at it, and then take small things out and wrap them up. And then they'd write things down. But we had no idea what they were doing. At first when we saw the gold we thought it was only sand. What could they possibly do with this? But later we realised its value.

"They said to us—you people like shells, that's why we're giving you shells. But if you liked this money, we'd give you that instead. They told us that the gold they were looking for is what you make money from. If someone found a piece of this gold we'd give it to the white man, and we'd get big shells for it.

"As more and more people learnt pidgin, things became clearer to us. We eventually realised that they came here looking for gold. They brought good things with them, we traded with them, and it became a way of life. Having the white men here too became a part of our lives."

Michael Leahy took a photograph of two men panning for gold near Bena Bena in 1932. Intent on the job, they seem indifferent to the great crowd of onlookers squeezed together. In the distance, more people approach. The white men would hardly have avoided giving some kind of explanation of their actions, and according to Dan Leahy they did this wherever possible.

"You'd pick up ordinary river stones," he says, "and break them up with a geological hammer, or we'd get a dish of gravel and start washing it. Well—they naturally thought we were looking for good axe material. And they'd indicate the stuff in the dish was no good at all. And they'd bring us a bit of axe stone, and say, 'This is the stone you'll be wanting.' And they'd try and point out where it would be a good place to get it. And we'd shake our heads and tell them we didn't want that at all.

"We told them we were looking for something that belonged to the white man. Sometimes we'd show them a shilling, and we'd say, 'Well, this is the same as your shell. This is our money, that's your money. And the gold is the same. You want a tomahawk, we want this. You can buy a pig with gold-lipped shells, or a wife or all sorts of things. And if we find a lot of this gold, we can buy ourselves all sorts of things too.' "

The Leahys began mining gold at Kuta in August and September of 1933, during their initial journey into the Wahgi. They were disappointed with the returns at first but the mine was to surprise them in later years by providing quite a good living until the 1950s. But in 1933 the takings averaged an ounce and a half a day, a modest haul compared with the twenty-five ounces a day mined by Michael Leahy seven years earlier at Edie Creek. For the Leahys, then, Kuta was a marginal proposition. What made it profitable was the unlimited source of cheap labour and food at their disposal. Their mining technique at Kuta was typical of the small-scale operation then popular in New Guinea. Gold-bearing gravel was washed through a sluice box about nine feet long, the heavier gold catching up against a series of wooden slats set at intervals along the bottom. More often than not the gravel was buried

Working the alluvial gold at the Leahys' Kuta claim on Ewunga Creek, Mount Hagen, 1934. Leahy's coastal men are wearing **lap laps,** *while the Hagen men wear the traditional back covering of leaves. The workers are removing boulders in order to get at the gold-bearing river gravel.*

beneath tons of overburden—earth and rocks that had to first be removed. Without access to machinery, this mining process was extremely labour intensive: shifting the overburden, digging trenches to redirect creek water for sluicing, shovelling tons of gravel through the boxes, carrying quantities of stores from airstrip to mining camp. And this was the work the Hagen people were called upon to do within a few months of their first contact with the outside world.

"The local natives all rolled up," wrote Leahy to NGG's Major Harrison in October 1933, "and we had an average of forty-six working . . . the whole time. They are really good workers as far as shifting overburden and moving the big boulders are concerned. . . . Only once did it look like we were going to have an argument. [It] started over the payment for a pig and we had to belt a couple over the head with a stick. I thought there may have been some hostilities after that but up to date they have been better than ever and there have been a surplus offering to work every day. . . . They are on the job ready to have their names put down before seven A.M., and work right through until five P.M. Sundays and Mondays all the same to them."[1]

The Hageners were no strangers to hard routine labour. Men worked periodically, clearing and fencing new gardens, digging drainage ditches, and with stone axes their major tool, this was intensive and time consuming. Women worked year round. Apart from child rearing, they shouldered the responsibility of producing food for themselves, their families and their pig herds. The labour was unremitting. Women had to plan and plant to ensure a constant supply of food, because nothing was stored against a time of shortage. Apart from routine gardening chores, the women harvested daily from vegetable gardens often a considerable distance from the homestead. Each day they would walk home, bent under heavy loads of sweet potatoes and firewood needed for the evening meal.

The Leahys initially employed mainly men. Women kept the camp supplied with food. For the men the physical effort of shifting overburden was not much different from their own work. What was novel was the notion of working at regular times, for an employer who determined the job and gave payment in return. For most highlanders their own work was their own concern and they did it when they wished, each person setting his or her own pace. But from the very beginning, Michael Leahy wanted the working arrangements on his terms. People had to come and work for a full day. He introduced and enforced these methods by rewarding those who conformed and punishing those who did not.

"It's amusing," he wrote in his diary in September 1933, "to see them running to work about 7:30 in the morning so as to get their names down for pay in the afternoon. They have realised they have to be on the job on time to get pay. The good workers I pay better than the lazy ones which is gradually influencing the slower ones and those who just get their names down and then duck off . . ."

At first the people were employed casually—picking up a handful of small shells at the end of each day. But from 1934 onwards, Dan Leahy says, they were engaged for three or six months at a time. Their names were written down at the beginning of the work term, and they were assigned to a gang supervised by a coastal man. With the help of

Sluicing gold-rich gravel and soil at Kuta, 1936. The heavier gold collects against slats in the bottom of the sluice box.

translators like Kopia Rebia, each of these coastal *bosbois*—there were about fifteen of them—controlled about fifteen to twenty men. "It was all fully explained from the start," says Dan Leahy. "We told them they had to work the full six months or they got nothing. We'd say, 'Now if you've worked *faipela mun* [five months] and two days to go, you leave, then you don't get any pay.' It was remarkable how many of them did stay on. The labour was very good then, more than I could ever use. They'd work for six months and get a couple of gold-lipped shells, two tomahawks, some sixteen-inch knives and small shells. Every Saturday they'd line up and anyone due for pay was paid. As their time expired they got paid that Saturday. It was a big day, all the Saturdays, after we got going for a while. The ones that had done their time—they'd get their pay and away they'd go."

The Leahy brothers' accounts of these early times suggest that everything went in their favor—that they had the upper hand and could dictate terms and conditions to the Hageners. They could certainly set the wage, because as the notion of work for pay was totally foreign to the people, they had no idea what to demand. But the power relationship existing between the Australians and the Hagen people was by no means one sided. Michael Leahy well knew that good relations with the local people were important, as in the long run he could not operate without their cooperation, in particular their constant supply of cheap food and labour. By the end of 1934 Leahy had a spreading reputation as a man who did not shrink from violence. "Some bastard around Salamaua or Wau," he noted in his diary on December 6 of that year, "has been telling the Papuan officials that we have been shooting natives in their territory on sight. They should have enough sense not to believe that, as a person would not get too far if he had a pot at all the natives, as they come into sight. He would have them all on the run and no one to bring *kai kai* [food] to his boys." It was not the slur on his honour he was commenting upon, but the insult to his common sense.

In their dealings with the Leahy brothers the Hagen people actually possessed considerable bargaining power, much to Michael Leahy's often-stated irritation. When he settled back among the people at Kuta and Wilya in March 1934, he was soon complaining about the high price of pigs. At Kelua in 1933, the white men began by paying the standard price of one *kina* shell per pig. But over the months the price went up.

Leahy in 1934 no longer enjoyed the patronage of the wealthy New Guinea Goldfields Company, and he had to be more frugal. Only two weeks after his return, April 2, 1934, Leahy wrote in his diary: "We have a price war on our hands . . . they are demanding two gold-lipped shells, or a gold lip and a tomahawk [per pig], which is impossible for us to pay and carry on. A gold-lipped shell costs two shillings and sixpence in Salamaua, and an additional four shillings and sixpence in freight, which unless we get a reasonably sized pig, is too expensive to use as trade. I think they will come around, but it's going to take time."

The final price seems to have settled around one pig for one shell, and for most of the time their fresh meat needs were satisfied from then on. But periodically the Leahys had to send their men further afield, where people with less access to the new flow of shells were more willing to part with their pigs for a cheaper price. In September 1934, Ewunga Goiba returned to Kuta from a pig drive in an outlying district, and

Leahy triumphantly recorded: ". . . Twelve good sized pigs, bought with *tam* or Bailer shells. The whole lot never cost more than three pounds in shells so we are set for boys' meat for a week or so." Compared with Mokei prices, that represented a savings of fourteen shillings—no mean sum in 1934. Michael Leahy needed the Hageners. No matter how much he might joke about their running to work, he had to accept the fact that without them he had no gold mine.

By the end of 1934 the Leahys had built themselves a timber cottage at Kuta, raised up on stilts for defensive purposes, and outlying accommodation for their labour line. There were storehouses for their trade goods and a pig pen covering almost an acre. Kuta had become a lively meeting place, as men and women from clans all over Mount Hagen were attracted by the wealth that could be obtained. Each day crowds of people arrived; the men occasionally leading pigs, the women laden with *bilums* of sweet potatoes and vegetables to be exchanged for the shells handed out by Waria men responsible for the food trading. As the Leahys began full-scale mining operations, more men were attracted to the new opportunities, and Kuta took on the air of a bustling boom

The Leahys' house at Kuta, 1934.

town. The Leahys were making a modest living, but by their own standards it was the Hagen people who were becoming truly wealthy in comparison to those with no access to the Australian shell boxes. The Leahys were handing out enormous quantities of shells and steel goods for mining work. Catholic and Lutheran missionaries—busy establishing their settlements before beginning the delicate process of proselytising their religions—were also handing out modest amounts of shell for labour.

One of the men who worked for the Leahys during these early times was Penambe Wia Tugl. Although the great war in the 1920s had dispersed most of the Penambe, leaving Kuta a no-man's land, some of them had gradually found their way back home, among them Penambe Tugl and his four brothers. At the height of the war, their mother had been killed, and the five boys, now orphaned, had been taken in by friendly clans. After a few years Tugl had managed several visits back to his homeland near Kuta to see relatives who had stayed on there. Finally they invited him to remain, and his brothers gradually joined him. When the Leahys began full-scale mining at Kuta, Tugl was about eighteen.

"Two men we knew," says Tugl, "had been working and got Bailer shells. When my brothers and I went to visit them they were cleaning and decorating them. They told us they were going back next day, so Wai and I decided to join them. We were very excited about going for the first time. We left everything and joined them.

"We had it explained to us what went on. Time didn't mean anything to us. We were just thinking about what we were going to get. We'd go home at night and sleep and first thing in the morning we'd go up there to work. The work was all to do with gold. Later when Father Ross [the Roman Catholic missionary] settled, there was other kind of work, like building houses. At Kuta it was all to do with gold. We'd work for three months, then get paid in the fourth month. When we saw the fellows who worked before us get their pay—which was *kina* shells, bailers or axes—we'd get excited and count the time, and hope it would pass quickly so we could get our own. Once we got our first payment we were really excited. We'd say, 'We really got something out of that!' And we were looking forward to the next pay. At first it was only one shell. Much later, he'd give them two axes, two *kina* shells and two knives. As time went on the payment increased.

"People who were sick of the job left, but there were plenty who just wanted to go on and on to get these things. They wanted more and

Penambe Wia Tugl (1984) remembers working the gold at Kuta.

more. It was up to us. If you wanted to work and get something and then leave, it was all right. But those who wanted to work on, they could.

They were good times. People were having big feasts, and Kuta was a crowded place. Life was good there. After you got those things, *kina* and bailer shells, how could you stop the crowd pouring in? They didn't even want to go home, they camped around the area and slept out there. Lots of trading went on. Women from other people were marrying the coastal men, people from long distances were marrying people from around here, all this sort of thing went on. With what we got out of working we were able to make our *moka* and increase the length of our *omaks*.

"I worked on the water race for the gold company. We went in with spades and shovels and axes and dug the ground. The work was very hard, very hard indeed for what we got. If it was nowadays we would have got more, but at the time we were satisfied with the pay. A *kina* shell was a much desired thing. Everyone wanted to possess one at the time! And the axe! You can imagine what amazing things it did."

Mokei Akelika Yaga of Kulumamp says many of his clansmen worked at Kuta, and he recalls the discipline: "If we didn't work, the ones who were bosses over us they would really beat us. They said we were being paid for the job, so we should do it. Some of us were frightened of them, but we put up with it and then we got paid. Some of the men if beaten would leave and run away to their homes. It was really hard work. Nowadays people get a lot of money for just little jobs. My hands

Michael Leahy was fascinated by the Hageners' response to western-made items—gadgets, guns, mirrors, record players, and, in this case, a celluloid doll.

were like iron! In those days we did everything by hand—building bridges, making airstrips, everything. My hands must have been like a bulldozer! But we were paid well in shells. Later we put our sticks together to show how many shells we had, and we made *moka*, bought women. We followed the traditions of our fathers. We made *sing sing* grounds, *moka*, all that kind of thing. When the whites came we had more and more of these shells to make *moka* with."

Penambe Tugl and his brothers worked hard at Kuta for as long as it took them to gain enough wealth to marry. Pooling their pay, they raised the bridewealth of the woman Ife for Tugl, and later Kuan married Jara, Wai married Koina, and two other women were married to their other clansmen. Tugl says the boys would have eventually married had the white men never come, but agrees it would have taken much longer. The family had been dispersed by the great war, and the boys were orphaned. Normally a young man's father and relatives contributed heavily towards the bridewealth, but these boys would have been forced to raise the whole amount on their own. Tugl admits he didn't like the work, and after being paid two axes, he never signed on again. But he did not need to stay on the job to take advantage of the new opportunities to accumulate wealth. He raised pigs and sold them to the Leahys for shells, and then accumulated more by wheeling and dealing in the traditional way with those who did work at the mine.

So in these early years, work at Kuta was not seen as an alternative to traditional life but as a means of enhancing it. It was something to be taken on in short bursts, to get valuables to use in traditional ways— primarily marriage and *moka*. The Hageners did not have to sell their labour; they could satisfy all their basic needs themselves, as they had always done. As Tugl says, work for the white man gave them something beyond the requirements for survival—a new chance to gain wealth and prestige. Of course their food surpluses had always been converted into wealth—food into pigs into shells—but here now was a new way to gain even more, and to extend the range of opportunities to make *moka*. Only two shells were needed to get a man started in *moka* exchange. Poorer men who could not previously have thought of participating could now join in.

Given the great demand for shells, it would seem logical that all the men would want to work full time for the Leahys. Some of them did, but the whole purpose behind accumulating shells was their distribution to others in *moka*. That involved a great deal of effort, organisation and skill, not only for the prime movers but for all the participants, and it was by these very skills that a man was partly judged. And there were other things to attend to—disputations, trading, marriage arrangements, gardening, decorating the body for ceremonies, funerals—in addition to the *moka*. Full-time mining work would have brought a harvest

The first gramophone in Mount Hagen, 1933. In the Asaro Valley, some informants told of their conviction when first hearing the music that their ancestors were inside the box, calling out.

of shells and left a man with no time to fulfill his proper role in life, taking away all reason for earning shells in the first place.

So these highlanders were still free to pick and choose whether or not they worked for the white man. In that sense they were independent, although in a long-term sense the erosion process had begun the moment the Australians walked into the valleys, a process that would have been accelerated had the white men brought in their trade stores to offer new and tantalising consumer goods and introduced cash as the means to pay for them.

In the 1930s the seeming independence of people who did not have to work for a living was a constant source of concern in colonised New Guinea outside the highlands. From the moment the Europeans settled New Guinea's coastline and outer islands, they had worked to reduce the independence of the villagers, knowing that to profit from the island's relatively meagre resources they needed unlimited, cheap and docile labour. If this labour was self-sufficient and could choose to take a job or leave it, then its regular supply was not assured. Hence such measures as the indentured labour system, which bound a man to his employer for three years; and hence the howl of protest from the white

A consignment of fresh fish has arrived at Mount Hagen by plane. Dan Leahy shows one to onlookers.

community whenever there was talk of watering down that system.

"One of the greatest contributing factors," pronounced the *Rabaul Times* in 1936, "to the unsatisfactory services rendered by native labourers in this country is their economic independence. For it must not be forgotten that every native is a landed proprietor, and nature has endowed New Guinea with a prolific soil, which provides adequate sustenance for a minimum of labour. Dismissal from employment, if he fails to carry out his duties, holds no terrors for the New Guinean native. It is the shadow of the sack, hovering over the white employee, which urges him on to render service. Unless and until our natives reach such a stage of development that they must work in order to obtain sustenance or a livelihood, they will never make suitable unindentured labour for the average white resident."[2]

Administration policy rested on the assumption that the New Guinean's rise from "savagery" to "civilisation" would be hastened if he went to work in the homes, docks, plantations, mines and carrier lines of the Australians. The Administration talked of improving village life, introducing education, establishing cash crops that the villagers could grow and sell themselves. But these initiatives wilted under pressure from the settler community, which wanted an unlimited labour pool, not educated, independent farmers. By the second world war, there was no Administration education programme to speak of, no government-supported cash cropping and almost total illiteracy.

The Administration's main activity in these prewar years was ensuring that village men went to work as labourers for Australian private enterprise. Following on from the Germans before them, the Australians imposed, and collected under threat of jail, a head tax. Every New Guinea man paid ten shillings annually in cash, and the money could only come, by and large, by working for a European. And gradually the white-owned trade stores exerted their seductive pull, creating a desire, and then a need, for tobacco, pots and pans, matches, torches and western clothes—all to be paid for with cash, which had to be earned. All these things combined to lock the New Guineans into the colonial economy.

New Guineans outside the highlands had shown themselves no less immune than anyone else to the seductive pull of western consumerism. And in time the highlanders would succumb the same way. That

---

OVERLEAF: *A ceremony at Mount Hagen. The pigs have been killed and will soon be cut up, cooked, and distributed to visiting clans.*

Michael Leahy is given a portion of cooked pork on the Wilya airstrip, 1934.

was inevitable from the moment the Australians strode into their valleys. But in the absence of large-scale European settlement in the highlands, there were no trade stores established there until the late 1940s, and no cash. The traditional economy held sway. For a brief time, then, those highlanders—particularly the Hageners—who found themselves within the European orbit lived out a kind of golden, insubstantial dream. Wealth that the people knew and understood and could absorb was there for the taking. The Australians may have opened the door to the highlands without knocking and had their passage occasionally disputed. But once inside, with their bags of traditional wares, they were made welcome. It was not conquest; it was seduction.

Chapter Fourteen

FINE MARRIAGE POTENTIAL

At Kelua in 1933 the sexual encounters between the coastal men and Hagen women like Dau and Meta gave the people an inkling of the essential humanity of the strangers—or at least the coastal New Guinean strangers. At Kuta from 1934 onwards, the surrounding clans picked up clues that the white men were made of flesh and blood as well.

At Kuta the Leahys were hard taskmasters and felt it essential they maintain an attitude of fierce aloofness to the people who surrounded them. There was no suggestion of social familiarity—their own notions of caste and the enormous cultural gulf made that impossible. If there was any meeting ground, any mutual acknowledgement of common humanity, then it was in their relationships with the women.

Throughout 1934, Michael Leahy made frequent diary references to the sexual activities of his men and the highland women, and in the latter part of the year, to his own as well. It seems that whenever a group of highlanders had time to familiarise themselves with the Leahy party, sexual relations quickly developed. This had happened at Bena

Bena and at Kelua the previous year, and when the prospectors walked back through the Chimbu on their return to Mount Hagen in March 1934, Leahy frequently referred to the nightly activities of his carriers and the Chimbu women.

A month back in Mount Hagen, among the Mokei at Kuta, the same thing was going on. "There are a good few black harlots hanging over the fence just now," Leahy wrote. "The only trouble now is the boys are getting too much fornicating and are tired of taking them away in the kunai but now want to bring them into the houses and sleep with them. We did not object to that either, but . . . the bastards did nothing else for the great part of the night, until we got out and spragged them. . . . Anyway, no molls are allowed inside now, and they have to come and ask Ewunga for the necessary payment when they have arranged an assignation with the girl of their fancy. Ewunga gives them five small common seashells, the price is stabilised and away they go."

"Had to chase off a few more harlots this morning," he wrote next day, April 13, 1934, "who had come in last night by stealth to get a few shells. They did not like getting chased. The old men I think must make them savvy [tell them off] when they come back without a good supply of shells."

Michael Leahy was still a practicising Catholic when he arrived in New Guinea at twenty-six, brought up in the rigid, conservative orthodoxy of the Irish Australian Church, which taught that sexual activity was forbidden outside marriage, and marriage to a good Catholic girl at that. But in New Guinea he had been sorely tempted, and while there is no mention of his own sexual activity in his diary until 1934, it had long been playing on his mind. In October and November of 1934, his confusion and ambivalence surfaced.

Following his retreat from the Enga, Leahy and his brother made another quick prospecting sortie through untried corners of the lower Wahgi and Chimbu. On October 20, camped near a Catholic mission outpost in the Chimbu, he learned that Lutheran missionaries in the Goroka Valley were complaining to the authorities about prospecting parties consorting with highland women.

Leahy had already had one dispute with the Lutherans in 1932, when the missionary at Kainantu, Pastor Willi Bergmann, took him to task over one of his shooting incidents in the Bena Bena Valley. Neither side had much good to say about the other. They were natural enemies on the highland frontier—German against Australian, Lutheran against Catholic, missionary against prospector. Leahy shared the widespread

Australian dislike for these German nationals and their constant, almost seditious criticism of Australian colonial rule, but the Australians were forced to tolerate the Lutherans under the freedom of religion provisions of the League Mandate.

Sitting in his tent on October 20, after another fruitless day of prospecting, Leahy's frustration boiled over. The Lutherans were allowed to bring their wives to Australian New Guinea, he wrote, and could not or would not understand or sympathise with the plight of the single white man, "whose occupation prohibits his having a wife accompany him, relieving his feelings by camping with one of the perfect specimens of womanhood to whom the sexual act is as natural and innocent an act as nature intended it to be."

This new sentiment stands out like a rock in Leahy's stream of almost obsessive denunciation of the highland character. He goes on to accuse the Lutherans of taking away everything that is natural and pleasurable to the people. They are blamed for blighting the highlanders' lives, so that their *"sing sing* grounds will no longer resound to their joyous celebrations and happy, carefree dances. Instead they may be desecrated by the bloody apologies for hymns and the monotonous tones of their endless prayers, for what and why the natives will not know."

It was not hymns and prayers per se that Leahy objected to, it was Lutheran hymns and prayers. There is no evidence that Catholics or Lutherans differed in their determination to eradicate "heathenism" but Leahy, naturally enough, was more comfortable with Catholicism. He was quite happy to see the Catholics come into the highlands, and he himself had invited a missionary priest he knew—the American Father William Ross—to set up near him in Mount Hagen.

On the next day, October 21, there is more in the same vein: "Mr. Bergmann—the Lutheran missionary—went to some pains to inform Father Schaefer [a Catholic missionary in the Chimbu] that the Bena Bena, Garfuku, Marifutiga were to a certain extent ruined for missionary work by the action of the first white men who came into these areas coercing the poor natives into selling their womenfolk for trade. . . . His statements re the first white men is a deliberate lie. . . . The natives are naturally inclined that way, which I really think and know is the case. Why not, they are essentially children of nature and have not been influenced by any missionaries which teach that sexual intercourse is a sin and in fact something of which they shoulld be ashamed. Bugger them anyway."

Leahy's vision of highland women swerved from "harlots" to "children of nature." He was unconsciously characterising them to suit the occasion. When he was finally able to write about his sexual activities, his conscience could only have been eased by the conviction shared by many white men in New Guinea that the virtue of "native" women counted for nothing.

"I am afraid this walking about among these kanakas," he wrote on November 1, "especially their good-looking womenfolk, has not been conductive [sic] to the persistent observances of my early religious training. And if I was to be bumped off suddenly, I would most certainly become a permanent resident of Old Nick's domain. . . . When I left Queensland for New Guinea I was full of high ideals and religious fervour. But a few years among the natives, with no chance of ever being able to make a home of one's own, where a person could settle down with a member of the opposite sex and justify his existence by perpetuating the race, very soon woke one up to the futility of trying to suppress one's urges to copulate, and the longer one looked at the black, brown and coppery coloured girls, with essentially feminine mannerisms, the prettier and more seductive they become. And I still think I done the best I could under the circumstances, and I am sure the Good Lord, who instilled the sexual urge in all of us, perhaps in some stronger than in others, will not be too hard on a poor sinner who has fallen by the wayside with one of these seductive damsels of this hinterland country."

Leahy was actually encountering a society with rules and codes as complex as his own. Codes regulating sexual behaviour were well defined everywhere, although sexual customs differed from region to region. But prostitution in any form was unheard of in all regions before contact.

What Leahy was observing, and now participating in, was entirely unorthodox behaviour—a response to the coming of large parties of strange men, outsiders, with unlimited means of paying for what they wanted. Leahy might have thought the women were partially responsible for what was going on, but most likely they were pawns in a transaction between the strangers and their highlander menfolk who brought the women along in return for shells.

At Kuta then, as in other pockets of Australian settlement, there were less arduous ways of obtaining shells from the white man than merely working in his gold mine. Like the Yamka and Ndika men in 1933, Mokei and other tribes around Kuta with an eligible daughter or sister saw fine marriage potential in these wealthy, unattached newcomers, and if not marriage, then a modified version of it.

A Hagen woman dressed for marriage, 1936 or 1937. As more shells flowed into the highlands a certain amount of devaluation naturally took place. Bride-wealth contributions of **kina** *shells increased.*

Leahy described 1934 in his diary as an "Arabian nights" holiday for his men in Mount Hagen. Today the Hagen people see it differently.

Those personally involved, or who know of women who were sent to the coastal men or white men, talk of it more in terms of marriage in the traditional sense. Mokei Kominika Kubal Nori married his sister to a coastal man. "That's when I got my first shells. We had so many young women then, but there weren't enough of these strange men to go around. For a woman we got a few big shells and a variety of small shells. Maybe an axe or two."

Mokei Kubal Nori does not mention the casual sex referred to by Leahy when the price was a handful of small shells. That of course does not mean that it did not go on, or that he is unaware of it. "When one of our women married a coastal man things weren't done quite as we normally do them. The woman didn't receive the bridewealth immediately. They might live together for a while, and then it would come. It wasn't the usual traditional exchange, where you gave pigs and things. During the marriage the coastals would be paid and they'd give things to their women, who'd pass it on to the relatives."

In this society the main characteristic of the marriage contract was the exchange of valuables between the two parties. The man's family presented bridewealth to the woman's family. In that sense, all the relationships between the highland women and the newcomers were deemed marriages of sorts, and therefore legitimate. Or at least that's how the Hagen men choose to see it today. "They were properly married," says Mokei Kubal Nori, "but they would leave the white man and then they would often marry again. The white man would marry one, and then another. He didn't have any women of his own kind with him." In Mount Hagen a man could take as many wives as he could afford. The white men were obviously very wealthy, and this could have helped to explain their unusual behaviour.

If Pastor Bergmann disapproved of the activities of the prospectors and their workmen, so too did Pastor Georg Vicedom, the Lutheran missionary who settled at Ogelbeng near Kelua in the latter part of 1934. In matters of sex, as in everything else, it is hard not to sympathise with the initial confusion of the Hagen people when the missionaries arrived on the scene. Just as they had begun to accustom themselves to one set of strangers, the Lutheran missionaries came with what seemed like totally different ways of behaving. "The natives simply could not understand," wrote Pastor Vicedom, "that we were so completely different from the others, and refused their womenfolk. Once they even asked whether the Ogelbeng people [the Lutheran mission] did not have any sexual organs because they acted so properly towards their womenfolk and also refused marriage. We were not able to contribute to the earnings of the natives from this source, like other Europeans . . ."[1]

Dan Leahy makes no secret of his activities in Mount Hagen in those days, although at the time both he and his brother did. It was not considered acceptable for white men to consort with "native" women in prewar New Guinea, although of course it had been going on from the very beginning. Dan Leahy draws an interesting comparison between the attitude of coastal women and their highland counterparts. "The highland women were more natural," he says. "The coastal women were timid as far as the Europeans were concerned, shy, and it would be hard to talk to a native woman on the coast. But in the highlands they were very friendly. And the men weren't watching them all the time.

"The women would come to Kuta bringing food, and they'd get paid the same as anyone else. And when they found that we wouldn't rush out and grab them, or wheel them off somewhere, that we treated them quite normally, the women got very friendly. The fathers or brothers—they'd sort of tee it up with the women before they came along. And they'd say, 'Well, my sister wants to come.' And as long as she was quite willing and everything. I mean, sex was a normal thing. There would be something wrong with you if you didn't want sex. That's the way they look at it.

"These women were around, you know. And you're out here—and that's all there is to it. There'd be a nice little sort and she'd be hanging round a bit longer, and that'd be it. There was no particular price—but you'd give them a present."

The rewards for sending women along to the white men were significant, and the fact that the whites were outside the traditional structure of society and its code of ethics made it easier for rules to be broken. Mokei Wamp Wan explains how it happened: "The Hagen man would say to his wife, 'I want some of those trade goods, which the white man is giving out. Go and sleep with him.' And she wouldn't disobey. She would go because he told her to. Some men didn't want their wives to go to the white men. Some women, when their husbands asked them to, refused. Nothing happened to them. Their husbands didn't make them go. If a married woman went to the white man behind her husband's back, or if someone else took her to the white man, she would get in a lot of trouble. The husband might beat her. If the husband himself sent her that would be all right."

Kopia Rebia—who had become one of Leahy's main interpreters—says young boys like himself were often used as go-betweens by the white men, taking messages to particular women or their male relatives. "The white men used to point out a woman to me and say go and tell her to come to me. I'll give her axes and shells and things. But I was frightened of the husbands, and I'd tell the white man I was going to do this, but often take my own time about it and not tell them. Sometimes I'd go back to the white man and pretend I'd spoken to the woman. I'd make something up and say: 'Oh that woman doesn't want to come to you.' I didn't like doing this very much. Sometimes when they'd ask I'd say no. But there were others who did it all the time.

"Generation and generation before the white man came," says Kopia Rebia, "there was no such thing—for a man to take his wife to another man in exchange for something—never. There were tribal fights over women, but men would never give wives to other men. They did this only with the white men. And they did it because of the shells. We would not do this with a wealthy man of our own race. That is certain. We did say that the white men were different."

As Mokei Wamp, Kopia Rebia and Dan Leahy imply, there was no set pattern or uniform response. People acted individually. Men had great control over their women and could compel them to do as they wanted up to a point. Many disapproved of prostituting their women-folk but others were overcome by their desire for what their wives could get for them. And sometimes this led to shame and suffering for those involved.

One young man suggested to his new wife, Yamka Amp Wenta from Korabug, that she go along to the white man. They lived close to Kuta so it was a short journey. "My husband told me the white men were giving out good things for women," says Wenta today, "and he asked me to go to them. He took me there at night. I went there three times, and when I got the things, my husband took them all.

"I didn't mind going. I was attracted myself to all the different things he had. Seeing the white man had paid for me I thought it was all right. My husband told me to go, so I had no choice in the matter, anyway. The white man liked me. He gave me a lot of shells and pork and things like that. He'd show me a place to sit down in his house, and put the trade goods in front of me. We just made sign language. He just thought about things to himself and I did the same."

Wenta says the white man was Michael Leahy. She remembers him taking photographs of her, and these exist today. She appears as a young

Yamka Amp Wenta, the mother of Clem Leahy. Taken at Kuta in 1936.

girl of fifteen or sixteen, alternatively apprehensive and smiling, wearing a necklace of giri giri shells, a woven string bag around her head.

Wenta's brief association with the white man would have passed unnoticed were it not for the fact that she later gave birth to a mixed-race son. "When I saw he was different," she says, "I knew that it must be the white man's son, from the times I had been there with him. When I was expecting the baby, everyone thought it was my husband's child. Then people said, 'She's had a white son!' She must have been with the white man! And my husband said nothing to defend me."

Wenta was upset by her husband's failure to declare that it was he who suggested she go to the white man. Now it looked for all the world as though she had gone on her own initiative and this she found utterly shameful, and so did others. There was much snide gossip. Humiliated, she left her husband and fled with her baby to her relatives in another village.

"I was hurt and embarrassed, and at the time it was very hard. My son was quite a grown boy when I went back to my husband. Other men wanted to marry me during that time, but if I had done that, my son would never have been a Kopia now [the clan of her husband]. When I brought him back my husband was good to him. He was quite grown then about three of four years old. But those early times when my son and I were separated from my husband created a scar which is lasting even now."

Wenta says she would never have confronted the white man with his child—she was too shy and embarrassed, but more importantly, this would have drawn even more attention to the fact that the child was not her husband's. There were two other mixed-race children born during these early years. Michael Leahy is acknowledged as the father of all three. The mothers are now dead. One was Marpa, who had been given in marriage to Towa Ulta in 1933, and the other was Kumbi, the sister of Mokei Korua Kolta. "Kumbi was married to a wealthy Ndika man," says Korua Kolta, "but he wasn't looking after her properly, so we took her back and she used to go trading up there at Kuta. Mick Leahy saw her, and said he wanted her. So we gave her to him. When Mick realised she was pregnant he gave her to another coastal man. Then Mick left. Kumbi gave birth to a son, and he was white in colour. We were wondering what had happened. Was this a real child, or was it some kind of spirit? We then looked after him ourselves."

By the time these children were conceived and born, around 1937 and 1938, the highlanders around Mount Hagen had grown accustomed to the white men, but they were still by no means certain about their origin. Some were still convinced they were spirits who had come from the sky. But there is no question that whatever their misgivings, the three children were as cherished by their mothers and highland relatives as any baby could be. The three boys were raised separately and lived a full traditional life until the end of the second world war. Each was accepted into his respective clans. As teenagers they attended mis-

A young Hagen boy.

sionary schools in the postwar years, and as will be told later the half brothers Clem, John and Joe Leahy—the sons respectively of Wenta, Kumbi and Marpa—are today prominent and wealthy planters and businessmen in the Western Highlands Province.

The births of these three boys did nothing to affect the relationships between the white men and the highlanders during those early years. Certainly they bridged no social gulfs. The young mothers were shy and kept their children away from the white men. Joe Leahy lived closest to the mining camp at Kuta. After Marpa had given birth to the boy, his stepfather Towa says he swallowed his rage and raised the boy as his own son. Joe says today that the white men were distant, aloof and even fearsome figures. The supposed father, Michael Leahy, made no effort then or later to single out the mothers or acknowledge his sons.

Quite the reverse, in fact. Dan Leahy says these things weren't broadcast because of the social stigma, and Ewunga Goiba recalls there was a conspiracy of silence. "We weren't allowed to say—that was Mick's child. Or anything like that, because it was forbidden by the government. All Mick's men sided with Mick, and didn't say anything about his having children. We thought it was a good idea to keep it secret, because if we hadn't he would have gone to court. If we had children, they had the same skin colour as the local people. We could look after our children. But the white people were the ones hiding theirs."

Ewunga Goiba and his highland wife now live in Goroka, supported by their prosperous sons and grandsons, who run trade stores in the town. Towa married another Hagen women when Marpa died a year or so after giving birth to Joe. Towa and his wife live on the coffee plantation of Towa's stepson, Joe Leahy.

Some of the Waria eventually went back to their home villages, but not many took their highland wives with them. The experience of Dau and Meta, the first two Hagen women to marry among the strangers in the early days of Kelua, perhaps explains why. Dau married Buassi, one of Taylor's policemen, and Meta one of Taylor's cooks. Both women followed their husbands back to the coast and then to various newly established patrol posts in the highlands. Living among people with foreign tongues did not bother them. "We used sign language," says the indomitable Dau, "and they were happy we were there. They pointed at us, laughed, joked and called us friends."

But after several years the young women tired of the itinerant lives of these government servants, always at the white man's beck and call. "When we travelled around with our husbands," says Dau, "we were like birds flying. We had no home, and we realised there would be no future in this. So we left them and came back, and married Hagen big men. We married men who would look after us."

Asked whether this angered their coastal husbands, Dau replied:

"No, why should they be angry? They didn't offer us anything. They just couldn't do anything. We came back to our own people and our own men."

"My coastal husband took me to court," says Meta. "I said in court he had no land, he has offered me no security. So I went back to where I'd come from and married a wealthy man who would provide for me and my son. So I left the coastal man."

Meta was asked how her own people reacted to her son by the coastal man. "My husband's people said I had brought a nice little boy with me. And they were very happy. My husband had several wives. He was pleased I brought a child with me, especially a son. So were his other wives. My husband Mokei Ninji gave bridewealth for me and the son. He gave the coastal man a lot of pigs and cassowaries and he gave more things to my own clan for me. He's dead now."

Meta married Mokei Ninji, who was to become one of Mount Hagen's most powerful and prominent big men. Dau married Mokei Wamp Wan, Ninji's clansman and a future big man himself. The coastal husbands might have been considered more worldly, but these two women had learned something about them and their status in the outside world, and they knew where their best interests lay.

Chapter Fifteen

CHURCH AND STATE

The end of 1934 marked the end of the Leahy brothers' central role in opening up the New Guinea highlands. Following the deaths of the two Catholic missionaries in the Chimbu, nonofficial Europeans were restricted to within a five-mile radius of their camps, which put an end, of course, to further prospecting. To relieve the boredom of mining routine at Kuta, Dan Leahy now took up his brother's favourite hobby and bought himself a large format Rolliflex. Dan's photographs lack the impact of Michael's—he did not have his brother's eye. But they are remarkable nonetheless for the way they reveal the profound economic impact the coming of the Australians was having on the highland people.

Already, in Dan's photographs, the Hageners appear more relaxed and confident. There is a greater familiarity between the photographer and his subject. But the most striking feature is the enormous number of shells the people are wearing or displaying. In scene after scene of weddings, feasts and religious festivals, men, women and children are shown draped and festooned with shells of all descriptions. In *moka* exchange ceremonies rows of *kina* shells carpet the ground.

Hagen children in 1936 or 1937. The photograph illustrates the vast amount of shellwealth the Australians brought with them and distributed in trade. Decorations like these were only worn on special occasions.

Shells and to a lesser extent steel tools paved the Australian road into New Guinea's interior. They cushioned the collision between the two peoples. Sanctioned by international law, motivated by high and low ideals, the Australians invaded the highlands, occupied them and proceeded to impose their colonial rule. The highlanders were given no choice at all as to who should rule them, how they should be ruled, or whether they should be ruled at all. Given the history of European colonialism elsewhere, this penetration and occupation of the highlands by the Australians could have been a much bloodier affair. There were casualties, of course. The Leahy brothers and their coastal offsiders were by no means the only prospectors who shot highland people in the 1930s, although the Leahys' toll was probably the highest. For one thing their interaction with the people was more prolonged and intense than that of their prospecting contemporaries. Total casualties to gunfire directed by white prospectors and patrol officers throughout the 1930s might conceivably have amounted to a thousand men, women and children.

It remains enduringly ironic that throughout that first crucial decade of the 1930s, the imposition of the colonial yoke was made immeasurably easier for the Australians because they brought with them those particular items of wealth and utility most valued in highland society. Simultaneous with their arrival, the Australians ushered in a brief but unprecedented era of prosperity for the highland people, more particularly those who came within their orbit of control and influence.

Whatever trauma they may have suffered with the coming of the Australians, there is no denying that by and large the highlanders made them welcome, and that by their own standards these first years of enforced contact and pacification were boom times indeed. And those highlanders who could do so revelled in them.

From the time they arrived, the miners, kiaps and missionaries in their outposts throughout the contacted regions used shells supplemented by steel trade to pay for their needs, and their needs were considerable. By 1936, for example, the Administration and missionary outposts in the Chimbu between them supported nearly five hundred people—policemen, labourers, interpreters, students. By 1937 the Lutherans and Catholics operated similar-sized establishments in Mount Hagen. The Leahy brothers alone employed about twenty indentured labourers and over two hundred highlanders.

All these people were paid in shells. Their food was bought with shells. Marriages and liaisons were paid for in the same way. An enormous number of shells flowed out from the Australian and Lutheran outposts into the surrounding communities. The Leahys alone in 1936 were flying in about five hundred *kina* shells a month to meet their food and labour bills. The geographer Ian Hughes[1] has calculated that between 1933 and 1942 at least five and possibly ten *million* shells of all types were brought into the highlands by the Australians—an enormous number when it is remembered how the arrival of one pearlshell in the time before contact was cause for great celebration. The steady influx of shells brought about a gradual devaluation, but basically there was no upper limit to the demand.

The Leahys got their shells from Australian pearling stations. The Lutherans and Catholics bought them along the New Guinea coast wherever they could. The Catholics augmented their supplies by putting school children to work, collecting cowrie shells along the beaches. But Hughes says the demand was so insatiable the missionaries even tried counterfeiting them. Father William Ross tried out imitation shells in Mount Hagen but the people refused to accept them. James Taylor

Nets of **kina** *shells being carried to a large* **moka**. *Photo, late 1930s.*

Mokei men display shellwealth in procession at their great **Amp Kor** *(amp = woman, kor = spirit) held in 1937 and witnessed by Father William Ross and Dan Leahy. High walls of woven grass exclude women and children from the climactic moments of this elaborate fertility ritual, held infrequently to enlist the help of the female spirit. In 1985 men of the Kawelka tribe near Mount Hagen held an* **Amp Kor,** *attesting to the continuing strength of traditional religious practice.*

says the Lutherans ordered up imitation cowries from England's Birmingham china factories, but customs officials in Salamaua refused them entry and dumped them at sea.

Without being aware of it the Australians were transforming traditional trade routes, creating new rich and new poor. In precontact times, shells had been traded into the highlands from the coast along well-defined routes. Communities on the highland fringe that had controlled the inward flow of shells now found them being traded back towards them, to their own disadvantage, while communities like the Hageners became the new rich. And none were richer than the tribes around Kuta.

In 1937 the Mokei displayed their new-won wealth in a series of great ceremonies photographed by Dan Leahy. First came the *kor* ceremony, held infrequently to honour certain spirits and to enlist their support to ensure continuing fertility. The missionary William Ross left an account of this: "One orator after another rose, and brandishing his stone axe, addressed the crowd . . . 'Let all Mokei unite in one grand effort to show our wealth and power. The feast today was to invoke the help of the spirits. The rest is up to us Mokei men!' This was the gist of the speeches . . . when some months after, the Mokei did hold their tribal feast, some seven hundred pigs were roasting on the coals, and the name and fame of the tribe had gone to the uttermost parts of the earth."[2]

But there was another side to this apparent flourishing of Mokei wealth and culture. There were other forces at work, which threatened to undermine the confidence of the people at the moment when their wealth and strength seemed at its height. For a start they owed their wealth to the presence of the Australians, and this in itself had created a dependency. The Mokei, and communities like them, eagerly accepted the wealth, and, along with it, step by tiny step, they also accepted the loss of their autonomy and the end of much of their way of life as they had known it. There was resistance, of course, particularly when the people were called upon to jettison customs and practices they thought intrinsic to their well-being. The resistance was overcome—by blandishments, persuasion, by force at times, but also by the

Mokei men holding gold-lipped pearlshells at their **Amp Kor** *in 1937. The man on the left wears a saucer as part of his head decoration.*

people's own desire to emulate these foreigners and gain some measure of their wealth and their power.

While gold prospectors like the Leahy brothers were in the forefront of the European invasion, the really profound changes were ushered in by those who followed—the representatives of church and state. Certainly the very presence of the Leahys and their mine was a powerful agent for change in Mount Hagen. But the Leahys were not intentionally seeking change—they were there to win gold, not hearts and minds and souls. In the postcontact phase it was the missionaries and *kiaps* whose business it was to challenge many of the foundations of traditional highland society and to begin imposing upon the people the values of the western world as variously interpreted by Catholic priests and Protestant parsons of several nationalities and Australian patrol officers. Despite their differing backgrounds, creeds and methodology, they all had one intention in common—the imposition of change.

The missionaries arrived in Mount Hagen halfway through 1934. First came the Catholics under the American priest William Ross. With Michael Leahy's encouragement he established himself among the Mokei at Wilya, alongside Leahy's aerodrome-on land owned by Wamp Wan's Mokei Nambuka. They were followed shortly afterwards by the Lutherans under Vicedom and Strauss, who set up their mission a discreet distance away at Ogelbeng, near the old Kelua airstrip, much to the satisfaction of the Yamka and Ndika, who had lost the Leahys to the Mokei.

The Lutherans and the Catholics disliked, mistrusted and avoided each other. The Lutherans also disliked the Leahys and had much to say against the Administration as well. The Leahys had little time for the Lutherans but admired William Ross, who went about armed, and once startled a visiting priest by telling him it was preferable the potential faithful learn about the gun before the crucifix the visitor carried. But to the highlanders they were all white men and they were all wealthy. In the second half of 1934 the two denominations radiated out into the surrounding communities, the Catholics building outstations that they would then periodically visit, the Lutherans installing coastal New Guineans—trained mission evangelists—to live among the communities within their sphere.

The Hageners showed their eagerness to accommodate these new white men by responding enthusiastically to their calls for labour, particularly those in outlying communities who had previously had less access to the European distributed wealth. Late in 1934 Ross wrote in

Father William Ross with his students outside the schoolroom, 1936.

his diary: "It would seem almost unbelievable, but one outstation . . . was completed in one day of thirteen working hours. . . . Two thousand native men, women and children like an ant colony, kept busy bringing *kunai* grass, ropes from the bark of trees, wild sugarcane for walls, saplings. . . . In this one day eleven houses were completed and ready for use."[3]

Ross bided his time for the first six months. There was no attempt at proselytising. He and his associates worked away at their housing and churches, administered to the sick and injured and cultivated the friendship of prominent big men—in particular Mokei Ninji, on whose land Ross was eventually to settle permanently. Like the Leahys and Taylor in 1933, the Catholics knew the quickest and surest way to gain influence among the people was through the authority of the big men.

Ross records that his immediate goal was to set up a school to train fifty young Hagen boys, convert them, and send them out into the communities as catechists. He writes that after six months, Mokei Ninji finally arrived to ask what the priest expected in return for all the favours Ross had done his people. Ross then put in his request for fifty boys, asking Ninji to organise them. The big man obliged and in January 1935 the priest began instructing his first class of twelve-year-olds.

Mokei Korua Kolta attended Ross's school but, to his eternal regret, his school days were short-lived. "My father and I were on a visiting trip to see some relatives up towards Kuta. Father Ross saw us on the way and he took me by the hand and he told my father to leave me with him. I was quite happy to go along. He'd taken a lot of other boys about my age. He gave me a book and a pencil and I slept the night there. He stood up in front of us and told us to write things. I was watching him and I was quite interested. The whites had killed Mokei Joea in Titip's fight, so my father didn't trust them, and was quite sure they would kill me. So he went and got an older, stronger man and they came for me, all covered in mud.

"Father Ross lifted their *omaks*. 'Probably this is what you want for your son,' he said. 'I have a different way of offering you wealth but if you want him, you take him.' To this day I always say my father was a fool for taking me away. School would have been good for me. Now I'm getting to be an old man. I've not got many teeth left and I don't know how to read and write. My father didn't know any better. He didn't realise that what the priest wanted me to do was a good thing.

Kominika Korua Kolta surrounded by family members.

"I'm very impressed with educated people, being able to live in a modern house, drive a car, sit on a chair, go places in an aeroplane. I'm very impressed with the things educated people do, and I think that's a better way than we have. I feel I missed out on a lot. It took us a long time to catch up with the world because I think we're on a high mountain. This is my theory. I've travelled now to Port Moresby, Lae, Madang and Wewak, and it always seems we are going downhill to get there. I'm sure our place must be very high, up near the clouds."

Korua Kolta's father was still in two minds about the white men. So was Mokei Titip. After the shooting incident in May 1933 which left his arm shattered, it was some time before Titip came to regard the Catholic missionaries as men of a different purpose to the Leahys. "Dan and Mick at Kuta were offering really good things," says Titip, "so I took my pig and got shells from them. But I wasn't friendly with them. I always feared them. We had nothing in common, not even a common language! When Father Ross came he made a temporary home on our ceremonial ground. Then he made a church there. Father Ross used to pull his beard and say: 'Come and listen to what I have to say.' He was a wild spirit. In this temporary house he used to ask children and people to gather in there. People used to take their children. Then he taught them religion. I didn't go there. Why should I? I was scared of spirits. That's how it was for quite a while. I didn't go near the whites, but then I got to know Father Ross."

Mass conversions did not come for another decade in Mount Hagen, although twenty-six of those fifty school boys were baptised by Ross in 1938—his first converts. But it is quite clear that before long men like Ross were exerting a powerful influence on the highland people they worked among. "Father Ross came," says Mokei Wamp Wan, "when the airstrip had been built at Wilya, and I was looking after it. He went into our cemeteries and saw the little houses we'd built on top of graves, for the dead person's spirit. We killed pigs for the spirit, and placed a hollow piece of bamboo from the spirit house down into the grave, into the middle of the body about where the heart was, so the dead person could get fresh air, and his spirit could come and go from the grave.

"Father Ross said all this was not so. The spirit didn't live there at all. Every dead person was with God because he was the creator. These things you do are wrong, there is a creator of everything and everyone. Some dead go to hell, where there is only fire, some go to limbo, which is really cold. Forget about the way you are doing things. You should follow only God."

Wamp says he readily took up Ross's ideas. "We believed him. We could never really understand spirits, or explain them. Father Ross said they don't live around the graves and we could never really prove they did. When Father Ross said they go back to the person that made them, his explanation seemed reasonable, but whether it was true or not we didn't really know."

Although many Hageners today are nominally Lutheran or Catholic, traditional religious belief and practice has by no means disappeared. Mokei Wamp Wan, however, remains a staunch member of the Roman Catholic church, a regular attendant at the wooden cathedral built by William Ross. He formed a close association with Ross from the day the priest arrived. Ross initially camped on Wamp's land, and the big man gained considerable prestige and material benefit from the connection. Today he still lives in a wooden cottage on the edge of the Leahys' old Mokei aerodrome on the outskirts of Mount Hagen township. The flat space is largely covered now by casuarina trees, garden plots and Wamp's several hundred coffee trees. Photographs of Catholic popes adorn the walls of his cottage, along with pinups of the British royal family, and pictures of a younger Wamp, dressed in the Australian colonial rig of shirt, shorts and long socks, meeting various visiting dignitaries in his preindependence role as a local government councilor. Mokei Wamp still commands respect, despite his often-expressed nostalgia for the days when the Australians were in charge and his criticism of the younger highlanders who now hold the reins of power.

Wamp Wan implies that his traditional religious beliefs were rather fragile—easily shaken by the arrival of the white man. The Lutheran pastor, Georg Vicedom, agrees. He wrote that when Hagen travellers first brought back news of the outside world—that there was no land of the dead, or place where the legs of the sky met the earth—the people's belief in their own cosmology and religion disintegrated.

But if the Hageners did not and have not given up their beliefs anywhere near as readily as Mokei Wamp or Pastor Vicedom suggest, they were undoubtedly vulnerable to what the missionaries had to say. There were certain similarities of belief—existence after death, the soul, nonhuman forces for good and evil, the notion of a supreme life giving force—that enabled them to graft onto their belief system, even if in a distorted form, some of Ross's religious concepts while still retaining much of their own.

But why did they accept any of it at all? "We were amazed by the white men," says Mokei Wamp, "and we believed everything they told us." Mokei Kominika Nembil adds, "It was because the white men had all the things, that we thought they must be the owners of all things, and that everything they said must be right."

The fact was that the Hagen people—particularly those close to the Europeans—simply could not ignore the great gulf that existed between them. The white men had wealth and power. They compelled people to do their bidding. And they could conjure up an unending array of astounding new things. Even when the Hageners made direct comparisons with their own possessions—steel axes as against stone ones—it was all too clear where the superiority lay. All this pointed to a material power—and therefore a spiritual power—vastly superior to their own. Spiritual power was the fundamental basis of material success, and material success was all important. The highlanders, then, were encountering for the first time men who forced them to question their abilities, their knowledge, their control over the physical and spiritual world, their position at the centre of things. The white men, not the highlanders, seemed to hold the key. So the highlanders automatically assumed that the white man's wealth and power came not from human endeavour, manufacturing expertise or intellectual ability but from spiritual ability, and there was little happening at the European settlements to contradict this view. Virtually nothing the Leahys or the missionaries had in Mount Hagen was made there. Guns, cloth, tins, record players, mirrors, aeroplanes, pearlshells—the endless cornucopia—were all either carried in or flown in. There was no evidence, then, to suggest they had not come from a spiritual source, a source that the white man had managed to tap by the correct application of spiritual knowledge. If the highlanders were also to gain access to this wealth, they would need access to the white man's spiritual knowledge.

In the initial period of contact, certain Mount Hagen tribes—the Yamka and Ndika at Kelua, and later the Mokei at Wilya—assumed their eventual access to this spiritual knowledge would be assured so long as the strangers remained among them. The white men had camped among them and seemingly aligned themselves with them. The tribes worked strenuously to cement the relationship, always anticipating it could only be fruitful. This was what motivated Ndika Opa to give Dau in marriage to Buassi. The Ndika big men were hoping that the alliance would ensure them access to unlimited wealth—the "shell trees" that they thought grew in the strangers' place. But as time went on it was clear the newcomers did not favour one tribe over another. They shifted camps. They refused to take sides against enemies in fights, despite their obvious ability to do so. In fact they made a point of dealing with friends and enemies alike, even to the extent of escorting enemy clans in and out to trade or work in their mine. There was no consolation then that one's own tribe was among those chosen by the all-powerful.

The gap between the highlander and the white man became even more incomprehensible as the evidence mounted that these strangers were human and not spirit beings. Direct comparisons could now be made between them all as mortals, and the inevitable acknowledgement of the white man's apparent spiritual superiority carried with it an acknowledgement of highlander inferiority. No one was immune from this—not even the big men. If anything it was those who were closest who were most aware of the gap.

This left the people vulnerable to anything the Australians might have to say that pointed in the direction of eliminating the gap between them. It was in this context that the missionaries and later the *kiaps* began their work. Both agents had no shortage of suggestions as to how the people might eventually transform their lives. The highlanders were receptive to much of what the missionaries and *kiaps* had to say because they hoped to benefit from it.

But when new ideas were perceived to be in direct conflict with traditional ways, they were naturally resisted. Whatever the pressure on them, functioning societies do not lightly discard what they believe is intrinsic to their well-being. "When the white man came and brought all these shells with them," says Mokei Nembil, "so that we had plenty of them ourselves, who could accept their religion and have only one wife when we now had potential to buy so many? But we did respect him, because of all the material things he brought with him. We had our own ways then—our own ways of getting more women and of trying to accumulate more things for ourselves. Everything we wanted the white man brought with him. And with these things the traditional way was to buy more wives. But the priest said one wife was enough! Who could listen to that?"

Without more than one wife no one could hope to become a big man or remain one. Extra wives meant extra gardens and so more pigs; it meant wider political influence and control, through in-laws. To renounce polygamy was to renounce a cornerstone of society. It was not done overnight. It was, in many cases, not done at all, and polygamy is still a feature in Hagen today among the men of power and wealth in the postcolonial society. The big man Ninji, the Hagener closest to Ross who attended his church for thirty years, preferred his six wives (Meta among them) to baptism—although Ross did manage a last-minute deathbed conversion in 1963, Ninji having seen to it beforehand that his six wives were cared for by clansmen.

By the end of 1934 the Hagen people were having to deal with three quite separate forms of the outside colonial power—private enterprise, religion and government—and to adjust their behaviour accordingly. "If we hung around the missionary yard," says Mokei Korua Kolta, "that was all right. But if we hung around the *kiap's* place, or the company place [Kuta] they would hit us. The company was tough. When they were working on the gold a lot of men got belted up. Mick and Dan were always grumpy and cross."

Despite the infrequent visits of the *kiaps*—there was no permanent Administration post until 1938—the Hageners seemed to have no trouble recognising where the ultimate authority lay. By 1935, with the closure of the highlands, it was the *kiaps* who were calling the tune. "The white men all looked the same," says Korua Kolta, "with their clothes and trade goods, but we knew that Taylor had more power than the others. We wondered often why he was respected even by the other white men. Father Ross—he was quieter. He used to watch us and never captured us or put us in jail. We figured Taylor must be above the others in some way. Whatever was said, matters were always referred to the *kiap*. We realised he must be the boss—as in our society, he was the big man. Mick and Dan were working, but we felt sure he was the boss over them."

Having effectively ended the expansion of mission and prospecting activity in 1935, the Administration soon came under pressure to reverse the policy again as the decade wore on. In 1937 the Administrator, McNicholl, rejected an application by a consortium of British and Australian businessmen to bend the rules and allow an exploring party into the region west of Mount Hagen again. This time it was oil, not gold they were after. But McNicholl soon found himself under pressure from Senator Sir George Pearce, the Australian cabinet minister in charge of overseas territories. Pushing the case of one of the rejected applicants, Pearce told McNicholl he was "keenly anxious that oil should be discovered in Australia or Australian territories . . ." Pearce said he did not want uncontrolled areas thrown open again until they were "safe and under real and effective control," but he requested McNicholl to concentrate his forces on "the penetration of any areas in which oil-prospecting companies are likely to be interested."[4] So now, in high Australian government circles at least, oil was the new impetus behind the imposition of the pax Australiana, the new pragmatic interpretation of the sacred trust. It was not a view universally shared, however, by the administration patrol officers nor by their leader, Director of the District Services Division E.W.P. Chinnery.

There were occasional oil-prospecting forays into uncontrolled regions in the late 1930s (they found nothing), but by and large this was a period of gradual consolidation as Chinnery's men, following in the wake of the missionaries, set about their appointed tasks. These men did not always see the missionaries as allies. They did not, by and large, share the Catholics' desire to eradicate polygamy, the Lutherans' disapproval of dancing and festivals, or the Seventh Day Adventists' earnest wish that the highlanders stop eating pork and start eating goats. Referring to New Guinea's coastal districts and islands, Chinnery claimed that missionary activity struck "killing blows at the very root of native culture, and in almost every district where missions have become firmly established, the old customs are rapidly disappearing whether all the people have been converted to Christianity or not." He was a man who had shared James Taylor's feeling prior to the penetration of the Wahgi in 1933 that the Australians' arrival there would be a mixed blessing. In a paper attached to the 1932–1933 report to the League of Nations, Chinnery described the Administration's procedure and commented: "The Government does not interfere with general culture, excepting in practices which come under the criminal law or are outstanding abominations."[5]

In point of fact the patrol officers were pervasive agents of change. From their highland outposts the *kiaps* with their armed police detachments fanned out in a continuous programme of energetic patrolling, visiting each village and settlement in turn. The *kiap* would call the people together, inform them they were now under the protection of the "gavman" (pidgin for administration, or government) and explain the new laws by which the people were to live. The *kiap* would conduct a census, build himself a hut for future visits, choose a man he thought influential, and appoint him the representative with the task of encouraging obedience to the new ways, keeping the village clean, clearing pathways between villages, adjudicating minor quarrels and reporting serious offences and disputes at the *kiap's* next visit, which the *kiap* would then adjudicate. So began the process of what the Australians called "pacification."

At the head of the list of priorities was the cessation of warfare. It was thought that until this could be achieved, no worthwhile advancement was possible. Throughout the 1930s a handful of *kiaps* gradually imposed their will upon these hundreds of thousands of people by various methods ranging from persuasion to brute force. What the *kiaps* were attempting to modify of course was the legal system by which the highlanders administered their justice and settled their disputes. Their initial efforts were by no means universally appreciated.

In the Bena Bena Valley the Korofeigu, who had clashed with the Leahys in 1932, were a powerful tribe and had long dominated the surrounding communities. Koritoia Upe describes his people's reaction to the call for an end to warfare: "Some of us dropped our bows and arrows, others didn't listen and hid them, to use later. Why should we give up carrying our bows and arrows? They were our bodyguards, a part of us, like our bones and muscles. We never went without them. We survived only because of them. Even now we keep them in our houses, but we don't carry them around as much as before. Our fathers brought us up with this tradition, and told us not to go without them. So we could not."

Further west of the Korofeigu, in the Goroka Valley, was Gavey Akamo's village of Asaroka. "Fighting didn't stop immediately," he says. "In fact we kept on for a long time, although they told us to stop. We just couldn't give it up. Only much later did we take notice of them, when they put us in jail and showed us they really meant business."

"If we caused trouble by fighting," says Sole Sole of Gorohanota Village in the Asaro, "we'd be punished—locked up and whipped. The missionaries warned us about this—that we would be punished by the policemen. One thing they did was to dig a hole and drop us into it. We'd have to urinate, shit and eat in there. And then the policemen would come and urinate on us. With this sort of punishment we gradually cooled off and stopped fighting. And then the second world war came."

Until 1938 the Administration presence in Mount Hagen was restricted to periodic visits from the patrol officer based in the Chimbu. So in these early years the Hageners' experience of the European concepts of law and order came primarily from their day-to-day dealings with the missionaries and the Leahy brothers. These had no authority to in-

These photos are from a roll taken by Michael Leahy in the late 1930s, most probably 1936. A Hagen clan has decided to burn its weapons, a gesture which was not completely without precedent in the Hagen area or elsewhere in the highlands about this time. Father William Ross witnessed the big man Mokei Ninji and some of his clansmen ceremonially burning their shields and spears in 1936, and the same thing is here occurring at Kuta. In the first photo a group of armed men approach on the road leading to Leahy's house. Next, they per-

form a mock battle with each other. They begin breaking spears and chopping up their shields, and finally they watch the conflagration with a certain air of pleased satisfaction. William Ross was somewhat alarmed at Ninji's gesture of unilateral disarmament, as it left those Mokei clans at the mercy of others who had not disarmed. Ross says he kept a store of weapons at his mission centre and had occasion to hurriedly redistribute them before a general peace was imposed over the area in the late 1930s. Warfare in the region has never completely disappeared, however, and is not uncommon at the present time.

terfere in fighting or any other disputes for that matter, but by their own actions they could not help ushering in revolutionary notions.

The people were already aware of the consequences of attacking the Leahys or their employees, and knew that neither they nor the missionaries would take sides in warfare. Gradually they began to look to the white men for adjudication in certain circumstances, and on one occasion they looked to Dan Leahy for sanctuary. "I was mining at Kuta and Mick was away," says Dan. His brother was actually in London giving his address to the Royal Geographic Society. "One lunchtime I came out from the mine and here's a whole tribe of natives around the house. I said to them, 'What do you want? What are you doing?' I picked out the head man [Ndika Mukuka Wingti*] and he said, 'The Ndika have just declared war on us and chased us. A few of us have been killed and we had nowhere to go, so we came here to you for your help.'

"I said to them, 'Well, you can't stop here.' And they said to me, 'If we go back they'll kill us.' At that particular time, there was plenty of food about and it was very cheap. And there were a lot of them wounded, cut up in a bad way. It was the whole clan—men, women and children. So I said, 'All right, you can stay here. But you'll have to do as I tell you and live as I want you to live.' And they said, "Oh, anything at all.' I told them they'd have to start building houses and gardens, that I would keep them in food and look after them until their gardens and everything got going. I told them, 'The people I've marked out to work on the gold, you can work in the mine. There'll be no pay for that, that pays for your food.' They were quite agreeable to work for nothing but later I did pay them. Well they all hopped in—some working in the mine, others in the gardens."

As highlanders began travelling long distances to work or trade at Kuta the Leahys extended protection to them as well. The paths cleared by the people under instructions from the *kiaps* had by 1937 become an almost continuous thoroughfare from Kainantu to Mount Hagen. Dan Leahy says that by 1936, groups of up to one hundred Chimbu men and women were travelling without Australian escort along the Wahgi Valley to work for him at Mount Hagen. "It was nothing to see fifty or sixty Chimbu arrive. If there weren't enough houses they'd go and make their own. They'd work for six months and at the end they'd get the gold-lipped pearlshells, tomahawks, knives, and enough beads and small

*Father of Papua New Guinea's present Prime Minister, Paias Wingti.

trade to buy food on the way home. It only used to take them a couple of days. The road they came on was fairly safe. The enemy tribes wouldn't molest them because they knew they had our protection." Because of the Leahys' efforts to ensure a steady labour supply, the notion gradually took hold that travellers along this twentieth-century Roman road were sacrosanct.

By the end of the decade the Australians were making their claims to the League of Nations that peace was gradually coming to the highlands, due primarily to the tireless efforts of the patrol officers. Had they been given a hearing at Geneva the missionaries would have presented their case as well. "The few government officials," wrote Pastor Vicedom in 1938 after four years at Mount Hagen, "were only partly successful in pacifying the natives in this vast inland area. Such masses do not allow themselves to be governed by a few patrol officers and a few dozen native policemen." Vicedom claimed the government had used the missionaries as an extension of its arm, and that they "soon exercised great influence upon the tribes around their stations, and these stopped fighting and became Christians."[6]

Explanations concerning the coming of peace vary according to who is giving them. There was no uniform pattern of events. Koritoia Upe seemed never to have given up fighting, while floggings and degrading punishment apparently discouraged some men in the Asaro. In the Chimbu Valley in 1939 the patrol officer, Ian Downs, says he confiscated the entire pig herd of one powerful and resistant fighting clan and the ensuing shock waves brought fighting in his region to an end almost overnight.

In Mount Hagen, Mokei Korua Kolta remembers the *kiaps* shooting pigs in reprisal raids for fighting, along with imprisonment for the fight leaders. "They came and took our bows and arrows," he says, "and burnt them on the ceremonial ground. After, all of us men were captured and taken as prisoners to Wilya. We spent the night in there. The next morning the *kiap* told us we were free."

Father William Ross, writing in his journal, was surprised one morning in 1936 when the big man Ninji led a group of Mokei clans to the Catholic mission where with speeches and due ceremony they voluntarily broke their shields and spears, piled them into a heap, and set fire to it. In a lengthy speech Ninji announced that henceforth there would be no more warfare. In fact, tribal fighting continues even today around Mount Hagen, but it was an extraordinary acknowledgement— three years after contact—of the white man's power, the missionaries' influence, and Ninji's own notions of pragmatic self-interest.

"I was one of the first to give up tribal fighting," says Mokei Yaga. "If my people said we had to go and kill one of our enemies to avenge one of our own dead people, I'd say, 'What for? He'll only end up in this place Father Ross is talking about.' That's our man who will end up there in the good place Father Ross is talking about. I'd killed a lot of people, and I told them we must not fight. I burnt the weapons— our shields and our spears. As for others, it's up to them. We Mokei won't have any more tribal fighting. If someone is killed in a car accident, or something like that, we get our compensation in the proper way—the lawful way. Even if women are raped we should let the law handle it. We Mokei are strong about that."

There is no question that peace was imposed largely by force in the highlands and that the highlanders initially resisted it. But Ninji's voluntary act of destruction was by no means an isolated case. The highlanders could recognise the practical advantages of peace—particularly the freedom of movement it opened up—an absolutely unprecedented situation. Many old people—particularly women—speak warmly of the gradual feeling of relief that came over them with the realisation that their lives were no longer at risk.

"When I was a young man," says Ndika Wingti, "just before the whites came, my father really pushed me into fighting. Our fathers would say, 'Come on! Go and fight!' Even today some of us are still enemies with each other. Maybe it's not obvious, but we still feel it today. But some of us, since we became leaders and councilors, we'd say, 'Fighting is not a good thing. Let's forget about it now.' And I told my clan we must not take part in any fight at all. I want to live a long time before I die. I don't want to have anything to do with fights. No fighting for me. Fighting is a bad thing. You can't rest at night."*

In the Eastern highlands by the late 1930s some of the communities were moving their villages down from the strategic crests of ridges and rebuilding them on better land along the valley floors. The end of warfare, together with the widespread adoption of steel tools, gave the men more leisure time, and this, coupled with the wealth of shells still pouring in, was put into greater and more frequent competitive gift giving.

"Long, long ago," says Kirupano Eza'e with poetic finality, "before the white man had ever come, we ourselves managed all things—fights, the time of feasts, the time of ceremonies, the marriages of women to

---

*Ndika Mukuka Wingti and his clanspeople were eventually able to resettle on their original clan territory.

men. When we grew to be young men they put us in the men's house and told us to look after our friends and our clanspeople. And in our land we toiled hard in the hot sun and we got all our needs. We beat the bark and made cloth, the women worked on certain plants and made their skirts and string bags.

"Our fighting with the enemies was changed when the white man came. When we wanted to fight he sent his policemen around. They shot us, jailed us, shot our pigs. Then we were afraid and we changed our old habits. And we had peace at this time and could sleep anywhere. Why hide in the mountains? We left our old fortified villages for good. The white man said, 'You throw away your ways of the past and come down and build your villages like this, and you live together and whatever we say to you can be more easily heard from there.' In the past each man was his own boss, but this came to an end when the white man came, because the *kiaps* and the *luluais* and the *tultuls** ruled over us. When they told us to work, we worked. They themselves selected the day when we would have to work and we made sure that we never failed to turn up."

In 1938, with much of the world on the brink of war, the Australians in Geneva could announce much of the highlands under colonial control on the brink of peace. And what's more, the final veils were about to be lifted from New Guinea's interior. James Taylor, at the head of a huge Administration expedition, was systematically exploring the ten thousand square miles of country west of Mount Hagen, much of it thinly populated, lying between the Papuan and Dutch borders and the Sepik River. Times had changed for Michael Leahy since the heady days of 1933. His participation in the Hagen-Sepik Patrol was restricted to filming its departure from Mount Hagen with his motion picture camera.

Coincidentally, Taylor's expedition covered the areas where the oil men had been clamouring to enter, and a patrol post was established in the middle of the Enga country at Wabag as a prelude to pacification. There was no oil there, but Taylor and the Administration had other ideas now for the highlands, and these were given full rein in his official report, published by the *Pacific Islands Monthly*. "A Second Kenya in Central New Guinea" announced the *Monthly* in August 1939. With the luxury of hindsight there is irony in Taylor's dreams of a white-ruled "middle kingdom," given what was about to happen to the European colonial world built up over the past five centuries. The notion

---

Tultuls were the *kiap*-appointed village officials. *Luluais* had wider powers and could, for example, be responsible for several villages each with its own *tultul*.

of an eventual withdrawal from New Guinea was a distant and remote possibility in Taylor's mind. New Guinea was going to stay a white man's country. Taylor could see natives growing cash crops for themselves, but the crux of it was, "I think we should adopt the policy of the government of Kenya, and reserve the highlands of New Guinea for Europeans, where climatic conditions are temperate and suitable for the European manner of living. . . . The almost uninhabited lowlands may be settled by natives from overcrowded areas . . . or perhaps by native-born Chinese, who it is said are increasing at a prodigious rate. . . . Asiatics flourish exceedingly in the warm climate of the lowlands and the coast . . .

"The country will lose some of its charm by this development," wrote Taylor, "but that has been the history of colonisation, I suppose, since Roman legions infested Britain and European governments began the emancipation and westernisation of the African." In conclusion, Taylor observed that "New Guinea is a much greater country than most of us have believed hitherto. That it has a golden future I have no doubt, and I trust that we may see it in our time."[8]

Europe was days away from war when Taylor's report was published. Pearl Harbour was two years away. The Australians carried on in New Guinea unaware of the looming Japanese invasion at the end of those two years.

In Mount Hagen, Daniel Leahy was now the sole *masta* at Kuta. With little faith in the claim's long-term prospects, Michael Leahy had sold Dan his share for a thousand pounds and left the highlands permanently, settling along the Watut River to mine a gold lease he shared with his brother Jim. At the end of 1940, both Mick and Jim had married Australian women and by the end of 1941 all three brothers—the once close-knit family partnership—were feuding. Both Jim and Dan resented the close interest Mick's wife took in the brothers' business affairs. Nineteen-year-old Jeannette Leahy née Best was the daughter of a Queensland sugar mill manager, and her husband turned a deaf ear to his brothers' complaints. On a visit from Kuta, Dan brought the matter to a head. He and Mick knocked each other down, and for several years neither spoke to each other. A reconciliation would eventually take place, but from this time onwards all three brothers would follow different paths and live in different parts of New Guinea.

Early in 1942 the Japanese Army came pouring ashore on New Guinea, routed the Australians, and by mid-1942 had occupied Rabaul, Wewak, Lae, Madang, Salamaua and Finchafen. With the Australians hanging on grimly in Papua, the coastal New Guineans found themselves for the third time in half a century under new colonial masters. After three years of savage and destructive warfare, the Australians and Americans prevailed, although the Japanese were still resisting when the bomb was dropped at Hiroshima. Along with 150,000 Japanese corpses rotting in the jungles were those of an estimated 50,000 coastal and island New Guineans—embroiled in a war they neither initiated, wholly sympathised with nor fully understood.

"We are just in the middle," said Yasa of Manam Island off the northern New Guinea coast, recalling the war. "First the Germans came— and the Australians pushed them out. Then the Japanese pushed out the Australians. Later, the Australians and the Americans forced the Japanese to go. It is beyond us. We can do nothing. When a *kiap* . . . tells us to carry his baggage, we have to do it. When a German told us to carry his baggage, we had to obey. When a Japanese told us to carry his baggage, we had to do it. If we did not we might be killed. All right, there it is. Take it or leave it . . . I didn't say anything, that's just how it is, that's life."[9]

The highlanders, secure in their remote valleys, emerged in 1945 largely unscathed from the experience. Largely, but not completely. Fearing an invasion of the highlands—which never occurred—all European civilians were evacuated. A handful of patrol officers stayed on, but the miners and missionaries went. There were military establishments at Kainantu, Bena Bena, Goroka and Mount Hagen, but these were kept supplied by air and were largely self-contained, so the level of white interaction with the highlanders was reduced.

This seems to have been responsible for an outbreak in the early war years, of a series of "cargo cult" (*kago*) movements—attempts to gain wealth by ritual means.[10] *Kago* is a pidgin word loosely meaning wealth and/or possessions; the cults aimed to attract the attention of the spirits through ritual and influence them to channel cargo to its rightful owners. There was one in the Nebilyer Valley a few miles west of Mount Hagen in 1943. The anthropologist Andrew Strathern studied this movement after the war and believes it arose in response to the departure of Dan Leahy and the missionaries in 1942.* When they left, the flow of pearlshells was drastically reduced.

---

*Michael Leahy worked for the American air force as an intelligence officer in New Guinea and distinguished himself by seeking out and constructing forward airstrips. Dan Leahy won fame escorting European refugees away from the invading Japanese. The Catholic missionaries were repatriated to Australia, while the German Lutherans were interned there.

The Hageners were less willing to trade off what they had with the outer communities, like those in the Nebilyer. In their frustration at the new shell shortage the Nebilyer big men developed a cult, claiming they could get hold of pearlshells again by ritual means. As was traditional, they made their services available for payment—in pearlshells. For a time, the Nebilyer men actually induced the flow of shells towards them again. But the cult was short-lived. Apart from the fact that after a while the rituals did not appear to work, the *kiap* in Mount Hagen burnt down the cult houses and jailed the leaders.

Ten years after contact, the cultists were still failing to realise that European goods were the product of human knowledge, intellect and endeavour, not spiritual knowledge. In some coastal areas this misapprehension had tragic consequences. On the Rai coast around Madang, for example, Europeans first arrived in the 1870s, and settled soon after. For fifty years the Madang people found themselves working on the fringe of the European world—observing its wealth, gaining virtually none of it for themselves, blocked by the unavailability of education from any real opportunity to understand the basis on which it functioned. In their frustration, the people were driven to a succession of ritual experiments to find the key, to tap the source of the white man's cargo. Always there was the belief that the whites were selfishly guarding the secret and diverting the cargo that had originated with the ancestors and by rights should flow to the people.

The results of these cargo cults were, naturally, frustration, disappointments, despair—as, decade after decade, they brought no results. The colonial authorities tried to suppress them in light of their undertones of rebellion and antiwhite feeling, but did nothing to alleviate their fundamental causes.

The cargo cults in the highlands during the 1940s were short-lived. Their end coincided with the end of the war, the return of the Australians—and with them the resumption of an even greater flow of shells—and the passing of an era. Mokei Wamp Wan says, "We thought that spirits created all the things the white man had, like the aeroplane and the gun. Even recently, in Madang, I heard that a black man and a white man had a fight, just after the war, over the things the white man had. The black man thought the white man's things were made by the spirits of our ancestors and they should have been sent to us black people. This black man believed the white man had somehow taken all the goods so that only the white people had them.

"Here at our place we were wondering whether the spirits made all these things and passed them on to the white people, or whether the white people had invented all these things for themselves. Then much later we saw white people pulling something apart and then putting it together again. I saw a white man mending a cup by sticking the handle back on. Once I saw a white man taking the tyre off a car. When I saw this, when our people saw these things happening, we thought—maybe the white men have invented these things that we have here. Nowadays we know this."

Chapter Sixteen

END OF
EDEN

We had plenty of food, and I never missed anything," says Joe Leahy, recollecting his childhood. "All the boys of my age would get together and go out chasing birds and rats, and sometimes we'd pretend we were big men. We'd see the big men killing pigs and giving them out so we'd copy them. We'd kill rats and birds and line them up and do the same things as the grown-ups, and put feathers in our hair."

Village life at Mount Hagen, with the white men off fighting their war, meant no mine work, no missionaries, just a small group of American airmen who kept to themselves. This was the low water mark in the ebb and flow of the colonial tide. And for Joe Leahy the first shadows of doubt. "When we put feathers in our hair, mine wouldn't stick. I'd have them falling off all the time and I was feeling a bit funny. When my parents dressed me up for the *sing sings* they glued the feathers on my hair, but they kept pulling. I started to realise something was wrong."

No one told Joe Leahy who he was, least of all his stepfather Towa

Ulta, who had swallowed his rage when Marpa gave birth and accepted the boy as his own. Marpa died about eighteen months later, Towa married another Hagen woman, and Joe was raised in the vicinity of the camp at Kuta. Towa and his new wife loved the boy and feared that one day he would learn the truth, and they would lose him to the white man's world.

The distraction of the invading Japanese proved a short-lived interlude for New Guinea's highlanders. In 1945 the Australians were back in force, administering a unified territory of Papua New Guinea, promising a new deal for the Papua New Guineans. They were not universally welcomed. During the war American and Australian troops came to rely on the coastal Papua New Guineans to carry their stores and their wounded, to help them fight in the frontlines. The soldiers in general did not adopt the colonial relationship of *masta* and *boi*, and their friendly egalitarianism astounded a people long resigned to the contemptuous paternalism of the prewar whites. Now those whites were coming back in, bringing their old attitudes with them, and for many of the people it was a bitter experience.

But in the highlands it was different. The outside world had touched the people lightly, had enriched them, and they wanted more of it. Father William Ross led the way back in 1944, getting a jump on the Lutherans. Soon after the war, various denominations were extending their influence at a furious pace. By 1947, Ross had several hundred converts. By 1953 he had ten thousand.

Gradually the Australians made their way back. Michael Leahy, now in his midforties, took up farming at Zenag, not far from Wau and the goldfields that first attracted him in 1926. James Leahy settled at Goroka in 1947, which had taken over from Bena Bena as an administrative centre because of its better airstrip. Leahy could recognise Goroka's commercial potential, but in 1947 his European neighbours consisted of nearby missionaries and James Taylor, now District Commissioner of the whole highlands region.

Dan Leahy came back to Kuta in 1948 after extensive medical treatment in the United States to help his eyesight and hearing, seriously impaired by prolonged privations suffered during wartime activity against the Japanese. Ewunga Creek began yielding up its gold again, and Kuta returned to its prewar level of hectic activity, while Dan resumed his title of *masta* over the surrounding communities.

In one of these lived young Joe Leahy, now approaching ten years old, product of a traditional Hagen upbringing, distinguishable from the other children only by his straighter hair and paler skin. "The mixed-race children were around all the time," says Dan Leahy today, "but the mothers used to keep them out of the road of the missionaries, people like that. They'd keep out of the way of strangers."

Joe Leahy's perspective on those early postwar days is slightly different. "When I was living near Kuta, Mick Leahy came up with his *misis*, and the *kukboi* at Kuta called out—we used to live about half a mile away—he called out, 'Take Humbug,' that was my nickname, 'off into the bush! A *masta* and *misis* are coming and we don't want to see him!'"

So the fiction was maintained to everyone's satisfaction. When explanations had to be made occasionally, "Humbug" was passed off as Dan's. Dan was living there; Mick was not. Mick was married now; Dan was not. Dan says today that his brother knew about the children but preferred to ignore the matter. "There was a terrible stigma about that sort of thing then," says Dan, "and after Mick got married, that sort of strengthened his attitude. I don't think he regretted it. I don't think he regretted anything he did."

"But I got funny feelings," says Humbug today. "Why did I have to go away when the others went to see the *masta* and *misis*? They'd run towards them, I'd run the other way. So I said bugger it, there must be something wrong with my hair that nobody wants to see. So I got an old towel and wrapped it round, and then went playing with the rest of the kids."

In 1949, Dan Leahy's mining foreman Bill Tracy took it on himself to reveal the truth to the growing boy. "This bloke told me I was Mick Leahy's son," says Joe. "I didn't like the idea. I wanted to be with the Hagens. Now they were saying I was Mick Leahy's son. We were frightened of whites—always hitting and bossing us. I thought I might lose my people. Towa brought me up as his son. He was really upset. He thought if I got to be a white man I might never look after him, might treat him like the whites did."

"The man asked me if I was going to send Joe to [Father Ross's] school," says Towa, "and I said he wasn't old enough yet. The man held me by the hair and said I needed a good smack. He said I had to send Joe to school, or he would belt me. Before, when whites came, they'd tell me to go away and take the boy and hide somewhere. They were frightened visitors would find out about the children. So now I stood by my words about the school. I didn't let him go. Why should I? They'd already made a fool of me, so I didn't listen to them. I was

Joe Leahy on his coffee plantation, 1983. Behind him stand a few of his plantation workers with their children.

ready to kill the man who pulled my hair and I got my axe ready. I was thinking if Dan took sides I'd kill him too.

"Then Joe asked me, 'Why aren't you sending me to school?' His words got to me. The white man had told him to ignore me and go to school. I thought about it. What would become of Joe if anything happened to me? If I died, what would happen to him? He'd have to be strong to hold a job. These thoughts came from my heart. So I sent him to Father Ross."

With similar pangs, Joe's half-brother Clem was given up by his mother Wenta and stepfather Kubal and sent down to the Catholic school. Wenta had shaved her boy's head to hide his pale coloured hair and says today her greatest fear was that the Australians would take him away. Joe and Clem Leahy began their education at Ross's mission school and learnt about the Catholic God. "Everybody had been believing the white people, whatever they said," says Joe. "We just had to believe them. It had to be true, how somebody created us. And when they talked of people living in America round the earth, we thought they must be living under the ground, but we didn't question them, we just believed it."

While the two half-brothers were wrestling with the concept of far-off America, more revolutionary change was coming to the highlands, in particular the cash economy. In 1947, District Commissioner James Taylor decided to begin paying his sizeable labour force in Australian currency as well as shells and axes. But in 1947 there was nothing to spend the money on—not even trade stores. Some of Taylor's workers burst into tears when they got their first pay packets, threw the money on the ground and demanded shells. "We said no," claims Mokei Yaga when the same thing was tried in Mount Hagen. "We don't want that. Just give us more shells. They told us they were giving us something of value and we should take it. And we said, 'What would we do with it? Thread it and wear it? What use is it to us? All we want is shells, nothing else!' "

Taylor set up display boards and the crowds gathered to stare at the pounds, shillings and pence. By 1948 quite a few thousand pounds had spread out into the communities. Asaro Valley men were hoarding nearly

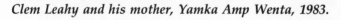

Clem Leahy and his mother, Yamka Amp Wenta, 1983.

Yamka Amp Wenta, Kuta, 1936.

three thousand of them for their part in building the road over the mountains separating their valley from the Chimbu. And then, in mid-1948, having been overshadowed by his brothers before the war, James Leahy entered the stage. Displaying the business acumen that would eventually make him a millionaire, Leahy got permission to set up a trade store beside the Goroka airstrip—the first in the highlands.

"When I first went to New Guinea," said Leahy with disarmingly cheerful candour just before his death in 1981, "I didn't think I would stay very long. I didn't like the climate, I didn't like climbing mountains, and I wasn't particularly mad about the people. I went there not for the natives' benefit but purely for my own. I was a colonialist from way back, and I didn't mind being one, either. I couldn't see anything wrong with it; it was the way things were in those days. But I did have a humane side to me, and I did try to help them. I had my one servant for fifty years, so I couldn't have been too bad a *masta*, wouldn't you say?"

Jim Leahy's trade store opened in June 1948, stocked with a thousand pounds' worth of axes, knives and other trade goods flown in from the coastal port of Lae. Within five days he had sold the lot. He brought in another thousand pounds' worth. Gorokans were waiting at the airstrip, cash in hand, when the plane taxied up, and the trade goods went in one day. Word had spread, and Taylor remembers Asaro Valley men running down the dirt road to Goroka, waving sticks with pound notes stuck in the ends.

"Cash," says the Australian historian Charles Rowley, "is the satanic power which breaches the limited cycle of desire and need in the village Eden. . . ."[1] If you had money, then any material possession could be yours. There was no need for a careful distribution of finite resources, no need for careful balance between trading partners. Money opened up the infinite, lifting expectations, creating the hunger for new things, and offering the means of getting them. It meant greater material comfort—who could deny the value of matches and candles, kerosene lamps and bicycles, torches and blankets, pots and pans and buckets and spades?

But it came with a hidden price tag. Villagers sold their food and their labour for the white man's money and then took the money to the white man's store to buy the foreign wares. The highland "Eden" had joined the world—but it was the Third World. And straight away, certain Gorokans were noticed buying up extra stock from Jim Leahy's store for profitable resale to outlying regions, or to breathless hopefuls who arrived at the store too late, to find the cupboards empty.

The Hageners, however, had not yet done with their shells, and when Dan Leahy followed his brother's example and opened Mount Hagen's first store, *kina* shells were his most popular line. "The most expensive one," says Kopia Rompinjimp Nangambia from Wilya, who sorted the shells in Dan's store and sold them over the counter, "was about ten pounds, and a big man like Ndika Wak would pay that. The prices ranged from ten pounds to one, and there were shells for two, three, three pounds ten shillings, and four pounds. And the people still fought to get at them."

Those prices are an exaggeration according to Bob Fraser, a Leahy nephew who had worked for Mick Leahy on the Watut just before war broke out and had returned to New Guinea in 1948 along with several other members of the Leahy family following in their uncles' footsteps. Fraser briefly manned the counter of Jim Leahy's Goroka store in 1948. "Jimmy charged a pound for a *kina* shell," he recalled, "and it cost him twelve and sixpence from Thursday Island plus freight, so he wasn't making that much. But he would open the store at daybreak, and they were all waiting. Jim was just handing out a *kina* shell, taking a pound note, handing out a shell, taking a pound. He had two windows. One was socially more elitist than the other. There was a coin window and a pound-note window. Anyone with coins who went to the note window was, well, discouraged."

"The shells," says Kopia Nangambia, "sold well from 1949 on to the early sixties, but then our children all started going to school and we lost interest. We started buying clothes for the children and things like that."

Large-scale *moka* involving *kina* shells were still going on in the early sixties, but then they quickly lost their prestige value. In 1965 the anthropologist Andrew Strathern watched men from the Tipuka clans, who lived in an outlying district of Mount Hagen, give more than eleven hundred *kina* shells in *moka* to exchange partners from the Kawelka people. In 1974, those shells were "forgotten" when the Kawelka came to reciprocate. They had gone out of fashion and lost their value. Pigs, money and motor cars were the featured items. Cash was the thing and what it could buy. "Nowadays," says Mokei Yaga, "we have forgotten about shells and our *omaks*. We like money. Before, we used these money notes for rolling cigarettes with."

The next great initiative of James Leahy was to experiment with coffee trees. By 1950 he had twelve acres growing on land he bought from villagers a few miles from Goroka. He picked his first crop in March, dried and processed the beans, and flew them out to Australia.

When news got out about the price he was paid, the rush began. Taylor had earlier resigned as District Commissioner to grow coffee next to Leahy, and these two were joined by a flock of white Australian families who went round the valleys buying land from villagers who were only too happy to sell.* They wanted the trade from the Australians, the Australians could also show them the ways of the world.

By 1954, extensive tracts of Michael Leahy's old prospecting country—the valleys of the Bena Bena, Dunantina, Goroka, Asaro and Wahgi—were fenced in and laid out with orderly rows of European-owned coffee trees, tended and picked by highlanders, who called the Australians *masta* and *misis* and took home two shillings a day.

In Goroka, where nearly four thousand acres of the valley's most productive land had gone to the Australian planters by 1954, the highlanders' initial enthusiasm often gave way to disillusionment. "Europeans who wish to settle on our land," complained one Gorokan in 1957 to a visiting patrol officer, "are initially very friendly to us who own or have rights to the land they wish to have. After they have the land and have planted their gardens and built their houses they do not seem to like us anymore. They do not let us near them. They do not give us enough pay for food we sell them. They shoot our pigs."[2]

By the late fifties there were well over one hundred Australian coffee plantations in the highlands. It had happened so quickly the government in Australia had been caught off guard. But the world was decolonising, not recolonising, and when the Australian metropolitan newspapers began headlining "a second Kenya", it was not Taylor's prewar vision they were talking about but the growing spectre of Jomo Kenyatta's Mau Mau, who were taking up arms against British coffee and tea planters in Kenya's highlands. Australia told its Administration in Papua New Guinea to curb the white plantation rush, and it did so.

The highlanders were keen to try anything that might earn them more cash, and, when offered the chance, they began planting their own coffee trees at a furious rate. By the end of the fifties the people had more coffee trees than the white planters, and a few wealthy men were emerging, like Goroka's Khasawaho Baito Heiro. While most white planters cared little for their highland neighbours, Baito had a friend in James Taylor, who had established his plantation on Baito's land, employed him as a foreman, and then helped set Baito up with a plantation of his own. In 1957, Baito's crop brought him four thousand pounds when the mass of the people were getting a few pounds a year from their handful of trees.

---

*More specifically persuading the owners to sell it to the Administration, which then handed it over to the prospective planter on a ninety-nine-year lease.

By the end of the fifties, men like Baito were emerging in increasing numbers, making money from coffee and then expanding into other forms of *bisnis*—trucks, coffee buying from the villagers, trade stores, eating houses. They were the new big men, drawing on their clans for money and cheap labour, bestowing in return prestige and favours. In the early years of contact the big men had sought to maintain their monopoly over shell wealth by acting as middle men between the Australians and the mass of the people. Just as Leahy and Taylor tended to deal with the big men at Kelua in 1933, their successors followed suit, appointing big men like Mount Hagen's Mokei Wamp Wan to official and unofficial Administration positions, and favouring men like Goroka's Baito in their business ventures. The big men still depended upon their clans for support, and emerging inequalities were tempered by the big man's old web of clan obligation. But the Australians were also encouraging the favoured few to borrow from the banks, to buy their own land, pay their clans cash for it and become sole proprietors.[3]

Money is the great unraveller. The Australians were selecting their favourites, creating a class of new rich, this time with money rather than shells. Astute white businessmen and planters knew that they could secure their own privileges by widening their group to include a few rich highlanders. And, once again, those highlanders with most to gain became the Australians' willing allies. The framework was being laid down for a postcolonial society of widening inequality, with a gap between the fortunate rich and the less fortunate masses.

In the 1950s, however, the widest gap was that which existed between white and black. "They had everything," says Joe Leahy. "We didn't argue with them. We never went near the place [of the white men]. If one of our people went to a white man, he would never go and sit down, person to person. He had to stand up in front of the door and get his order. We never had the chance to eat with them and get the taste of European cooking and all these things.

"The whites bossed the local people and pushed them around. The best belonged to the *mastas*, and the *kago boi* jobs, the low jobs, they belonged to people like us. They never had any friends among the local people. They never eat together. They were up there and the locals down here. It was the same for all white people—miners, missionaries, planters or *kiaps*—there was no difference, they were all the same."

But Joe Leahy's mixed blood set him apart, pushed him into the ranks of the favoured few. In 1958, he and Clem, like Meta, Dau, Narmu and Rebia nearly three decades earlier, took their first look at the world outside the highlands. The circumstances were very different—two Hagen youths chosen for further training by the Catholic missionaries at their school for mixed-race boys in far off Rabaul. Their circumstances were also very different to those thousands of highlanders who joined the Highland Labour Scheme, set up by the Australians in the 1950s to ease the chronic labour shortages in the less populated but more highly developed regions outside the highlands. By the time Clem and Joe began their journey, seven thousand highland men were working along the coast and in the outlying islands, mostly for white Australian planters and settlers, on eighteen-month contracts at twenty-five shillings a month. The worst abuses of the prewar indenture system had been done away with, but the scheme still served white interests rather than black-menial labour with no chance of learning skills that might serve a man at home.

"A monotony of work, sleep and wages,"[4] wrote Ignatius Kilage of the Chimbu, now the government ombudsman, with wages soon swallowed up by the trade stores, leaving nothing to show for the work. In a fictitious account of a young highland man's experience based on his own observations of what was happening, Killage writes of how the returning labourer's clanspeople in the Chimbu looked to him for help in starting business ventures but "to my shame, my experience on the coast did not teach me anything new. Business ideas never entered my head and I was still handicapped by my illiteracy." So were the vast majority of highlanders in those days, with only the missionaries offering any education, and then to a tiny few. And a rudimentary education at that. Killage's character threw away his fancy trade store clothes and taught himself to read and write. There, he knew, lay a key to the white man's cargo.

Dan Leahy paid for Clem's and Joe's passage and tuition in Rabaul, and sent them pocket money as well. Ewunga Creek had yielded up far more gold after the war than either he or his brothers ever imagined, and when the gold eventually gave out in 1953, Dan turned to coffee. By 1958 he had a well-established plantation at Korgua in the nearby Nebilyer Valley. He had also married two Hagen women, Ndika Mogumand Amp Biam and Ndika Komp Amp Mancy.

"Biam's mother and father, they were well up in the community," says Dan. "They weren't 'rubbish men' or little people. Nor were Mancy's people. Biam and Mancy just came one day with their fathers and brothers. They picked me! There was no arguing at all. They just took it for granted there would be a good brideprice. That was one of the compensations you got for always being honest with the kanakas, and always paying exactly what we thought a thing was worth.

"It was unorthodox in European eyes—the way I lived—but in the way of the country that I lived in it wasn't so bad. I was a big man and I had plenty of money. I could afford it.

Biam and Mancy maintained a background role in Dan's social life, a situation which seemed to sit easily with them, but these two sturdy Ndika women would rear ten of Dan's children as the years rolled by, becoming nurses as well as wives as Dan's eyesight and hearing grew steadily worse. There is an inevitability in the way they were brought to Dan by their relatives. The Hageners were reaching out to embrace this white man, who had been among the first to arrive, had spent more years among them than any of his compatriots, and had no wife of his own. Less demanding and judgmental than his older brother, less conscious or prideful of his white heritage, Dan was quite amenable to the process.

But Dan was, as Joe Leahy says, a tough *masta*. Even today, elderly and frail, his moral certitude and iron will remain a palpable force. Crippled by a stroke in 1979, he forced himself into remedial exercise, and in 1986 was still spending hours each day striding around his coffee plantation, which he could not see. There is no suggestion that he or his fellow Australians were not in the country to rule, to show the way. "I don't think," he says, "that there was anything in the native way of life that was better than what they have now."

But of all the Leahy brothers, Dan has lived closest to the highland people, and his life has been enriched because of it. "I like the people," he says. "Biam and Mancy, my two meris, have been wonderful, and I've got a wonderful family with them. I have no regrets and if I were to start all over again I'd do the same things I did this time in the next life."

At Zenag, between Lae and Wau, Michael Leahy began the 1960s still struggling to build up his farming and grazing property. It was a difficult business. The landscape at Zenag is bleak, the soil thin, and the returns were a long time in coming.

Had he settled in the highlands, Leahy would undoubtedly have prospered. But he did not, and his nephew Bob Fraser believes that this cast a pall over the rest of his life. The two men became very close during the war, and Fraser says Leahy confided in him about the existence of his mixed-race children. "He said it was a source of great trial to him, and that he could not possibly mention it to [his wife] Jeannette.

Of course it was a horrific thing in those days, for a man of such reputation to have black children. If you'd had a native child in the Administration in those days they'd have probably kicked you out if they knew.

"His going to Zenag," continues Fraser, "was a compromise, because he couldn't go to the highlands. He felt he couldn't go with those children there, because it wouldn't be fair to his wife and family. He used to say he wanted ten thousand acres in the highlands and they [the Administration] wouldn't give him a land grant. There was no doubt in my mind that every time he looked out the window he saw the highlands."

Fraser's first memories of Michael Leahy were during the early thirties, the days of adventure and exploration. "He would come down [to Toowoomba from New Guinea]," says Fraser, "and I used to listen to his stories. He was absolutely inimitable, he had great charisma. The change after he left the highlands—it was as if he faded, like a flower after it had been transplanted. He wanted some fief, some domain. He became a married man, a petty bourgeois. Before that he was an explorer, his horizons were wider. He wanted to stay in the highlands. It was as simple as that, as plain as day. It soured his whole bloody life." And the photography urge went. They bought him a new Leica and I said, "Why don't you keep it up, Mick?" He said, "Oh, well, I've been through all that. There's not much here to do."

As the years rolled by, Michael Leahy seemed incapable of recognising that New Guinea was now a different place, that the prewar days had gone forever. His differences with the Administration would grow increasingly rancorous with the passage of years. At Zenag there were frequent clashes with the local people as well. "Mick had scant regard for the capacity of the village people who were his neighbours," wrote James Sinclair, a patrol officer in the Zenag region in the 1950s, "and he was usually at loggerheads with them. They returned the compliment. He accused them of spearing his cattle and stealing from his market garden; they countered with claims that his cattle were trespassing on their land. The local patrol officer at Mumeng was continually being called in to adjudicate."[5]

"At Zenag," adds Bob Fraser, "I was saddened by the way Mick kept going on and on about the injustice of the Administration, the stupidity of the *kiaps*, the lack of discipline in the community, the fact that they'd [the Australians] all be kicked out on their arses, that the country was too good for the people in it, that they were going to ruin it and slide back into barbarism. There was some sort of mental block. I think he sat there at Zenag and brooded so much that in the end he started to believe what he was saying. He was listening to the news eight or nine times a day. He had an idée fixe. It was disappointing to go there, because he never stopped fuming about it. When he did stop fuming he was his old charming self."

When Clem and Joe Leahy went to the Rabaul school for mixed-race students, Michael and Jeannette Leahy were seeing to the education of their children at respectable Protestant boarding schools in Sydney. Dan's domestic situation was not publicly discussed. Robin Leahy, the Australian wife of Michael Leahy's eldest son Richard, says that for years after her marriage she was not even told that Dan was married to Hagen women and was rearing their offspring. She knew nothing of Joe, Clem and John Leahy until after Michael Leahy's death in 1979.

In Goroka, Jim Leahy's marriage had ended in divorce soon after the war, and he was never to remarry. James Taylor, however, surprised many of his peers by marrying Yerema, daughter of the Nongamp big man Maasi Pinjnga, whom Taylor had met when he first walked into the Wahgi in 1933. In the early 1960s the people of Goroka, black and white, became accustomed to the sight of Yerema at the wheel of the plantation Land Rover, driving home the fact that she was Taylor's wife, not his out-of-sight black mistress. Her family became his family. "Only his skin is white," says Yerema. "The way he thinks, the way he mixes, the way he handles his household affairs is just like a man from our place. The people don't see him as a *masta*." In 1986 the Taylors are familiar figures around Goroka, regarded with universal affection. Taylor is 86 and greatly relies on the care and support of his wife, a woman of commanding stature and personality.

Jim and Yerema Taylor's daughter Meg would eventually study law, but Joe and Clem Leahy were more suited to business pursuits, as they soon discovered at Rabaul. They made other discoveries as well. Before leaving Mount Hagen, Towa took them aside and told them they were half-brothers and should stick together in their new adventure. Towa also told them of their half-brother John. After John's mother Kumbi had conceived him, she married an employee of Michael Leahy at Kuta. On Kumbi's death, John was brought up by relatives at Goroka. Joe and Clem were told to look out for him at Rabaul, as he had also been sent there from Goroka.

The two half-brothers were given shoes and trousers for the first time for their flight out to the coast and then to Rabaul. When they arrived they were quick to seek John out. "We saw him," says Joe Leahy, "and he was different from all the other mixed races. I said to him, 'Where are you from?' He didn't understand *tokples* ["talk of the place," i.e., Temboka] so I started with broken English, couldn't make myself clear, and then talked pidgin. He said, '*Mi bilong Goroka. Nem bilong mi John Goroka.*' Clem and me both had local names at first but when we went to Rabaul old Dan said, 'Put them down as Clem and Joe Leahy.' So the Catholic sisters at Rabaul called us Clem and Joe Leahy. And we told John, 'You're from Hagen. Your name's not John Goroka, it's John Leahy. 'You understand?' "

The three brothers quickly learnt in Rabaul the caste divisions of a colonised society in contact with Europeans for almost a century. In Mount Hagen there had been very few mixed-raced children born, and the boys had been cherished and accepted by the communities that had reared them. "But in Rabaul," says Clem, "the mixed-race people were classed as Europeans, some sort of *masta*, and all the mixed races thought we wanted to be like them. But we'd never been like that, so we went around with the Tolais [indigenous people of the Rabaul region] and ate with them."

Joe remembers, "A lot of the mixed races said, 'You shouldn't go round with the *kanakas*, stupid! You're not allowed!' They called us names—bush *kanakas*, cannibals, Chimbus."

"All the highlanders," writes Ignatius Kilage, "were known under the name Chimbu. The coastlanders looked down at us as coolies, and men of mediocre mentality and ability. For this reason we stuck together. . . . Whenever our *wantoks* [friends, clansmen] got into trouble . . . all of us would go there and help."[6]

But Joe Leahy was soon doing what came naturally. "I went to a Manus bloke's house and he had some *kina* shells lying under his bed. He told me he sold the small ones to Tolais to scoop out coconuts with. They didn't like the big ones, and they'd been lying round for ages. I was getting three pounds ten shillings a month. Smokes cost a pound a month, so I thought I'd sacrifice the smokes. I offered [the Manus Islander] a pound for four shells, and he accepted right away."

Joe buried the shells, waited for the weekend, and borrowed a pushbike. Forty-five miles away was a plantation and a line of Hagen labourers. "I dug up the *kinas*, tied them on the bike, started pedalling in the hot sun, three, four hours pedalling. This was the time highlanders began accepting money. They would take it and buy *kinas*. All these Hagen boys, they were gambling—boxes full of money. But they didn't want money, they wanted *kinas*. One of the blokes saw one of the *kinas* in my raincoat and he grabbed it and took it.

"I said to him, 'That's not mine! A boat captain told me to sell it for him. He wants five pounds each.' 'Five pounds!' said the Hagen, 'I'll take the lot! How many did you bring? Ten? Twenty?' 'No, only four.' 'Then bring some more!' So the bloke grabbed the whole lot and they started fighting over them. They gave me forty pounds—ten pounds each. So I took the money and went back to school. I didn't tell Clem. I told the Manus boy I sent back all the *kinas* to the highlands but they probably got lost or something, so I better try sending another four. I bought another four for a pound. I sold them again and I soon had almost a hundred pounds buried in the ground, and nobody knew it. We used to buy Three Cats smokes—the cheapest you could find. I'd buy Craven As and put them in the Three Cats packet, chuck out the Three Cats. People thought I was smoking Three Cats. I didn't want anyone to know I was getting plenty of money.

"I asked the Brothers if I could buy a pushbike. 'Where'd you get the money?' I told them a *wantok* had helped me. I bought a brand-new bike, and the mixed races said, 'Shit! All these Chimbus, we thought they were cannibals! Where'd you get that bike?' I just put it at the door and walked in, listening to all these blokes saying, 'Where'd you get it? Where'd you get it?' "

In Papua New Guinea's polyglot society, highlanders today have a reputation for aggression and energy. Perhaps they owe these characteristics to their schooling in a dynamic, competitive society. Perhaps also the deadening hand of colonial occupation touched them lightly and briefly. Whatever the reason, the highlanders are respected, even feared by coastlanders today for playing the game too roughly as they begin to flex the political muscle their numbers have given them.

At Rabaul in 1960 the Catholic brothers decided that twenty-three-year-old Joe Leahy was too much to handle. "We were getting a bit fast. The Brother tried to pin down what had been going on but he never found out." Early one morning Leahy was roused out of bed, bundled into clothes and sent packing back to Mount Hagen and to years of menial work on Dan Leahy's plantation. So ended Joe Leahy's formal education. He managed to tell his brother about the shell business, but Clem by then had his own operation going. The school's Catholic nuns sold polished shells to the tourist trade—particularly mother-of-pearl shell, and Clem had been helping out with the polishing. He had also been keeping and quietly selling the best shells.

Chapter Seventeen

INDEPENDENCE

In 1960, there were highlanders less worldly still than those business customers of Joe and Clem Leahy. Tens of thousands of them lived in what was to become known as the Southern Highlands, and they were the last significant uncontacted population then remaining in central New Guinea. Assistant District Commissioner James Sinclair led one of the last major exploratory patrols carried out by the Administration into their territory, and with a professional film crew going along it was an extraordinary opportunity to capture definitively on film one of history's final encounters. But the film crew's objective was propaganda, not realism.

In this film, *New Guinea Patrol*, the shock and wonder of contact is submerged beneath an endless montage of sturdy white men going about their colonial business, shooting at pieces of wood, extracting arrows from grateful bodies; their *lap-lapped* offsiders blow bugles, raise and lower the Australian flag and scamper after packages dropped from the air.

In other films the progress is shown in more settled regions. Youthful Australian patrol officers explain western law and order to assembled villagers, census the population, tend to the sick. Agricultural officers lecture apparently spellbound highlanders on the care of coffee trees. Engineers build roads and bridges and airstrips. Great play is made of the local government councils—"nurseries for democracy"—where middle-aged highlanders—they were men like Hagen's Mokei Wamp Wan, Goroka's Kirupano Eza'e, Bena Bena's Isakoa Hepu—listen to the *kiap's* talk of voting procedures, ballot boxes, candidates and electoral rolls.

The film *District Commissioner* has as its star Mount Hagen's Tom Ellis. Made in 1963 at the height of his reign, the "DC" arrives at his district headquarters by chauffeured jeep. Uniformed policemen stiffen in salute as Ellis stalks to his office and tells the camera the scope of his kingdom—the Western Highlands. District Commissioner, proconsul of the Wahgi—such was the flavour of postwar colonialism: efficiency, authoritarianism, paternalism. They were earnest men and women, these thousands of Australians, sent north, as they saw it, to civilise New Guinea. Many of them were devoted and dedicated in their desire to impose upon the people the Australian vision of how things should be.

Their policies were gradualist. The people were primitive and had much to learn. "Look what we face," *New Guinea Patrol* was subliminally saying to those impatient with what the Australians were doing. "How can you press us when there are such as these still living in the southern highland valleys?" Less publicity was being given to those Australian monopolies selling the Papua New Guineans their pots and pans and matches, luxuries becoming necessities, or to those sending abroad the proceeds of Australian plantations and mines, or to the shooters who were steadily decimating the crocodile populations of the Sepik and the Fly to make handbags and purses.

New Guinea Patrol went to New York when completed for screening before the United Nations Trusteeship Council, postwar equivalent of the Mandates Commission of the League of Nations, but a different forum altogether to that which the Australians faced at Geneva in the 1930s. By the 1960s the Council was becoming very impatient with the pace of change in Papua New Guinea. Most of Asia had been decolonised in the 1940s and 1950s, much of Africa by 1961. Indonesia had removed the Dutch from the island's eastern half by 1962. The Australian colonial presence in Papua New Guinea was becoming something of an historical anachronism.

The Englishman Sir Hugh Foote, head of a visiting United Nations mission in 1962, told the Australians to change their thinking, readjust their timetable to properly prepare the place for early independence. It was not good enough that out of nearly three million Papuans and New Guineans, a bare twenty-four hundred were in secondary school and none had graduated; that there was no university; that the Legislative Council's indigenous members were completely dominated by Administration officials, businessmen, planters and settlers, all of them white-skinned Australians.

The United Nations report was ammunition for those Australians in the Administration who had long been anxious to push ahead with reforms. In fact most of the specific changes suggested by the United Nations' team had been fed to them by progressives within the Administration, which was now stung into action. The crucial requirement of education was at last taken seriously, and crash programmes were established to train an indigenous elite.

But Jim Leahy in Goroka, by now running a plantation and retail business empire in the highlands, says the United Nations mission was greeted skeptically by his fellow expatriates, who refused to believe highlanders could do without them and could not see the point of higher education for a people they thought incapable of absorbing it. The United Nations simply did not understand. So went the talk in the whites-only clubs and pubs in Goroka and Mount Hagen—by now established towns—echoing the sentiments of an earlier age. Some of these sentiments found official, if more subtle, expression at the United Nations.

When the Trusteeship Councillors were told by the Australian representatives that the highlanders did not actually *want* independence, or at least not in the near future, they were highly skeptical and flew out to see for themselves. At public meetings in all the population centres, highlanders gathered in their thousands, and told the visiting mission they wanted more schools, faster development, overseas travel to learn more ideas, a university, factories. But they also wanted the Australians to stay.

"I am very happy with the Australian government," announced the Chimbu leader Kondon Agaundo, "and with all the laws they brought to New Guinea. . . . Just one thing you have said make me unhappy. I have heard you want to give us self-government. I ask you not to give it. When I feel strong enough I will ask for it, but I do not want you to force it on me. . . . Before we can have self-government we need six things: pilots and aircraft factories; an arms factory; an ammunition factory; a mint to make money; factories to make glass and iron for houses; meat and clothing factories. All the work in these factories must be done by Papuans and New Guineans. When my people make these things I will know I am ready for self-government."[1]

Everywhere the mission went the message was the same, and it finally got too much for Liberia's Nathaniel Eastman, vehemently opposed to colonialism in any form and for whatever reason. At Laiagam in the Enga, an administrative post established only eleven years before, five thousand people assembled in full ceremonial dress. Kombo, a hospital orderly, told the United Nations mission he did not want self-government. "This gentleman," said Eastman in exasperation, "who wants this everlasting colonialism. Why?" Kombo replied that Australia had given his people many good things, and as they still had much to learn it would be better for Australia to remain.

A former fight leader named Paglin took up the theme, praising Australia for bringing peace, schools and hospitals. He wanted them to remain until his people were advanced enough to "join" with Australia. Eastman jumped on this. Did the man not know that the Australians did not allow blacks to settle in their country and that such a union was therefore unthinkable?* Paglin had nothing to say. At Wabag, a medical orderly named Amean repeated the theme and talked of the territory becoming Australia's seventh state, believing this would bring industry and finance into the highlands. When a mission member queried Amean's right to speak for others, another man rose to his feet, indicated the long double rows of fellow local government councillors, and said, "He speaks for our people. It is our fashion to talk together and then appoint a spokesman. These are the views of eighty-three thousand Engan people."[2]

Nathaniel Eastman was a citizen of Liberia, founded last century by former slaves from the cotton fields of the southern United States. He was confounded by what he was hearing. How was it possible in the mid-1960s for a colonised people to cling to their colonisers? Eastman's perspective had been shaped, of course, by his own people's collective memory of horror and outrage, the highland people's by three decades of a different form of invasion. The benefits of that invasion had so far

---

*Australia at that time had a restrictive immigration policy which discriminated against non-Europeans. This is no longer the case.

been more obvious than the drawbacks. First shells and axes, and now money, know-how and enormous material and social changes. There were aeroplanes, roads and motorcars, bridges, schools, cash crops, medical aid posts, trade stores, freedom of movement. And if the material gains from all this had not been flowing out to the mass of the people, it was all highly visible. For those few who had managed to tap into the available wealth or gain the prestige of appointed colonial office there was certainly nothing to gain from the departure of the Australians. What everyone wanted above everything else was development— the objective being the same material prosperity the Australians in their midst so obviously enjoyed. They had to stay until more development had come, until local factories and industry were in place, run by Papua New Guineans, which could provide what the people needed. Was that not why, after all, the Australians said they were there—to bring progress?

Progress was one thing, economic independence quite another. The highlanders' brief colonial experience had so far not taught them that colonial status and economic independence do not go together. Colonies serve the interests of their occupiers—raw materials for their factories, a compliant market for their products. White Australians knew that well enough. Their own country—the "Pastures of Manchester"— had been feeding Britain's mills and buying back their products for nearly two centuries.

Before the war the only development Australia permitted in New Guinea was that which assisted in its plunder. After the war it did not encourage development on any scale that might threaten its own economic interests. Here was an emerging market for Australian business. There was virtually no manufacturing in Papua New Guinea in 1965. There is very little now. The country exports the rawest of raw materials. And Australia's farmers tolerated coffee growing in the highlands only because they could not grow their own.

Perhaps more comprehensible to Liberia's Eastman was the highlanders' frequently expressed fear of what the coastlanders would do if the Australians left before the highlanders were ready. They were more familiar with the modern ways and might channel development their own way, grab the best jobs, relegate the highlanders to the low paid unskilled ones. As long as the Australians were around, the Chimbus might have a chance to catch up.

When the United Nations mission toured in 1965 it found only isolated voices calling for independence in Papua New Guinea. That does not mean that all those outside the highlands shared the views that left Eastman so disturbed; the Australians were resented by many for their sins of the past and their continuing presence. But to articulate and channel that resentment effectively, the Papua New Guineans needed higher education and political organisation. In 1963 only seven students had graduated from high school. In 1965 the first university graduates returned from Australia. The crash education programme produced, in the late 1960s, the small elite from which the first stirrings of an independence movement began. Educated public servants formed the first black political party—the Pangu Pati—and began calling, rather tamely, for "home rule leading to independence." They were promptly labelled dangerous radicals by many of the Australian colonists. But the message was beginning to sink home in Canberra that early independence was the only feasible policy to adopt in Papua New Guinea.

The lessons of Africa had convinced these metropolitan Australians that it was in their best interests to dismantle their political presence, but the white *mastas* in the highlands and elsewhere would take more convincing. The highlander response to the United Nations mission in 1965 had been music to their ears, and they were still convinced they had an indefinite future on their plantations in the cool and beautiful highland valleys. But the fledgling Pangu Pati was becoming a force to be reckoned with, and the whites now organised politically to push their own case, which was to delay independence as long as possible, preaching economic advancement before political independence, assiduously exploiting highland fear of the coastlanders. "We are here to stay," declared the Highland Farmers and Settlers Association in its magazine. The association had no trouble gaining support from highlanders, one of whom, Anton Parao, had already formed an organisation in Goroka warning against early independence. Parao's main fear was that coastlanders would take all the jobs and exclude highlanders from advancement.

But the desire to delay independence was not unanimous among the highlanders, and some of them organised in the late 1960s their own National Party, supporting early independence along with more opportunities for highlanders in *bisnis*. National Party strategists were also careful to play down regionalism and highlander/coastlander antagonism for the sake of national unity and development.

The indigenous drive towards independence gathered momentum.

At the University of Technology in Lae, the students had formed a political club, and in March 1970 it was addressed by a leading Pangu Pati
politician and labour leader, Albert Maori Kiki. Young students from all
over Papua New Guinea, highlanders among them, packed the class-
room, crowded the halls outside and hung through the windows to
hear Maori Kiki tell them that Papua New Guineans were no strangers
to independence, that they had enjoyed it hundreds of years before the
white man came. "Of course that independence was localised," went
on Maori Kiki, "with our people governing their own small villages or
valleys in the country. But it was self-government in its own small way.
Why should we be terrified of independence now?"[3]

It was hardly inflammatory, but that was the way many in the white
community saw it. "Mr. Maori Kiki is quite correct," wrote an elderly
Michael Leahy to the national newspaper from his farm at Zenag, "when
he states that Papuans and New Guineans are not strangers to independence." Leahy then launched into his detailed version of the way of life
of the highland people in the days of what he termed "their savage,
pre white man INDEPENDENCE."[4] The capitalised letters* of the word
gave evidence of his fury over its possible future implementation. He
wrote of highland children maimed by disease, of suppurating arrow
wounds, of rape and murder. "INDEPENDENCE," he went on, "as it
was known and endured for thousands of years by these primitive, stone
age people."

Leahy termed the political activists "idealistic visionaries, prestige-
seeking demagogues, ambitious soldiers transient opportunistic politicians," and predicted the chaos of Biafra if they had their way and the
whites, "the most cultured and civilised people of our world since bib-
lical times," departed.

It was all to no avail. The diehard expatriates were becoming an
anachronistic minority. In the 1972 national elections the United Party
(the anti-independence party which represented most white opinion)
and Pangu won most of the seats in the one hundred member parlia-
ment. But by forming coalitions with the smaller indigenous parties,
Pangu, under the leadership of Michael Somare from the Sepik region
of New Guinea, formed a majority. The popular will of the people had
been expressed, and, in any case, Canberra was now set on getting out
of Papua New Guinea as soon as possible, politically if not economi-
cally.

*Capitalised in his original letter but reproduced in small type in the Papua New Guinea *Post
Courier* of March 31, 1970.

Dan Leahy taking his daily constitutional through the coffee trees of his plantation at Korgua, near Mount Hagen. Leahy established Korgua in the 1950s when Kuta had yielded up all its gold. He is guided here by an employee and accompanied by his grandson.

In 1973, the new Labour government in Canberra under Prime Minister Whitlam granted home rule to the Papua New Guineans under Chief Minister Somare and decreed that full independence would follow in 1975. Realistic expatriates like Jim Leahy in Goroka sadly and quietly accepted the inevitable. "I thought they'd always have to have us," he recalls, echoing the sentiments of his fellow white planters, "because we had the know how. I couldn't imagine independence happening that soon, I said that quite often and I was wrong. I said it wasn't going to happen in my lifetime. The schools and universities were really only started after the war." Leahy's statement embraced all of Papua New Guinea, but he was thinking primarily of the highlands. He had, after all, accompanied his brother Michael on that first flight out over the Wahgi Valley in March 1933.

For Michael Leahy the years following that great adventure had been marked, as Bob Fraser says by anticlimax, disappointment and frustration, and enlivened by his bitter and destructive differences with an Administration that saw no great value in honouring what he had done. He had sold off his share in the Kuta gold mine to Dan before the war, only to see it come good. His business ventures had not made him rich, and he lost half his farm in the 1970s to local villagers after a long and expensive legal battle over original ownership. A crowning irony was to come later when Jim Taylor, who had taken up a gold lease at Porgera, in the Enga after the war, sold it to developers in the early 1980s for more than a hundred thousand dollars.

But most of all, Michael Leahy was implacably opposed to the political emancipation of the Papua New Guineans. The dull rage had flowered as the unbelievable happened, and the scales of power tilted inexorably the black man's way. No one wanted his advice, so he wrote a succession of vituperative letters to the newspapers. His published vision of independence had black cargo cultists squandering and despoiling all the good work done by "hardworking, frugal and generous Australians."

All this did him no good. While many of his fellow expatriates might privately agree with some of what he had to say, they could see the way events were going and tended to keep a judicious silence. Jim Leahy began to entertain black politicians and civil servants in his home. While Michael Leahy could on several occasions hold student classes spellbound on the subject of his highland explorations, charming them with his wit and eloquence, he could still refuse to admit a black university student into his home because it might upset his servants.

So this fearless, inflexible man tilted against unstoppable forces, like Pinketa in his mad dash down to that waiting Mauser way back in 1934. That was where Michael Leahy still lived in the 1970s. That was the sort of black man he could understand, not the well-dressed sophisticates who gradually, as the official date for independence drew near, assumed the reins of power.

As they did so, the Australians began to depart. The white planters, the thousands of *kiaps*, medicos, teachers, policemen, horticulturalists, tradesmen, civil servants—all yielded place to their black counterparts. Many of these Australians congregated along the tropic Queensland coast—it reminded them of New Guinea—to mourn, to drink, to reminisce on the Australian Raj, to wish the fledgling nation well or balefully predict its imminent descent into chaos.

And now, for those Papua New Guineans astute enough to seize the new opportunities, there were bargains to be picked up in the wake of the departing Australians. Joe Leahy, son of Marpa, Clem Leahy, son of Wenta and John Leahy, son of Kumbi, had prospered in the sixties and early seventies. Joe and Clem both learned the coffee business on Dan Leahy's plantation and then made money buying village coffee on the roadside and selling it to the Australian processors. By the seventies, Joe was processing coffee himself, and ran a fleet of trucks. He took up a parcel of land and began planting coffee trees. Clem borrowed money and bought a plantation at a bargain price from a departing Australian. So did John.

By the early seventies the three half-brothers were on their way to becoming wealthy and prominent men. Their relationship to Michael Leahy was an open secret in the highlands, but after all these years Leahy simply could not bring himself to acknowledge them, to bridge the gulf opened up by nearly forty years of silence. All three half-brothers had acquaintances among the large clan of white Leahys living in various parts of Papua and New Guinea—younger people who admired the half-brothers' business acumen and saw no great stigma in acknowledging the blood relationship. But not Michael Leahy or his immediate family.

In these circumstances it was inevitable that one day their paths should cross. "I was there the time Mick Leahy bumped into one of his [mixed-race] sons in Lae," recalls Bob Fraser. "Mick was very polite to him, but made no sign of recognition. He knew who he was. Well, my respect for Mick fell through my boots. He had come down from his pedestal. He was just a bloke. I said to him afterwards, 'Jesus Christ, Mick . . . !' And he said, 'Well, Christ! What can I do?' "

Fraser says that as the old man walked away, he saw that the other white Leahys who had witnessed events were laughing. "The laugh wasn't in derision," he says. "It was a laugh of astonishment that Mick didn't recognise him, acknowledge him."

On September 15, 1975, the Australian flag came down in ceremonies across the country, and at Kainantu, Goroka, Kundiawa, Kerowagi, Mount Hagen, Wabag and Mendi in the Southern Highlands. The new national flag was raised the next day. In the Chimbu diehards tore down the Papua New Guinea flag, and somewhere else a highland sorcerer called down rain to spoil the day (and it rained), but these were exceptions. In the capital of Port Moresby, brass bands from the Royal Papua New Guinea Constabulary and the armed forces serenaded visiting dignitaries. James Lindsay Taylor, a naturalised citizen of the new nation and a close friend of Prime Minister Michael Somare, was an honoured guest. The Leahy brothers were not invited.

The new head of state of Papua New Guinea, Governor General Sir John Guise, talked of lowering the colonisers' flag, not tearing it down, and it was true. There had been very little violence. The Australians were leaving before being pushed, departing willingly and peacefully, with a promise of continuing financial aid to help the new nation face the world.

When the Brazilian coffee crop failed in 1976—a birthday present to the new nation—highland coffee prices doubled almost overnight, and none were better placed to take advantage of this than the three Leahy half-brothers. As large-scale coffee planters, they joined the new rich. They built European-style houses, started families, bought expensive cars, invested in real estate, booked their children into Australian boarding schools and built up their plantation labour lines with highland men and women less favoured by circumstances. Just like their departed Australian mentors.

A handful of Australians could not bring themselves to leave, and among them were the elderly Leahy brothers, Michael, Daniel and James. Jim Leahy, suffering from a heart condition, sold his plantation back to the original clan landowners but retained, with their agreement, the use of the homestead in retirement. Dan, with two wives and sturdy children, had no intention of pulling up roots after more than forty years in New Guinea. Nor could Michael Leahy bring himself to leave, although as none of the three brothers had taken Papua New Guinea citizenship, they were now guests in a country they had once treated as their own.

Contrary to all his expectations, the cargo cultists did not grab Michael Leahy's assets and land holdings when the Australians departed. An orderly change of government in the first postindependence elections of 1977 might have given him reason to rethink, but by then Michael Leahy was beyond change.

"I last saw him at Zenag in mid-1977," writes former District Com-

Jim Taylor, wearing a handkerchief on his head as a sunshade, is given a prominent seat at a 1981 wedding near Banz in the mid-Wahgi Valley. His wife Yerema stands by his side. She is from the mid-Wahgi and now farms there. Sides of cooked pork have been laid out as part of the gifts to be offered at the wedding.

missioner Jim Sinclair, "when he was recovering from a stroke, a sad, disappointed man, a shadow of his former robust self, unable to leave the house without assistance, depending upon Jeannette to run the farm. But still he was 'agin the government,' and still refusing to give in. A man of indomitable spirit, of evident faults and equally evident virtues."[5]

Sinclair talked of Leahy's early explorations in the highlands as "his monument," and that is unquestionably the way Michael Leahy saw things. And the concrete expression of that monument was his collection of photographs. As his life drew to a close, the metamorphosis from prospector to explorer was complete. To Michael Leahy the photographs immortalised the pinnacle of that exploratory achievement, his

"discovery" of a hidden race. As Papua New Guinea refused to slide
into chaos, as the country began to participate as an independent nation
in the modern world, as the highland people began to exercise the political power their numbers warranted in a vigorous parliamentary democracy, the photographs became Leahy's palpable link to his bygone
world, the only world where he could find comfort, meaning and self-
realisation.

Even after independence, when a more judicious policy might have
dictated silence, Leahy could respond to criticism of Australia's colonial
rule by writing: "Many are still alive in the highlands and I am sure
much more appreciative of what the white colonialist has done to rescue him and his *wantoks* from the centuries of barbarism which were
their lives before the white man came."[6]

"Melanesia," writes the Papua New Guinea lawyer Bernard Narokobi from quite a different perspective," has been invaded by a huge
tidal wave from the West, in the form of colonisation and Christianisa-
tion. Like any tidal wave the West came mercilessly, with force and
power, toppling over our wealth, destroying our treasures, depositing
some rich soil, but also leaving much rubbish."[7]

Michael Leahy died in 1979, and when Joe and Clem Leahy heard
the news they drove from the highlands to say their farewells to the
father they never knew. Joe had met him once, casually in the street
with a group of Leahy relatives. "He didn't say much, didn't acknowledge I was his son, didn't want to talk to me, but he was caught there.
And when he went away, the others laughed at his back. But I didn't
like their laughing."

The mourners converged on Michael Leahy's farm at bleak Zenag.
Riding in Clem's Mercedes the half-brothers set out from Mount Hagen
uninvited. Mokei Wamp—now Sir Wamp Wan—rode with them, and
so did Towa and Tupia, who lived on Joe's plantation. Down the flat
expanse of the Wahgi, past the great plantations and the roadside sell-
ers, past Baklaka where the first two Hageners fell to the strangers'
guns in April 1933; past Banz where James Taylor mimicked an aeroplane to his future father-in-law's threatening tribe, while Michael Leahy
watched with his camera and his gun; past roadside markets, where
the women sit with their home-grown produce and their men lounge
and smoke and stare with narrowed eyes at Clem Leahy's luxury car.

Into the Chimbu and over the Korin River, where women wept and clung to Porte, their anguish immortalised by Michael Leahy's Leica; past the Chimbu capital Kundiawa, with its stores, post office, betting hall and luxury hotel—the Chimbu Lodge, enclosed within barbed wire, watering hole for the Chimbu elite.

Past Ulka Wena's house, where fifty years ago he watched his dead relative Konia Taglba walk towards him; past Oknel Village, where the people took Taylor to be Bare returning from the dead and then attacked him on his second visit. Down into the Asaro Valley of Gavey Akamo and Sirizo, Sole Sole, and the late Kirupano Eza'e; past Koritoia Upe's village and the people of the Bena Bena, past Finintegu and Kainantu, down the Kassam Pass to the Markham and on to Lae. Then back into the mountains straddling the coast and up to Zenag on the road that leads to the rusting gold dredges of Bulolo.

The service was held in the open air, and most of the mourners had gathered when Clem drove up. Dan Leahy was there, and Jim Taylor, and Ewunga Goiba from Goroka. "A lot of Mick's relations," says Joe, "and a lot of his friends, old timers, and a lot of people who didn't know us, looking at each other, wondering who we were.

"Some of them said we were Danny's boys, because he was always getting the blame. We never seemed to get together with Mick's family, so I don't know if they knew. I think he'd been hiding these things, because he was married to a European woman and didn't want to offend her and his family and friends.

"They already had white blokes carrying the coffin—Richard and Phillip and Tim [Michael Leahy's adult sons], but they didn't make room for me and Clem. We were really upset. It was my father, and I'd never see him again, and I thought I was going to see him sometime and have a talk with him. But things just happened, and that was the last time, the last respect. I knew he was my father, but he didn't take me as his son.

"Some of the boys, like Towa and Tupia and Ewunga, they were crying. We were all crying, couldn't help it. After the burial we all went in the house and everyone was talking, but no one from Mick's family came and asked us where we were from or what we were doing there, so when everyone went off we went off too. Tradition said we should cry. We cried more than all those Europeans. Nobody but myself and Clem and the old boys were crying. The old boys were probably thinking of the old times."

First contact, Mariefuteger/Chuave region, February 1933.

• • •

Fifty years earlier, at Kuta, Korpore accuses *Masta* Mick of feeling nothing at the death of Lik Lik. "Tried to explain to him," wrote Leahy in his diary, "that we felt sorry but did not always cry when we had any sorrow. But Korpore is still almost as primitive as these people, and wants to see outward evidence of my emotions."

Human beings, groping in the darkness, never quite managing to touch each other. Epitaph for Michael Leahy and the era that ended with him. Clem and Joe, Towa and Tupia, grizzled Ewunga who says he killed twenty-seven black men in his *masta's* service, portly old Mokei Sir Wamp, blind Dan Leahy and frail old Jim Taylor went their separate ways back to the highlands. And from village to village, settlement to settlement, valley to green and beautiful valley of this last hidden place on earth, the word slowly spread. Michael Leahy had finally returned to the place of the dead.

Note on Sources

This book is based primarily on interviews with highlanders and Australians who took part in the events described and on the diaries and other written records of the Australians.

The interviews were recorded in Papua New Guinea and Australia between 1981 and 1985. In the case of the highlanders, the authors always relied upon interpreters and translators—men and women of various ages and walks of life but primarily educated highlanders whose first language was that of the informants whose stories they were translating.

The primary intention at all times was to keep faith with what the people were saying, and wherever possible the transcribed interviews are reproduced verbatim. However, in some of these and in the interviews conducted with the surviving Australians, the authors felt it necessary, in the interests of precision and clarity, to edit the transcripts by eliminating repetition, supplying punctuation and occasionally correcting grammatical errors.

Notes

CHAPTER ONE

1 The concept of the "sacred trust" was embodied in the 1919 Covenant of the League of Nations and found later expression in the *Final Report of the Royal Commission on Late German New Guinea*, Commonwealth of Australia Parliamentary Paper 29, 1920, p. 77.
2 J.H. Johns to his parents, dated September 7, 1930, J.H.W. Johns Letters.

CHAPTER THREE

1 Source for the response by the Mikaru people is Ian Willis, "An Epic Journey: The Journey of Michael Leahy and Michael Dwyer across New Guinea in 1930," pp. 128–29.
2 The story of Hefioza is taken from Glenys Köhnke, *Time Belong Tumbuna*, p. 84.

CHAPTER FOUR

1 For information about New Guinea Goldfields, we are indebted to Peter Munster, in particular his doctoral thesis, "A History of Contact in the Goroka Valley, 1930–1952."
2 The notion of the highlanders being "on active duty" all the time was suggested by James Lindsay Taylor.
3 Letter from Assistant District Officer Taylor to District Officer at Salamaua, December 23, 1932, James L. Taylor Letters, Australian Archives, Canberra, A.C.T.

CHAPTER FIVE

1 Taylor to District Officer at Salamaua, December 23, 1932, James L. Taylor Letters.

2 Letter from G.A. Harrison at Wau to Michael Leahy at Bena Bena, dated January 28, 1933, Michael Leahy and Party Letters, New Guinea Goldfields Co. Offices, Sydney.
3 Letter from Ken Spinks at Bena Bena to G.A. Harrison at Wau, dated March 26, 1933, Michael Leahy and Party Letters.

CHAPTER SEVEN

1 Letter from Hector Kinsbury at Kelua to Mrs. Kingsbury at Wau, dated April 30, 1933. Reproduced with the permission of Mr. Kingsbury's son, Professor Donald Kingsbury, Montreal, Canada.
2 For more information on the moka, see *The Rope of Moka*, A.S. Strathern. Professor Strathern is the leading authority on the anthropology of the Melpa-speaking tribes of the Hagen area.

CHAPTER NINE

1 Letter from Michael Leahy at Kelua to G.A. Harrison at Wau, dated July 29, 1933, Michael Leahy and Party Letters.

CHAPTER TEN

1 Letter from Michael Leahy at Kelua to G.A. Harrison at Wau, dated July 29, 1933, Michael Leahy and Party Letters.
2 Levien's comments are found in R. Radford, *Missionaries, Miners and Administrators in the Eastern Highlands*, p. 94.
3 Georg Vicedom's observations are taken from the monumental three-volume ethnographic study of the Hagen people *The Mbowamb*, by Georg F. Vicedom and H. Tischner, vol. 2, p. 613.

CHAPTER ELEVEN

1 The reference to the seriousness of the Finintegu affair is quoted from the *Report to the Council of the League of Nations on the Administration of the Territory of New Guinea 1933–34*, p. 28.
2 The quotes from District Officer Melrose and Acting Director of District Services Taylor come from a letter written by Territory Administrator W.R. McNicholl to the Prime Minister in Canberra on January 28, 1937, regarding the outcome of the investigation into Leahy's shootings in uncontrolled areas, Investigation into Shooting by Michael Leahy and Parties, The Australian Archives, Canberra, A.C.T.

CHAPTER TWELVE

1 Goodenough's opening remarks at a meeting of the society on November 21, 1935, to hear Michael Leahy read his paper "The Central Highlands of New Guinea," which was published by the Royal Geographic Society, 1936.
2 Letter from Lord Lamington to the Australian High Commissioner, Court of St. James, dated April 1936, Correspondence Relating to Michael Leahy's Address to the Royal Geographic Society, Australian Archives, Canberra, A.C.T.
3 Letter from John Harris, Secretary of the Anti-Slavery and Aborigines Protection Society, June 22, 1936, Correspondence Relating to Michael Leahy's Address to the Royal Geographic Society.
4 Michael Leahy's statement to J.L. Taylor on October 6, 1936, Investigation into Shooting by Michael Leahy and Parties. The Australian Archives, Canberra, A.C.T.
5 Letter from Administrator McNicholl to the prime minister, Canberra, on January 28, 1937, Investigation into Shooting by Michael Leahy and Parties.
6 Minutes of the meeting on June 14, 1937, Permanent Mandates Commission 31st Session.
7 Frantz Fanon, *The Wretched of the Earth*, p. 32.

CHAPTER THIRTEEN

1 Letter from Michael Leahy at Kuta to G.A. Harrison at Wau, dated October 2, 1933, Michael Leahy and Party Letters.
2 *Rabaul Times*, September 25, 1936.

CHAPTER FOURTEEN

1 Quote is drawn from Georg F. Vicedom and Herbert Tischner's *The Mbowamb*, vol. 2, p. 247.

CHAPTER FIFTEEN

1 Source of information about the shell economy in the highlands is Ian Hughes, "Good Money and Bad."
2 William Ross, quoted by Mary Mennis, *Hagen Saga*, p. 195.
3 Diary of William Ross, reproduced in part by Mary Mennis, *Hagen Saga*, p. 63.
4 Letter from G.F. Pearce, Minister of Territories, to Administrator McNicholl on August 27, 1937, Correspondence Relating to an Application for a Mining Lease in Uncontrolled Area 1937, The Australian Archives, Canberra, A.C.T.
5 Chinnery's remarks appear in a paper he attached to the official Report to the Council of the League of Nations on the Administration of the Territory of New Guinea 1932–33.
6 Georg F. Vicedom and H. Tischner, *The Mbowamb*, vol. 1, pp. 11–12.
7 Taylor's comments appeared in the August 15, 1939, edition of *Pacific Islands Monthly*.
8 Taylor's comments appeared in the March 15, 1940, edition of *Pacific Islands Monthly*.
9 The islander was quoted in Edward P. Wolfers' *Race Relations and Colonial Rule in Papua New Guinea*, p. 110.
10 Cargo (in pidgin *kago*) here refers to wealth and/or possessions. For further information, see Peter Lawrence's *Road Belong Cargo*.

CHAPTER SIXTEEN

1 From Charles Rowley's *The New Guinea Villager*, p. 99.
2 The Goroka complainant is unknown. The patrol officer was J.R. McArthur, who quoted the complaint in his Patrol Report No. 11 of 1956–57, Goroka Department of District Administration. The passage also appeared in Ben Finney's *Big Men in Business*, p. 22.
3 For further information about the development of business in the highlands during this period see Ben Finney's *Big Men and Business*.
4 Taken from I. Kilage's *My Mother Calls Me Yaltep*, p. 35.
5 Sinclair's comments formed part of his obituary to Michael Leahy published in the May 1979 edition of *Pacific Islands Monthly*.
6 I. Kilage, *My Mother Calls Me Yaltep*, p. 49.

CHAPTER SEVENTEEN

1 Highlander response to the United Nations Mission appears in its publication *The People Speaking: New Guinea Nauru*, p. 8. Also quoted in H.C. Brookfield's *Colonialism, Development and Independence*, p. 174.
2 *The People Speaking*, p. 8.
3 Maori Kiki's speech was reported in the March 12, 1970, edition of the *Papua New Guinea Post Courier*.
4 Michael Leahy's reply to Maori Kiki was published in the *Papua New Guinea Post Courier*, March 31, 1970.
5 From Sinclair's obituary of Leahy in the May 1979 *Pacific Islands Monthly*.
6 Michael Leahy's letter appeared in the July 30, 1975, edition of the *Papua New Guinea Post Courier*.
7 Bernard Narokobi, *The Melanesian Way*, p. 8.

Bibliography

BOOKS, ARTICLES, AND THESES

Amarshi, Azeem; Good, Kenneth; and Mortimer, Rex. *Development and Dependency*. Melbourne: Oxford University Press, 1979.

Berndt, R.M. "A Cargo Movement in the Eastern Central Highlands of New Guinea." *Oceania* 23: parts 1 and 2 (1952–53).

———. "Reaction to Contact in the Eastern Highlands of New Guinea." *Oceania* 24 (1953–54).

Brookfield, H.C. *Colonialism, Development and Independence*. London: Cambridge University Press, 1972.

Brown, Paula. *The Chimbu*. London: Routledge and Kegan Paul, 1973.

———. *Highland Peoples of New Guinea*. Cambridge: Cambridge University Press, 1978.

Dening, Greg. "Ethnohistory in Polynesia." *Journal of Pacific History* 1–2 (1966–67).

Downs, Ian. *The Australian Trusteeship: Papua New Guinea 1945–75*. Canberra: Australian Government Publishing Service, 1980.

Epstein, T. Scarlett. *Capitalism, Primitive and Modern*. Canberra: Australian National University Press, 1968.

Fanon, Frantz. *The Wretched of the Earth*. Translated by Constance Farrington. New York: Penguin, 1967.

Feil, Daryl K. "From Pigs to Pearlshells: The Transformation of a New Guinea Highlands Exchange Economy." *American Ethnologist* 9 (1982).

Finney, Ben. *Big Men and Business*. Canberra: Australian National University Press, 1973.

Gitlow, Abraham L. *Economics of the Mount Hagen Tribes, New Guinea*. Seattle: University of Washington Press, 1947.

Golson, Jack. "Kuk and the History of Agriculture in the New Guinea Highlands." *Melanesia: Beyond Diversity*. Edited by R.J. May and Hank Nelson. Canberra: Research School of Pacific Studies, Australian National University, 1982.

Griffin, James, ed. *Papua New Guinea Portraits: The Expatriate Experience*. Canberra: Australian National University Press, 1978.

Griffin, James; Nelson, Hank; and Firth, Stewart. *Papua New Guinea: A Political History*. Melbourne: Heinemann Educational Australia, 1979.

Healey, A.M. "Bulolo: A History of the Development of the Bulolo Region, New Guinea." New Guinea Research Bulletin No. 15. Canberra: Australian National University. 1967.

Howlett, Diana. "Terminal Development: From Tribalism to Peasantry," in *The Pacific in Transition*, edited by H.C. Brookfield. Canberra: Australian National University Press, 1973, pp. 249–73.

Hughes, Ian. *New Guinea Stone Axe Trade*. Canberra: *Terra Australis* no. 3, Department of Prehistory, Australian National University, 1977.

———. "Good Money and Bad: Inflation and Devaluation in the Colonial Process." *Mankind* 11 (1977–78).

Jinks, B.; Biskup, P.; and Nelson, H. *Readings in New Guinea History*. Sydney: Angus and Robertson, 1973.

Kilage, I. *My Mother Calls Me Yaltep*. Port Moresby: Institute of Papua New Guinea Studies, 1981.

King, D., and Ranck, S., eds. *Papua New Guinea Atlas*. Port Moresby: Robert Brown & Associates (Australia) in conjunction with University of Papua New Guinea, 1982.

Köhnke, Glenys. *Time Belong Tumbuna*. Port Moresby: Robert Brown & Associates with the Jacaranda Press, 1973.

Lawrence, Peter. *Road Belong Cargo*. Melbourne: Melbourne University Press, 1964.

Lawrence, P., and Meggitt, M.J. *Gods, Ghosts and Men in Melanesia*. Melbourne: Oxford University Press, 1965.

Leahy, Michael. "The Central Highlands of New Guinea." *Journal of the Royal Geographic Society*, London, 1936.

Leahy, Michael; and Crain, Maurice. *The Land That Time Forgot*. New York and London: Funk and Wagnalls Company, 1937.

Maclay, Mikloucho. *New Guinea Diaries 1871–1883*. Madang: Kristen Press, 1975.

Mennis, Mary. *Hagen Saga*. Port Moresby: Robert Brown & Associates, 1982.

Munster, Peter. "A History of Contact in the Goroka Valley 1930–1952." Ph.D. dissertation, University of Papua New Guinea, 1984.

———. "Three Men from Morobe," *Morobe District Historical Society Journal* 3–4 (1975–77).

Narokobi, Bernard. *The Melanesian Way: Total Cosmic Vision of Life*, edited by Henry Olela. Port Moresby: Institute of Papua New Guinea Studies, 1980.

Nelson, Hank. *Black White and Gold*. Australian National University Press, Canberra, 1976.

———. *Taim Bilong Masta: The Australian Involvement with Papua New Guinea*. Sydney: Australian Broadcasting Corporation, 1982.

O'Faircheallaigh, Ciaran. *Mining in the Papua New Guinea Economy 1880–1980*. Occasional Paper in Economic History; no. 1, University of Papua New Guinea, 1982.

O'Neil, Jack. *Up from South*. Edited by James Sinclair. Port Moresby: Robert Brown & Associates, 1979.

Ongka. *Ongka: A Self-Account by a New Guinea Big Man*. Translated by Andrew Strathern. London: Duckworth Publishers, 1979.

Radford, Robin. "Missionaries, Miners and Administrators in the Eastern Highlands." *Journal of the Papua and New Guinea Society* 6, no. 2 (1972).

———. "Highlanders and Foreigners in the Upper Ramu: The Kainantu Area 1919–1942." Master's thesis, University of Papua New Guinea, 1979.

Radi, Heather. "New Guinea under Mandate 1921–41." *Australia and Papua New Guinea*. Edited by W.J. Hudson. Sydney: Sydney University Press, 1971, pp. 74–137.

Read, K.E. *The High Valley*. London: George Allen and Unwin, 1965.

Rowley, Charles. *The New Guinea Villager*. Melbourne: Cheshire Publishing Company, 1965.

Ryan, John. *The Hot Land*. Melbourne: Macmillan Publishing Company, 1969.

Sahlins, Marshall. "Poor Man, Rich Man, Big Man, Chief: Political Types in Melanesia and Polynesia." *Comparative Studies in Society and History* 5 (1963).

Said, Edward. *Orientalism*. London: Routledge and Kegan Paul, 1978.

Salisbury, R.F. *From Stone to Steel: Economic Consequences of Technological Change in New Guinea*. Melbourne: Melbourne University Press, 1962.

Shineberg, Dorothy. *They Came for Sandalwood*. Melbourne: Melbourne University Press, 1976.

Sinclair, James. *Wings of Gold*. Sydney: Pacific Publications, 1978.

Souter, Gavin. *New Guinea: The Last Unknown*. Sydney: Angus and Robertson, 1963.

Strathern, Andrew. *The Rope of Moka: Big-Men and Ceremonial Exchange in Mount Hagen, New Guinea.* Cambridge: Cambridge University Press, 1971.

———. "Despots and Directors in the New Guinea Highlands." *Man* 1966, 1.3.

———. "Gender Ideology and Money in Mount Hagen." *Man* 1979, 14.3.

———. "Cargo and Inflation in Mount Hagen." *Oceania* 61, no. 4, June 1971.

Strathern, Marilyn. *Women in Between: Females' Roles in a Male World.* London and New York: Seminar Press, 1972.

Trégance, Louis. *Adventures in New Guinea: The Narrative of Louis Trégance.* London: Crocker, Low, Marston and Co., 1876.

Vicedom, Georg F.; and Tischner, Herbert. *The Mbowamb: The Culture of the Mount Hagen Tribes in East Central New Guinea.* German language original published in three volumes in Hamburg, 1943–48. Our source was the unpublished English translation in two typescript volumes held at the Menzies Library, Australian National University, Canberra, A.C.T. Vol. 1 translated by Helen M. Wurm; vol. 2 translated by F.E. Rheinstein and E. Klestadt.

Whittaker, J.L. "New Guinea: The Ethnohistory of First Culture Contacts" in *The History of Melanesia: Papers Delivered at the Second Waigani Seminar.* University of Papua New Guinea and Australian National University Press, Canberra, 1969.

Willis, Ian. "Who Was First? The First White Man into the New Guinea Highlands." *Journal of the Papua and New Guinea Society* vol. 3, no. 1., 1969.

———. "An Epic Journey: The Journey of Michael Leahy and Michael Dwyer across New Guinea in 1930," Master's thesis, University of Papua New Guinea, 1969.

———. *Lae City and Village.* Melbourne: Melbourne University Press, 1974.

Wolfers, Edward P. *Race Relations and Colonial Rule in Papua New Guinea.* Sydney: Australia and New Zealand Book Company, 1975.

MANUSCRIPTS AND PRIVATE PAPERS

Canberra. Australian Archives. A518, L841/1/1 part 2. Correspondence Relating to Michael Leahy's Address to the Royal Geographic Society, London, 1935.

Canberra. Australian Archives. A518, BB 840/1/3 part 1. Correspondence Relating to an Application for Mining Lease in Uncontrolled Area 1937.

Canberra. Australian Archives. A518, L841/1/1, part 2. Investigation into Shooting by Michael Leahy and Parties.

Canberra. Australian Archives. AS/13/26 Q836/3, part 2 (56). James L. Taylor Diary and Mount Hagen Patrol Report, 1933.

Canberra. Australian Archives. AS 13/26, 30. James L. Taylor Letters.

Canberra. National Library of Australia. Michael Leahy Diaries 1930–1934.

Melbourne. University of Melbourne Archives. J.H.W. Johns Letters.

Montreal. Privately held by Donald Kingsbury. Hector Kingsbury Letters.

Sydney. New Guinea Goldfields Company Offices. Michael Leahy and Party Letters.

Sydney. The Australian Museum. Charles Marshall Diary 1933.

GOVERNMENT AND OFFICIAL PUBLICATIONS

Australia, Parliamentary Papers. "General Brief for Australian Parliamentary Delegation to the South Pacific." July–August 1983. W. Standish.

Australia, Parliamentary Papers. Report of the Committee to Review the Australian Overseas Aid Programme, Jackson Report 1984, Canberra.

Laws of the Territory of New Guinea 1921–1945 (annotated) vols. 1–5, Menzies Library, Australian National University, Canberra.

League of Nations. Permanent Mandates Commission, Geneva. *Minutes of the 27th Session, 3–18 June 1935.* Held at the National Library of Australia, Canberra, A.C.T.

League of Nations. Permanent Mandates Commission, Geneva. *Minutes of the 29th Session, 27 May–27 June 1936.*

League of Nations. Permanent Mandates Commission, Geneva. *Minutes of the 31st Session, 31 May–15 June, 1937.* Report held at the Menzies Library, Australian National University, Canberra.

———. *Reports to the Council of the League of Nations on the Administration of the Territory of New Guinea, 1930–31 to 1939–40.* Commonwealth of Australia.

Territory of Papua Annual Report 1937–38.

United Nations. Trusteeship Council. *The People Speaking: New Guinea Nauru.* Texts of daily progress reports covering the work of the 1965 Visiting Mission from the United Nations Trusteeship Council to New Guinea and Nauru.

BROADCASTS

Australian Broadcasting Commission. Radio series. *Taim Bilong Masta: The Australian Involvement with Papua New Guinea,* produced by Tim Bowden, 1981.

Photography Credits

By ROBIN ANDERSON:

Pages 42, 54, 57 *(right)*, 71 *(left)*, 83, 87 *(left)*, 101, 107, 108, 119, 133, 137, 143, 145, 161, 164, 277, 278, 297, 301, 302, 304

By DANIEL LEAHY:

Pages 123, 125, 141, 165, 186, 234 *(courtesy Michael Leahy collection)*, 239, 245, 249, 251, 253

Photographer unknown:

Pages 15, 21, 57 *(left)*, 81, 87 *(right)*, 189 *(courtesy of the Michael Leahy collection)*

All other photographs by Michael Leahy, reproduced with the kind permission of Mrs. Jeanette Leahy